The Blue Sweater

Bridging the Gap between Rich and Poor
in an Interconnected World

Jacqueline Novogratz

RODALE

Rodale books may be purchased for business or promotional use or for special sales. For information, please write to:
Special Markets Department, Rodale Inc., 733 Third Avenue, New York, NY 10017

Printed in the United States of America
Rodale Inc. makes every effort to use acid-free ♾, recycled paper ♻.

Book design by Joanna Williams

Library of Congress Cataloging-in-Publication Data

Novogratz, Jacqueline.
    The blue sweater : bridging the gap between rich and poor in an interconnected world /Jacqueline Novogratz.
        p.   cm.
    Includes index.
    ISBN-13 978-1-59486-915-0 hardcover
    ISBN-10 1-59486-915-4 hardcover
    1. Poverty.   2. Economic assistance.   3. Charities.   4. Microfinance.   I. Title.
HC79.P6N69   2009
339.4'6—dc22   2008043621

Distributed to the trade by Macmillan

2   4   6   8   10   9   7   5   3   hardcover

We inspire and enable people to improve their lives and the world around them
For more of our products visit **rodalestore.com** or call 800-848-4735

My family helped make me who I am . . . and they join me
in dedicating this book to our larger family, those countless
millions around the world who lack money and security
but possess dignity and an indomitable spirit.
For their time is coming, and this story is for them.

CONTENTS

PROLOGUE

They say a journey of a thousand miles begins with a single step. I took mine and fell flat on my face. As a young woman, I dreamed of changing the world. In my twenties, I went to Africa to try and save the continent, only to learn that Africans neither wanted nor needed saving. Indeed, when I was there, I saw some of the worst that good intentions, traditional charity, and aid can produce: failed programs that left people in the same or worse conditions. The devastating impact of the Rwandan genocide on a people I'd come to love shrank my dreams even further. I concluded that if I could only *nudge* the world a little bit, maybe that would be enough.

But nudging isn't enough. The gap between rich and poor is widening across the world, creating a dire situation that is neither socially just nor economically sustainable. Moreover, my work in Africa also taught me about the extraordinary resilience of people for whom poverty is a reality not because they don't work hard, but because there are too many obstacles in their way. One very sick child or the death of a husband can wipe out a family's savings and throw it into a vicious cycle of debt that keeps those with the least in poverty forever.

It doesn't have to be that way. Indeed, the idealism of my twenties has returned in my forties, not simply from unfounded hopefulness, but from optimism grounded in a deep and growing pragmatism. To address poverty in a more insightful way, in 2001 I started a nonprofit organization called Acumen Fund. We raise charitable funds, but instead of using the money for giveaways, we make careful investments in entrepreneurs who are willing to take on some of the world's toughest challenges. The entrepreneurs we seek have the vision to deliver essential services like affordable health care, safe water, housing, and alternative energy to areas where governments or charities are often failing. We measure our results in social as well as financial terms and share lessons and insights learned with the greater world.

We've seen what can happen when an entrepreneur views the market as a listening device that reveals how to tailor services and products to the preferences of low-income people who are viewed as consumers, not victims. The entrepreneurs are driven to build systems that can eventually sustain themselves and, ultimately, serve a wide swath of the population.

The returns on such investments can be enormous. At Acumen Fund, we've worked with an entrepreneur who built a company that provides safe water to more than a quarter million of India's rural poor, contrary to all conventional wisdom that truly low-income people would never pay. We've supported an agricultural products designer who has sold to more than 275,000 of the world's small-holder farmers drip irrigation systems that enable them to double their yields and income levels. We've invested in a malaria bed net manufacturer in Africa that now employs more than 7,000 people, mostly low-skilled women, and produces 16 million lifesaving, long-lasting bed nets a year.

Today, I believe more strongly than I did as a young woman that we can end poverty. Never before in history have we had the skills, resources, technologies, and imagination to solve poverty that we do now. I'm also a believer because I've seen that fundamental change is possible in a single generation.

My grandmother Stella was born in 1906. Her parents lived on a farm in Burgenland, Austria's wine region on the border with Hungary, and came to live in a little town called Northampton, Pennsylvania—like so many other Austrians, Czechs, and Hungarians—to seek their fortune. They couldn't afford to care for Stella, so when she was 3 years old her parents sent her back to Austria with her little sister, Emma, promising to bring their daughters to the new country as soon as they could manage it.

For more than a decade, the two girls were trundled from family to family, never fully belonging. They lived the lives of domestic servants, were sometimes abused, and each was allowed to wear her one pair of shoes only on Sundays. They were given no real education except how to work hard, believe in God, and keep looking forward.

The women of my grandmother's generation expected to start birthing children as soon as they married, do manual work outside the home for income, and take care of all household matters. My grandmother toiled under oppressive conditions as a pieceworker in a textile factory, cooked all day on Sunday, and waited until the men had eaten before she sat. And she never, ever complained. She buried three of her nine children before they were 5 years old, went to church every day, and had a beautiful, shy laugh accompanied by downcast eyes. I would come to see that same smile on so many women on the African continent.

In America, my grandparents raised 6 children, who then brought another 25 individuals into the world. My cousins and I stand on the shoulders of our grandparents and people like them who never asked for handouts, but supported one another and shared suffering and, through hard work and determination, gave their children better futures in a country that assured them hope and opportunity, if nothing else.

Today, poor people the world over are seeking opportunity and choice to have greater dignity in their lives—and they want to do it themselves, even if they need a little help. Today we have the tools and technologies to bring real opportunities to people all across the world.

The time has come to extend to every person on the planet the fundamental principle that we hold so dear: that all human beings are created equal. Rather than seeing the world as divided among different civilizations or classes, our collective future rests upon our embracing a vision of a single world in which we are all connected. Indeed, maybe this notion of human connection is the most important—and complex—challenge of our time. Markets play a role in this vision, and so does public policy. So does philanthropy. We all play a role in the change we need to create.

But where to start? Like so many young people with skills today, my desire to contribute to changing the world a quarter century ago wasn't matched by a proper game plan: I had no idea how to do it. I was a middle-class kid who paid my way through university. Pursuing a non-profit life seemed like an enormous challenge at the start, and I didn't know anyone at the time who did the kind of work I craved. Almost all of my role models were characters in books—or dead.

So I did what I now tell young people to do: I started where I could and where I was given a chance. This book is about my journey, one taken with gusto, if not always with wisdom. Indeed, as I look back at the adventurous young woman who left banking to pursue a life focused on a more global, connected vision, I see someone with guts, education, and skills, but also someone who had to learn time and again that those factors alone don't always lead to success.

This book is for people who do not seek easy solutions or insist on a singular ideology for the world. It is for individuals who care less about the amount of money people earn and more about whether they can access basic services and live with the freedom and dignity that are their inherent rights as human beings. It is for readers who seek simple truths while recognizing that today's problems are complex and often require equally complex solutions.

My own path has challenged even my most basic assumptions. Going to Africa for the first time only to meet with threats of voodoo and poisoning made me question an outsider's role in development. Seeing a group of women with whom I had worked for years both suffer as victims and act as perpetrators in the Rwandan genocide made me reconsider the very nature of what it is to be human. Watching the Berlin Wall fall, which resulted in a widespread belief in the "victory of capitalism," while also experiencing the cruelty an unbridled capitalist system can inflict on the very poor made me seek alternative solutions that could include all people in the opportunities presented by a global economy. Meeting and working with some of the world's wealthiest individuals made me explore the role of philanthropy and private initiative in bringing about large-scale change, especially when it comes to poverty.

My story is really composed of the stories of others, the extraordinary people who have shaped my life. They came from all corners of the world—a Cambodian monk and an elder American statesman; a man who lived his entire life in a mud hut in Africa and a president of the Rockefeller Foundation; Kenyan women dancing in a hut; a little girl who'd lost her home in Pakistan; and a genocide survivor who fought back to claim her life again with just 4 liters of milk. Each of these individuals and so many more have given me an incredible education about the human capacity to overcome enormous obstacles, how alike we are in the most fundamental ways, and that what is most important is our individual and shared sense of dignity. To a person, these unforgettable individuals, many of whom endured impossible suffering, never lost their sense of life or humor.

It is from them that I gained the confidence and sense of possibility that sustained me. They allowed me to believe we could—and therefore must—create a world in which every person on the planet has access to the resources needed to shape their own lives. For this is where dignity starts. Not only for the very poor, but for all of us.

CHAPTER 1

INNOCENT ABROAD

*"There is no passion to be found playing small in settling for
a life that is less than the one you are capable of living."*

—NELSON MANDELA

It all started with the blue sweater, the one my uncle Ed gave me. He was like Santa to me, even in the middle of July.

Of soft blue wool, with stripes on the sleeves and an African motif across the front—two zebras walking in front of a snowcapped mountain—the sweater made me dream of places far away. I hadn't heard of Mount Kilimanjaro, nor did I have any idea that Africa would one day find a prominent place in my heart. Still, I loved that sweater and wore it often and everywhere. I wrote my name on the tag to ensure that it would be mine forever.

In our neighborhood in Virginia in the 1970s, new clothing was a once- or twice-a-year event. We would shop in September for school and at Christmastime and then make do for the year. As the eldest of seven children, at least I didn't have to wear many hand-me-downs, and I liked choosing my own clothes; still, I loved that blue sweater. I wore it for years—right through middle school and into my freshman year in high school—though it started to fit me differently then, hugging adolescent curves I fought mightily to ignore.

But then my high school nemesis (who would burn down the school in our senior year by throwing a Molotov cocktail into the principal's office) ruined everything. At our school, the cool kids and athletes hung out in "Jock Hall," the area right outside the gym. During football season, the cheerleaders would decorate the hall with crepe paper streamers while the guys strutted around like peacocks in green and gold jerseys. Only a freshman, I was breathless just to be admitted to the scene. One Friday afternoon, the captain of the team had asked me on a date right there in the middle of the hall. The very air seemed to crackle with expectation.

And there was that mean kid, standing right beside me, talking to boys from the junior varsity football team about the first ski trip of the winter. He stared at my sweater, and I gave him the coldest look I could muster. "We don't have to go anywhere to ski," he yelled, pointing at my chest. "We can do it on Mount Novogratz."

The other boys joined him in laughter. I died a thousand deaths.

That afternoon, I marched home and announced to my mother that the vile sweater had to go. How could she have let me walk out of the house looking so mortifyingly bad? Despite my high drama, she drove me to the Goodwill in our Ford station wagon with the wood panels on the sides. Ceremoniously, we disposed of the sweater; I was glad never to have to see it again and tried hard to forget it.

FAST-FORWARD TO EARLY 1987: Twenty-five years old, I was jogging up and down the hilly streets of Kigali, Rwanda. I'd come to the country to help establish a microfinance institution for poor women. With my Walkman playing Joe Cocker singing "With a Little Help from My Friends," I felt as if I were in a music video. On the road, women walked with bunches of yellow bananas on their heads, their hips swaying in time with the song's rhythm. Even the tall cypress trees at the roadsides seemed to shimmy. I was in a dream on a sunny, big-sky Kigali afternoon, far away from home.

From out of nowhere, a young boy walked toward me, wearing the sweater—*my sweater,* the beloved but abandoned blue one. He was perhaps 10 years old, skinny, with a shaved head and huge eyes, not more than 4 feet tall. The sweater hung so low it hid his shorts, covering toothpick legs and knobby knees. Only his fingertips poked out of baggy sleeves. Still, there was no doubt: This was *my* sweater.

Excitedly, I ran over to the child, who looked up at me, obviously terrified. I didn't speak a word of Kinyarwanda, nor did he speak French, the language on which I relied in Rwanda. As the boy stood frozen, I kept pointing to the sweater, trying not to become too agitated. I grabbed him by the shoulders and turned down the collar: Sure enough, my name was written on the tag of *my* sweater that had traveled thousands of miles for more than a decade.

The blue sweater had made a complex journey, from Alexandria, Virginia, to Kigali, the capital of Rwanda. It may have gone first to a little girl in the United States, then back to the Goodwill once more before traveling across the ocean, most likely to Mombasa, on the coast of Kenya, one of Africa's most active ports. It would have arrived after being fumigated and packed into 100-pound bales along with other pieces of cast-off clothing, everything from T-shirts sold at bars at the Jersey shore to overcoats to evening gowns. The bales would have been sold to secondhand clothing distributors, who would allow retailers to discard the useless pieces and buy what they thought they could sell. Over time, many of those secondhand clothing traders would move into the middle class.

The story of the blue sweater has always reminded me of how we are all connected. Our actions—and inaction—touch people we may never know and never meet across the globe. The story of the blue sweater is also my personal story: Seeing my sweater on that child renewed my sense of purpose in Africa. At that point in my own journey, my worldview was shifting. I'd begun my career as an international banker, discovering the power of capital, of markets, *and* of politics, as well as how the poor are so often excluded from all three. I wanted to understand better what stands between poverty and wealth.

It had been a long and winding road getting to Rwanda in the first place—an unimagined outcome of choices made, sometimes with a sense of purpose, at times with reason, and sometimes simply by choosing the less traveled paths.

WHEN I WAS 5, our family lived in Detroit. It was the mid-1960s and the city was plagued by race riots and protests against the Vietnam War. My dashing father, a lieutenant in the army, had the unenviable job of helping the mothers of dead soldiers bury their sons. I remember hearing my father's strained voice as he told my mother about the injustice of so many young soldiers being economically disadvantaged. My mother, young and beautiful, would hug me close when I'd ask so many questions about why people weren't all treated the same way.

The next year, my father was serving his second of three tours in Vietnam and Korea, and we'd moved to a town outside of West Point, New York. I would walk to school early to meet my first-grade teacher, Sister Mary Theophane, and help her clean the sacristy. She was a jolly woman with round, wire-rimmed glasses that matched her apple face, and I adored being near her. I'd run past little mom-and-pop shops on the quiet streets, dressed in the dark green pleated skirt and pressed white cotton blouse I would have laid out the night before to ensure I wouldn't be late.

Sacred Heart was an old school, right next door to the church, with little wooden desks for the students and a concrete playground outside. Sister was known as one of the kindest of the nuns, though she had high expectations for content—and handwriting. If we earned a perfect test score, she'd hand us a card with a summary of the life of a saint printed on it, and I studied diligently to collect as many cards as I could. I found their lives an inspiration, even if some of them did end up in vats of boiling oil.

A poster of two hands holding a rice bowl hung on the classroom wall, making me think about faraway places, trying to imagine the lives of children in China, wanting to see it for myself. When I told Sister Theophane I wanted to be a nun, she enfolded me in her thick black robes and told me I was just a child, but it was a lovely idea.

"Regardless of what you become," she said, "remember always that to whom much is given, much is expected. God gave you many gifts and it is important that you use them for others as best you can."

Though we moved again and again throughout the United States until I was 10 years old, my mother and father masterfully created a sense of home, making us feel safe and rooted no matter where we lived. By the time I entered high school, our brood was living in a four-bedroom house in suburban Virginia: It was the place all the neighborhood kids wanted to be. Dreams of the convent had long passed, and I thought much more about boys and parties, though I still expected to change the world.

In summertime, my uncle Ed who gave me the sweater would throw big parties for our extended family, which meant my grandmother and her five sisters, their children, and their children's children. We were a tribe of hundreds made larger by close friends who came to feel like they shared the same blood in their veins. We called my grandmother and her sisters, all from good peasant stock in Austria, the Six Tons of Fun. They worked hard, but they knew how to enjoy themselves, dancing with full glasses of beer balanced on their heads and laughing as they whispered stories to one another. Meanwhile, their offspring would play competitive games and drink and dance till the wee hours of the morning. If there was a family ethic, it was to work hard, go to church, be good to your family, and live out loud. We learned from our elders to be tough, to not complain, and to always show up for one another. I didn't understand then how much about tribe and community I learned from this American family.

The strained finances at home meant that my siblings and I had no choice but to be scrappy and enterprising. At 10, I babysat and sold Christmas ornaments door-to-door. By 12, I was shoveling snow in the winter and mowing grass in the summer. At 14, I spent the summer working the midnight shift behind the ice cream counter at Howard Johnson's until a toppled bucket of boiling water sent me to the hospital with third-degree burns. Not long after, I was bartending, earning $300 in tips on a good night.

These jobs—plus a series of student loans—allowed me to finance my education at the University of Virginia. As I was about to graduate, I remember feeling a deep sense of pride in knowing that I would forever have the tools to support myself, no matter what happened in life. But I wanted a break and hoped to take some time off to tend bar and ski and then figure out how I would change the world. My parents agreed to the plan, provided that I promise to go through the interview process—"just for practice."

At the University Career Center, I dutifully dropped my résumé in all of the boxes labeled for job seekers in international relations or economics, and I was surprised when the center called to tell me I had an interview with Chase Manhattan Bank. I walked into the first interview of my life, dressed in a drab gray, masculine wool suit that made me feel like an imposter, and met a young man with sandy blond hair and piercing blue eyes who didn't look much older than me.

"Tell me why you want to be a banker," he suggested after introducing himself.

I looked at him for a moment, not knowing what to say. Being a terrible liar, I told him the truth.

"I don't want to be a banker," I said. "I want to change the world. I'm hoping to take next year off, but my parents asked me to go through the interview process. I'm so sorry."

"Well," he said with a grin, shaking his head, "that's too bad. Because if you got this job, you would be traveling to 40 countries in the next 3 years and learning a lot not only about banking, but the entire world."

I gulped. "Is that really true?" I asked, my face completely red. "You know, part of my dream is to travel and learn about the world."

"It is really true," he sighed.

"Then do you think we might start this interview all over again?" I asked.

"Why not?" he shrugged, raising his eyebrows and smiling.

I walked out the door and closed it, counted to 10, walked back in, and introduced myself with a big handshake.

"So, Miss Novogratz," he smiled. "Tell me, why do you want to be a banker?"

"Well, ever since I was 6 years old, it has been my dream . . . ," I started. And it went from there.

Miraculously, I got the job, and thus began 3 of the best years of my life. I moved to New York City and, after completing the credit training program, joined a group called Credit Audit, a division of 60 young bankers, most just out of university, who would fly first-class around the world and review the quality of the bank's loans, especially in troubled economies. The first time I ever left the United States, I landed in Singapore; the second, Argentina. Life had become a dream.

In Chile, we would spend the day reviewing loans made to copper mines and industrial concerns. In Peru, I came to understand the danger capital flight presented to already unstable economies. In Hong Kong, we studied the great trading houses such as Jardine Matheson and saw firsthand how Asia was rapidly changing. It was a stunning, privileged education. I began to see myself as a wanderer and a wonderer, a true citizen of the world. But no place changed my life like Brazil.

The minute I landed in Rio, I felt I'd arrived in a magical place that somehow already lived inside me. We walked off the plane and across the tarmac in a light summer rainstorm while just beyond us there was not a cloud in the bright blue sky. Though our job at the bank was to write off millions of dollars in debt that would never be collected, the Brazilians there were friendly and warm, never taking themselves, or us, too seriously. I worked till late during the week, always to the dismay of my Brazilian colleagues, who tried hard to explain that "Americans live to work while we work to live." I used the weekends to explore.

I remember walking along Ipanema Beach with a friend, both of us wearing black bathing suits with colorful wraps around our waists. We came across a woman dressed completely in white, wearing a turban, standing at the edge of the ocean. She was cracking eggs on the sand and then throwing flowers into the waves to see if they would come back or float out to sea—part of a fertility ritual. I loved that these rituals lived alongside an economy with such potential for growth and change.

That same weekend I wandered the hillsides of Rio, talking to whomever I met in the favelas, or slums. Though I felt people staring at me, some with anger in their eyes, I wanted to know this country, not just its wealthy places. The chasm between rich and poor was stunning. I'd never experienced such poverty alongside such wealth before, and I'd also never felt such a strong desire to make a difference or felt so fully alive.

A few weeks later, still in Rio, I met a 6-year-old boy named Eduardo who lived on the streets. I brought him to my hotel room, gave him a bath, and then treated him to a hamburger at the hotel's fancy poolside café. The hotel manager approached and asked me firmly to take the child outside and never do such a thing again. Street kids were one of Rio's biggest problems, he told me disdainfully, and I had to be careful or they would find a way to steal everything from the hotel and hurt its residents. I told the manager I'd take full responsibility and Eduardo and I stayed until he had finished eating, though it was clear that just the sight of the child made the manager uncomfortable.

The street kids were a perfect embodiment of the poor as *outsiders*, as throwaway people in a world that didn't want to see them. I wondered what I could do to change that in some small way. The bank doors were closed to the poor and working class. Because the commercial banks were writing off millions in bad debts to the richest sectors of society, they were in no mood to try lending to the poorest. I suggested to my boss that an experiment, even a small one, to lend to Brazil's working class might actually provide better results than lending to the rich. He patted me on the head and reminded me of the poor's lack of collateral, the high transaction costs of making small loans, and the culture of poverty, which would result in no one repaying—insinuating that I was naive and misguided.

The conversation went from bad to worse. I disagreed with him on the culture of poverty and repeated my idea for an experiment. He told me the point was moot and that I should think about how and if I wanted to pursue my long-term career goals at Chase. I was among the most productive of the young bankers, he told me, but added, "You laugh too loudly and dress like Linda Ronstadt. You are friendly with everyone, and I worry that executives might mistake you for one of the secretaries."

The conversation boosted my determination to explore a different kind of path, one where I could take my newly learned skills and use them to help people who would never have the opportunities this man had. I didn't want to become old at 35 and knew instinctively that a combination of service and adventure could lead to a life of passion and constant renewal.

"If you don't change," my boss added, "in time, the culture will change you anyway. So make it easy on yourself and combine your work ethic with a more professional style."

I swore to myself that I would never acquiesce to mediocrity—and I couldn't imagine stifling my laugh in order to succeed. The problem was that I loved being a banker. I just wanted to find a way to influence the bank to give more people a chance to become customers.

Since that wasn't going to happen anytime soon, I began exploring in earnest the possibility of working internationally in banking for the poor. A friend told me about Grameen Bank in Bangladesh, founded by an economist named Muhammad Yunus in 1976, which lent poor women tiny amounts of money—sometimes as little as a dollar—to improve their businesses.

Since they had no collateral, poor women would form groups of five and guarantee that all would pay. If one did not, then all five would lose the privilege of borrowing. To address the question of high transaction costs, Grameen Bank charged higher interest rates. And it enjoyed nearly a 100 percent repayment rate, a lot higher than we were seeing in our collateralized portfolio to the wealthy!

Twenty years after I first heard of microenterprise, Yunus and Grameen Bank were awarded the Nobel Peace Prize after successfully loaning billions to the poor and starting a social movement around the world. Many commercial banks now also have a part of their portfolio dedicated to microfinance and are doing it successfully and profitably. None of this was thought possible 20 years ago; change doesn't happen overnight.

In exploring other organizations involved in microenterprise, I chanced upon a nonprofit microfinance organization for women based in New York City. Run by a woman investment banker and a powerful, global board of women professionals, it seemed perfect, except for one thing: I'd never seen myself as focusing on women's issues. I'd been raised in a rough-and-tumble family with four brothers whom I would wrestle to the ground until they grew bigger than me. When I was 9 and living in Kansas, my dad once had me race the players on his inner-city football team. In short, my worldview had little place for complaining about women's status. I was expected to fight to be just as good or better than the boys.

I tried to imagine myself telling my uncles that I was leaving a well-paying job on Wall Street to work for a nonprofit women's organization that would send me overseas. They would think I'd lost my mind. Why would I give up a chance at making it? I admitted that the title "international banker" had a nice ring to it, and a small part of me feared risking my career and giving up my job title. But the promise of adventure and making a real difference had always been the internal force driving me. And there is no time like the present to start living your dream.

The woman who started the nonprofit microfinance organization had worked on Wall Street herself and had a reputation for being tough. I wrote her a letter, telling her that I believed one important way to solve poverty was to link grassroots organizations to the resources and skills of mainstream corporations. I wanted to be a bridge, I explained earnestly, an instrument of peace wrapped in a love of financial statements, of telling stories through numbers, of trying to build companies through strategic financing and management support.

In retrospect, I think she must have laughed at the dramatic description of my dreams, but she agreed to meet. As I sat in her office, surrounded by richly textured tapestries from around the world, I realized that I wanted to grow up and be much more like her than like my boss in the brown polyester suit. She was committed and passionate, visionary and strong. And her world was fascinating.

"I would love to work with you somehow," I told her, adding that I would do almost anything to be sent to Brazil to help build systems to make loans to low-income women. She listened carefully, said she would think about it, and told me that the organization was in an expansion mode but still learning. I went home with no job offer, but with dreams of working in Rio.

After a few days, she called me to have lunch. At a fancy Midtown restaurant, she told me she had good news and bad news. The good news was that she would like to hire me. I just about jumped out of my chair to hug her. The bad news, she said, was that there was no place for me in Brazil. Instead, I was needed in Africa.

Africa? My heart sank. This wasn't in my plan at all. I loved the passion of Latin America. Africa?

I knew nothing about Africa, hadn't even studied it at university. My impressions of the continent were from the movies *Born Free* and *The African Queen*—beautiful animals and spectacular vistas or hot and steamy jungles where missionaries worked. Africa? I didn't think so.

I must have looked like a deer caught in the headlights, for the woman quickly added that my job would be very prestigious. I would be an ambassador to African women with an office at the African Development Bank. My job would be helping local country organizations across West Africa get started. There would be travel and building things and working with people across national lines. That all sounded good.

Still, I couldn't help but feel queasy. "I think I'd like to do this, but I need to consider it for a few days," I said, unable to hide my mixed emotions.

"You will love it there," she assured me.

To complicate matters, my boss's boss at Chase offered me a "once in a lifetime opportunity," a position working closely with him that would be challenging and visible. He didn't care that I dressed in pleated cotton skirts instead of blue suits with bow ties; in fact, he seemed to like the renegade part of me, the bartender who liked talking to people and the Catholic girl who knew how to scrub a kitchen floor, making sure every corner shined.

The opportunity appealed to my ego, though I knew somehow that if I took the job it would delay for years my dream of changing the world. When we were in our teens, my younger brother and I had a recurring conversation about how best to make a real difference. He thought you should make a lot of money and then move from a place of power and influence. I argued that you had to start early, understand how change happens, and build relationships and credibility over a long period. Over the years, I've watched in awe as his life plans have unfolded, but I had to be who I was.

I gave notice to Chase and accepted the job in Africa. I still didn't really understand what being an ambassador meant, nor did I have a clear picture of what the organization did except lend to poor women for small businesses. But I was confident I would figure something out when I got there; and if I didn't, I would come back.

The truth was, I knew I couldn't return to New York until I'd done something real. I'd turned down one of the most powerful officers in the bank. And if it wasn't the Chase executive, then it was my parents I didn't want to let down. I loved them for accepting my choice even if they didn't understand why I'd traded a job they were proud to describe to their friends for something in Africa I could barely articulate myself.

I began reading everything I could find on Africa and studied the microfinance organization's global offices. I discovered how little was actually happening on the ground, and it challenged me to think about how much I could do. In the meantime, I gave away nearly everything I owned, including the antique furniture my mother had given me. Of course, I kept my guitar and a boxful of poetry books, both of which I deemed essential for saving the world.

Though I was supposed to go to Côte d'Ivoire, my new boss informed me that I was to first fly to Nairobi to attend a women's conference, where I would meet a lot of African women in the network and get a better sense of the organization itself. I could imagine Kenya much more easily than Côte d'Ivoire, especially since the film *Out of Africa* had recently been released (I didn't have a clue about how little Kenyans cared for it at the time). Starting in Nairobi might be a gentler introduction to the continent.

I remember making my way through the streets of Nairobi for the first time, stunned by the gentle shower of purple jacaranda flowers floating around me in Uhuru Park. Nairobi looked much more modern than I'd imagined, with its tall buildings and wide streets. What struck me most was the feeling of the air around me, which seemed to swirl gently and kiss my knees as I walked. In only a few hours, I had fallen in love with this place, too.

I entered the Intercontinental Hotel where some of the most powerful women on the continent had gathered and were talking and dancing together. Mary, the first woman bank manager in Kenya, more than 6 feet tall with a regal but kind air, welcomed me. She told me to try and meet as many of the women in the room as I could, emphasizing that it was important that they accept me. A Ghanaian woman with a tiny face under a brightly colored turban danced beside her. She'd started in business by making a dozen jars of marmalade and was now one of the wealthiest industrialists on the continent, focused on improving women's situations. An enormous Senegalese woman wrapped in pale pink silk, wearing huge rings and radiating confidence, completed the picture. What a different world from the nearly all-male bastion of Wall Street!

I found the swirl of color and music and the confidence of the African women exhilarating, overwhelming, exciting, and unsettling. Compounding my anxiety and uncharacteristic shyness was the inescapable drabness of my Wall Street navy jacket and skirt in comparison with the gorgeous dresses worn by the women who filled the room with such flair that it looked like a butterfly convention. No one seemed able to distinguish me from the only other white woman in the room, a shorter, more fulsome Italian with black curly hair and Abyssinian eyes. I was taller and more slender, with longish brown hair and blue eyes. Still, everyone confused us, thinking we looked exactly alike—poetic justice.

I found myself standing against the wall like a timid girl at a high school dance. Finally I asked the requisite introductory question of a tall African woman standing next to me who looked as awkward as I felt:

"Where are you from?"

She just looked at me. I tried asking again, this time in French.

She answered, "Rwanda."

"Uganda?" I asked. "How exciting—what an amazing place!" I'd read all about Idi Amin and the revolutionary Yoweri Museveni, who had just taken over the country and was promising peace and prosperity, and about the country's reputation for poetry and a more open media.

"No," she repeated in a heavy African accent. "Rwanda."

"Oh, Luanda," I said, "the capital of Angola."

"No," she said patiently. "Not Angola. Rwanda."

I was stumped. Though I'd been studying "Africa" for months now, I knew little about most of the continent's 54 diverse countries.

"Oh, Rwanda, yes," I muttered as my brain went into overdrive sorting, sifting, trying to find the country somewhere in the disorganized flurry of names and places in my head. Finally, I remembered: *Rwanda, a thimble-size country at the center of the African map; one of the poorest countries in the world; known for its beautiful geography and mountain gorillas; tribal tensions flare periodically between the majority Hutus and minority Tutsis.* Whew.

I was a typical American: Give me a few facts about a country and I felt perfectly comfortable commenting on the place. I remembered that Rwanda was right next to Burundi, a country that had seen mass killings of educated Hutus by the ruling Tutsis in 1972. Since this didn't seem like a good conversation starter, I opted to skip it and simply asked her name, this time in French.

She looked at me again, always waiting before answering.

"Veronique," she said slowly, enunciating each syllable, perhaps now thinking I was hard of hearing or a little daft. Though she was probably not much more than 34 or 35, maybe a decade older than me at the time, somehow she reminded me of my grandmother, with her thick hands, broad shoulders, and feet settled in sensible shoes. She wore a brown and green cotton, African-print dress with billowing sleeves. Oversize, boxy plastic glasses accentuated her square face. Her hair stood on end, flopping this way and that in cadence with her exuberant speech. I liked her immediately.

My grandmother Stella once wore a housedress to the wedding of one of her sons because she'd forgotten her fancy dress back home in Pennsylvania. I could imagine Veronique doing the same sort of thing.

She waxed eloquently about her country. "It is called the Land of a Thousand Hills, and that is what it *is*." She paused to smile. "Hills grow on hills, and it is a very green place. You would like it there."

As it turned out, Veronique was a midlevel official in Rwanda's Ministry of Family and Social Affairs, one of the weaker ministries in the government, which focused on women's status, family planning, and other "soft issues," and thus was the one where women across Africa usually found themselves. She was attending the conference in order to explore what other countries were doing to bring women into the economic mainstream.

As was the case in a number of African countries at the time, Rwandan law prevented women from opening a bank account without their husbands' written permission, Veronique explained. The country was still governed by the Napoleonic Code, a colonial holdover written in 1804 that gave women the status of minors and the mentally impaired. The idea of women borrowing money on their own terms was simply out of the question. Only recently had Veronique and other leaders made any movement on the issue at all.

"We are changing the laws now," she assured me, "and need to be ready for this." She had the confidence of someone who knew she was making history.

We spoke for a long time about her hopes and dreams, and it was clear that Veronique was more activist than academic.

"You will see one day that our women are so strong! They do so much of the work and take care of the children, but they are kept too far down by the fact that they have so few rights. You know, we need to find a way to let them borrow money for their businesses, to send their daughters to school, to be able to dream of the things we know they can do. If Rwanda is to develop, then its women must have more opportunities, don't you think?"

I laughed and said, "Of course! The question is how to change the environment so that women can be seen by both men and women alike for what they can contribute."

"Yes," she said, "and you will help us."

"That would be wonderful," I responded. In truth, though her blend of ambition and earnestness appealed to me, I assumed we'd never follow up after this chance meeting. Little did I know that her country would come to play a leading role in shaping my life, my views on human nature, and my ideas for what it takes to solve the big problems of world poverty.

The rest of the conference was a nightmare. The African women made it clear in a public way that I was neither wanted nor needed as an ambassador in West Africa. A woman from Côte d'Ivoire was introduced as someone who could be of assistance to me once I'd moved to her country to set up the regional office, but she clearly had no interest in talking to me. She snapped, "We have women who can and should staff that office and help us build the West Africa region. I don't understand why anyone thinks we should have a young girl who is not even African!"

The public nature of the conversations was humiliating. I knew the women had a point about it being preferable to have an African in the office, though I understood that I was to be a liaison between Africa and America, and I also knew that after several years of trying, not a single West African office had been built. I'd been hired to jump-start the actual work, to make sure offices were put on the ground. I knew I would work hard and include whoever wanted to work with me. But I didn't know how to confront their fears head-on and instead tried being sweet and sounding smart, hoping the West African women would come to like me.

They didn't.

The morning after the conference ended, I was told that plans had changed and I'd now be staying in Nairobi for a few weeks. The ultimate plan was the same. I was still to go to the African Development Bank in Côte d'Ivoire, but the office wasn't ready—or at least the women weren't ready for my arrival.

Had I known what was really in their minds, I might have terminated my foray into Africa then and there. As it was, I had some time to fill.

Since I had no place to live in Nairobi and no map for the work I was going to do, I decided to go to Lamu for the weekend. I'd heard it was one of the most beautiful places on Earth.

Lamu, a tiny island just off the coast of Kenya, had been a stopping-off point for Arab traders over the centuries. I roamed the island's narrow streets under a bright blue sky, looking out at the ocean, exploring the trinkets and spices and woodwork in little shops owned by Arab traders whose wives floated like shadows, fully veiled in black. A woman's black chador opened to reveal a sheath of bright red silk underneath. Overhead, a parrot flew, as if to show that even bright red silk was no match for his beauty.

At night, I ate a plate of fresh barracuda and rice with a glass of lime juice, all for less than $2. My dollar-a-night room at the Hotel Salama was cramped, so I climbed the stairs to the roof, where I found a little bed among brightly colored bougainvillea. As I lay in the light of a full moon, listening to a group of young people a few rooftops over strumming guitars and singing Cat Stevens songs, I fell asleep thinking about what I might do to improve my situation.

I was awakened before dawn by the call to prayer, and in the cool of the morning, realized I had no choice but to do the only thing I knew how to do well—I would just work. And then work some more. And try to pay attention to whatever the work was teaching me.

Two experiences in particular changed the way I thought about the world in those first months in Africa. The first had to do with befriending a wonderful young woman named Marcelina—Maz for short—who was a junior office girl in the place I was working. She wore her short hair in little braids around her head. Her uniform was a blue skirt and a white blouse with a navy V-neck sweater over it. She lacked all pretentiousness, and her good nature hid whatever hardships she had at home.

We had little in common, but we found ourselves stealing time to talk each day. Maz loved coaching me in Swahili. She would point to an object around the office and ask me the word for it, always with the patience of Job.

I often talked to her about the work we were trying to do to strengthen women's economic opportunities and about the importance of women having their own bank accounts.

"I've never walked into a bank before," Marcelina told me shyly. "They don't want people like me in there, and I don't even have enough to start an account anyway."

I promised to give her the minimum balance of $50 if she agreed to save regularly. The next morning, we walked through the doors of one of Kenya's largest financial institutions, an old-fashioned bank with tellers behind barred windows. The Kenyan bank manager approached me with a welcoming look, but my attempts to move the conversation to Maz—who apparently had not entered his field of vision—failed completely. Though obviously fluent in Swahili, he refused to talk to her directly, speaking only to me.

When we finally opened the account, Marcelina told me she would cry tears of joy to fill the Indian Ocean. I began to see what it meant to put into practice the idea of extending basic services as simple as bank accounts that the middle class took for granted to people who are often invisible to those in power.

The other experience that affected my worldview came during a visit to Uganda. I had gone there to meet a wonderful woman named Cissy, one of the nation's first women bankers. Uganda's president, Museveni, had come into power after a brutal guerrilla war in January 1986, and the country was still in shambles. I tried to push down my nervousness about what I might find there by focusing instead on what I'd heard about its artistic community, its poets and intellectuals who were famous in East Africa.

As the plane flew into Entebbe Airport, I looked out the window at its green lushness, thinking of Winston Churchill's words that this was "the pearl of Africa." But minutes after landing, all I could see were guns in the hands of young boys, bombed-out buildings, streets filled with potholes and broken glass. I wondered how a nation could plunge so quickly from being a paragon of success to becoming a cauldron of despair. Twice young boys dressed in fatigues and carrying machine guns stopped Cissy and I for "routine checks," searching bags and looking through the trunk of Cissy's car.

Despite the destruction in Uganda, the people were divine. Cissy herself was elegant, focused, and determined to create an organization to help women lift themselves out of poverty. She spoke for nearly the entire hour it took to drive to her family's home, thanking me all the while for ignoring the international media's warnings about Uganda and coming to see her country anyway.

Cissy and her husband lived in a modest three-bedroom house with their two young daughters. When we arrived, the little girls were dressed in white frilly dresses that looked like little brides' gowns.

"Why are you so dressed up?" I asked them. The elder daughter, 8 years old, replied that the soldiers had taken all of their dresses in the war; now they wore their very best dresses for every day because you never knew when you might lose them.

The girls did their homework at the kitchen table, one of the few pieces of furniture in the living room. It was really more of a card table, but as Cissy said, it would do. Twice already, the soldiers had ransacked their home and taken everything. There were still bullet holes in the broken bedroom doors, and every window had been smashed. Not a single picture hung on a wall. The plumbing didn't work, but there was a well outside where we could get water and take a cold bath with a bucket. As Cissy explained everything to me, she smiled with no hint of apology: This was simply part of her everyday reality.

We set the table with a hodgepodge of plastic plates and cups that Cissy had purchased at a gas station in Kenya.

"I'm not ready to invest in anything permanent yet," she told me, pausing before adding, "but nothing really is permanent, is it?"

Dinner was simple but abundant: *matoke,* a green plantain staple; millet; a bit of fish; bitter eggplant; and fruit.

"The most we can offer you is our food and hospitality," Cissy told me. "But nothing else has much value, anyway," she laughed. "Especially not here, especially not now."

There wasn't a speck of despair in her voice.

Everyone in the family ate several plates of food. Cissy urged me to eat more, reminding me that you never know when you might eat again.

That night, I slept with my passport under my pillow, hearing gunshots in the night and anticipating the arrival of soldiers, though I knew it was unlikely. In the morning, I took a bucket bath, wrapped in a brightly colored cotton wrap called a *kikoi*, sitting on my haunches and squealing as the freezing water cascaded down my back. I ironed my blue silk dress with an old-fashioned iron filled with hot coals, watching my hand tremble with the weight, knowing that letting the iron get too close to the fabric would result in disaster. I couldn't recall ever feeling so fully alive getting ready for a day except during those first weeks in Brazil. There was a rawness and a beauty here that brought every emotion right to the surface, and I loved the feeling, loved being in this place where the best and worst of everything seemed to coexist.

After a quick breakfast, we met with exuberant, optimistic women who were clear about contributing to peace and helping to build individual and community prosperity in this country so abundant in natural resources and in human spirit. Mostly I just listened to them as they told me the things they dreamed of doing. We also visited some of the women's newly sprung projects—poultry raising, a new kiosk for selling sundries, a tailoring business. Ugandans were putting their lives back together piece by piece, and clearly there was potential to support them in their efforts.

The trip to Uganda renewed and strengthened my sense of urgency. I wanted to feel useful. I was stunned by the resilience of everyone I met and returned to Nairobi awestruck by the Ugandans' ability to endure suffering and still embrace great joy. That first night back, I slept like a baby, acknowledging the privilege of a secure night of sleep, wanting to live in a world where basic security would not be considered a luxury, remembering again why I loved working in the developing world—if only I could find the right place for me.

I couldn't stay any longer in Kenya looking for things to do. I asked again if it might be time to test the waters of Côte d'Ivoire. Despite my anxiety about what might await me there, I knew it was time to go—and to go with enthusiasm. The regional director agreed, and I started packing, dreaming of all I would do to help women help themselves, not thinking for a minute of all the things that were soon to throw water—as cold as that in the bucket at Cissy's house—on my dreams.

CHAPTER 2

A BIRD ON THE OUTSIDE, A TIGER WITHIN

*"You gain strength, courage, and confidence by every experience
in which you really stop to look fear in the face.
You must do the thing which you think you cannot do."*

—ELEANOR ROOSEVELT

I arrived at the Abidjan Airport on a hot and sticky afternoon, and the sweet-sour smell of sweat permeated the thick air. My stomach was aflutter, though I also arrived confident I'd be accepted once the women there understood my serious intent and how hard I could work. But I was rattled even before I passed through customs. At a white wooden desk, everyone entering the country was instructed to drop his or her passport into a glass-encased box; then we waited while a man in a uniform gathered all the little booklets and took them somewhere out of sight. No one around me seemed to know what was happening, but within minutes, the man in the uniform reappeared and began returning the passports as if this were normal procedure.

All around me people were shouting and running, though it wasn't clear where anyone was going. Four men in brown uniforms approached me near the baggage belt and grabbed my boxes and suitcases. I found myself in a push-pull match and finally shouted to them, "Please stop!" One of the men laughed loudly as the others joined in, and I focused on holding back tears.

At customs, two men knifed open my boxes, making a mess of everything inside. By now I was soaked with sweat, though I tried to compose myself, knowing that the women who had rejected me at the conference in Nairobi were waiting for me on the other side of the door.

As I pushed my cart full of now-mangled boxes out of the terminal, I spotted the three women standing side by side, like extravagant mannequins, in long dresses of African print, with turbans on their heads and heavy jewelry around their necks and arms—a picture of beauty and composure in the midst of anarchy. I recognized a woman I'd met in Nairobi—let me call her Aisha—who had barely had time for me at the conference once she'd learned I'd inhabit the prized office at the African Development Bank (ADB). As I look back, I can only imagine what had been going through her head when I first approached her, shivering with excitement to "help" her country through my privileged job, when all I seemed to offer was unbridled, naive enthusiasm.

At the time, I didn't think the ADB office was a big deal. I'd told myself that I'd turned down a much bigger opportunity at Chase. What I didn't understand was how important the office was to the West African women. Given that the ADB was making a bet on women in Africa, no doubt it would have made sense to have an African lead the office, especially from the perspective of these women. At the same time, it was an office given to an international nongovernmental organization (NGO) that wanted to prove something to itself and the world by getting something done quickly. Regardless of why I'd been sent, the African women still weren't happy.

"Welcome to Côte d'Ivoire," a tight-lipped Aisha said in French before introducing me to her colleagues, a tall woman from Mali with wire-frame glasses and a shorter, more exotic-looking Senegalese woman with extravagantly braided hair and outrageous jewelry. "How was your trip?" she asked.

"Fine, fine, thank you" was all that came out of my mouth. Though excited to be there, I was also filled with a deep sense of ambivalence. I wanted to please, to show them how much I could contribute. But I still had no language for sharing my concerns or my aspirations, or any idea how to start a conversation about what they needed and wanted and what I hoped to do. The experience at the conference had weakened my confidence, both in speaking French and in speaking directly. I'd been asked some of the same questions before about why I was there, and I had no better answers now. When I wasn't quiet, mostly I mumbled.

We walked together to the parking lot, where we met an airport van. I thanked them for coming to welcome me. It meant so much, I said.

They shook their heads politely as we climbed into the van headed for the Hilton. As soon as we got into the vehicle, the women stopped speaking directly to me and began a conversation among themselves in rapid-fire French. I couldn't keep up with their words and heard only fragments, which made me feel even more the outsider:

"She is so young . . . too young. . . ."

"Not married?"

"She doesn't know Africa." "Where is her French?"

"She needs better French to work here in West Africa."

"Tell me why, again, *you* have the position with the African Development Bank. That is an important place, a visible place. . . . It requires someone very serious, not an American. . . . "

"Little girl . . . "

The women's sharp voices pecked at my heart. This wasn't going to be easy.

After we arrived at the Hilton Hotel and had a coffee outside by the pool, the women left. I retreated to my hotel room, where I planned to live until I found a permanent home, having no idea then that I'd be departing again in less than 2 months. That first night, I fell into bed in a pool of tears.

The next morning, I ran through the city's wide streets lined with tall palm trees, filled with a familiar sense of awe from my wanderings. Women were selling baguettes and African stews by the roadside in front of the imposing St. Paul's Cathedral that towered over the city, its white, modern architecture enormous and soaring. I stopped to look in wonder, but realized I felt more of God's presence in the eyes of the women sitting outside on the street than in the concrete edifice.

Later, I would visit the president's home village of Yamassoukro, where the avenues are as wide as the Champs-Elysées. Around the grand presidential palace was a moat apparently filled with crocodiles fed live chickens each day at 4:00 p.m. The palace's opulence stood in stark contrast to the desperate conditions of so many living within its environs, nearly always in mud huts without electricity. Côte d'Ivoire became a place where just walking down the street filled me with questions about justice and compassion, power and money, and the randomness of where we are born and how much that determines who we become.

In those first weeks, I worked from dawn to midnight every day, organizing a conference for women from 52 African countries that would be translated into four languages. Mr. A, my spineless contact at the ADB, who seemed to have a crush on the sensual Aisha, was always blaming me for anything that went wrong. When the minister from Zaire checked herself into the presidential suite at a cost of more than $400 a night, he called me and began yelling that I better do something about it. When I knocked on the minister's hotel room door, she refused to open it, citing security concerns, adding that she was a minister and so needed a proper room. Because I had no real authority, I turned around and crept down the hall to the elevator, feeling I couldn't do anything right.

Meanwhile, Aisha insisted that I not send any correspondence without her approval. "You don't know Africa," she kept saying. Of course, she was right: I hadn't a clue how Africa worked, but knew enough already to see how different Côte d'Ivoire and Kenya were. I was too intimidated to do anything but keep my head low and hope she would finally appreciate my work. Before long, Aisha moved herself into the office; suddenly we were sharing it. She never introduced me to a soul and tried often to separate us, insisting that I make copies of a research report only when other officials from the bank were there so that she could demonstrate who the real boss was while I played the part of her secretary.

I'd never met anyone so sure of herself. She seemed to do everything deliberately, even the way she crossed her legs and held her hands, the way she swung her body when she walked, as if knowing everyone was looking at her. I hungered to step out more fully in some way, just as she seemed able to do.

One day out of the blue, Aisha invited me to her home for dinner. Quickly I accepted, hoping we could find a way to talk—to start getting some real work done. Maybe we could even take a step toward friendship, since we would be working with one another for the foreseeable future.

In her white Peugeot, we drove through streets lined with contemporary buildings and endless palm trees. Her home was modern and refined without being ostentatious, decorated entirely in white with neutral accents and wooden African carvings. As we sat down to dinner—fish for me and a plate of pineapple for her—she said, "I am on a diet, though I'm not unhappy with the way I look, not like you skinny American girls."

I just smiled and sipped my wine, glad for something soothing.

After dinner, she suggested we take a tour of her home, after which we'd watch a movie. "Come, follow me," she said.

She guided me through the kitchen and past her designer bathroom, stopping in the bedroom, where she announced she wanted to change into something lighter because the heat of the day had been so intense.

When I offered to return to the living room, she responded. "No, no, just take a seat on the bed. I'll be out in a minute."

With that, she sashayed into her walk-in closet, where she'd just shown me an enormous photograph of herself that was surrounded by dozens of beautiful, colorful beaded necklaces hanging on the wall. I sat at the edge of her big bed on the white satin coverlet, hands folded in my lap, fully conscious of my wire-rimmed glasses, pressed linen suit, and swept-up hair, a perfect librarian of sorts.

A few minutes later, Aisha returned wearing nothing but a white bra and panties, arms stretching as she yawned like a cat, telling me that in fact it was too hot to put *anything* on just yet. She turned on the television and an old French film blared from the screen, more fuzz than picture. Aisha lay on the bed and began to question me as she gently caressed her enormous breasts: "Tell me, why did you come to Côte d'Ivoire in the first place? What was in your heart?"

I stammered that I wanted to do something good for the world, wanted to be of use. What I really wanted to do was flee, but out of politeness or numbness, I answered her questions as best I could, inserting a comment about how much work I really had to do.

As much as I wanted to see the film, I told her, I really had to get back to the hotel.

"Ah," she said, "you really are a boring girl. Time to go home so that you can work some more." Laughing in a pitying way, she stood up, pulled on a short satin robe, and walked me to the door.

After thanking her, I joined the driver, who returned me to the hotel. As I watched the city pass by, my head spun with a whirling stream of words and visions from the short evening I'd just experienced. I wondered whether Aisha had been seducing me, testing me, or just seeing how far she could push me to the edge. Maybe it was a bit of all three. I thought of the poster-size photograph in her closet: I was clearly out of my league. I'd imagined myself in Africa sitting on the ground with women in a rural village, talking about their hopes and dreams, not sitting on satin sheets trying to justify to a nearly naked woman why I'd come to Africa in the first place.

The next morning at the Bank, I arrived to discover that Aisha had changed the lock to the office. My own key was useless, but one of the guards knew me and let me in. I confronted Aisha about the new lock, and she answered coldly that she feared someone might have been tampering with our things. I never did get another key.

A Nigerian woman named Mrs. Okoro who worked at the ADB befriended me in the hall that same day. Having seen me at the conference in Nairobi, she wondered what I was doing here. She invited me to lunch, and though I'd only just met her, I spilled out much of what was going wrong without mentioning the prior evening.

She smiled knowingly, saying that this wasn't totally unusual behavior: "Those women understand that power in Africa is as important as money, maybe *more* important. They want that office because they want power, and *you* are standing in the way." She warned me to avoid drinking or eating in front of the women.

"You know, they're talking of poisoning you, not to kill you, but to scare you, and let me tell you that they are serious."

A friend in Nairobi had once told me how she ate food only at the homes of family members or the closest friends. "When you're successful, not everyone wishes you well," she had explained, though at the time, this concept was so foreign to me that I hardly believed it. Now here was another woman I barely knew telling me to watch what I ate, especially in front of people who didn't like me.

"You might tell them that it is your family practice to share food together if they want to give you something that they are not eating, too."

The Nigerian woman also advised me not to dismiss voodoo in West Africa, but to heed the warning it brought.

When I laughed, she grabbed my hand and looked at me with a steely gaze. "Trust me," she said. "You don't want to be cursed here in Côte d'Ivoire."

"I promise I don't like the idea of being cursed by *anyone*," I responded.

"Listen to me," she said, more gravely now, looking me squarely in the eyes. "If in the middle of the night you wake up feeling the cold hands of voodoo spirits clasping your neck, you must promise me that you will pray to Jesus Christ."

She paused to look at me and then asked, "Do you believe in Jesus?"

I just looked at her, not believing what I was hearing.

She rushed on, not waiting for an answer: "Do you have a crucifix in your hotel room?"

I shook my head no. "There is a Bible and a Koran in the hotel drawer."

"Then you must pray very hard, but it must be to Jesus, and He will fight the spirits for He is more powerful than voodoo."

I thanked her for her advice, not knowing if I should laugh or run away. I had never felt so lonely. At 25 years old, I was thousands of miles from home in a place with no close friends. I tried to convince myself that I was as strong as ever, but a noise in the night would cause me to jump out of bed in a cold sweat. I hadn't expected to encounter poisoning and voodoo among women bankers in Africa. Having no skills on which to draw, I simply pretended that everything was normal and tried not to recognize that there might be shadows dancing around me.

About 2 weeks after Mrs. Okoro's warnings, I attended a reception with all of the women and began feeling ill an hour or so afterward. Sharp pains seared my stomach, and by the time I stumbled to the hotel, I had begun projectile vomiting accompanied by a raging fever and the runs. For 3 days, I lay on the bathroom floor, shivering and nauseous as I wept, feeling miserable and sorry for myself. My mind would bounce from half-believing terrifying visions of imagined voodoo gods to brushing off any idea of witchcraft or poisoning as gossip and threats meant to scare silly girls. Regardless of the cause, I couldn't take a sip of water without the vomiting starting all over again.

The person I most wanted near me—my mother—was the last person I could call. I knew she could do nothing to help and that hearing my voice would just cause her to worry. My fever refused to break. I was too afraid to let anyone local know what was happening. The sheer sense of despair kept the same question spinning over and over in my aching head: *I left a promising banking career for this?*

By the end of the week, I'd recovered physically, though my face was gaunt and pale and my clothes hung on my body, making me look more waif than woman. Thoroughly exhausted, I felt like a failure. I wanted to be myself again, wanted to wake up in the morning excited about the day and to walk down the street feeling strong in my body.

First thing the next day, I called the three African women who had greeted me at the airport and asked them to meet in my office. We chose a time before noon, and I spent the morning thinking and rehearsing what I would say to them. As I walked to the African Development Bank, I waved at the popcorn vendor and the shoeshine man whom I passed daily, and they both greeted me with big smiles. When I'd first arrived, I'd thought I'd have more time with people like them. I'd wanted to know who low-income people were so I could be of greater service, but I had spent most of my time in big institutions with people who chattered and hobnobbed at conferences and did very little listening. It was time for me to go.

The women walked into the office dressed even more elaborately than usual in their long multichromatic robes crowned with towering turbans. They seemed to span half the wall as I stood alone in front of them, all skin and bones, a woman disappearing, arms crossed protectively over my chest. I wore a blue cotton skirt and a short-sleeved white blouse and looked more schoolgirl than banker. I told them I was leaving, fumbling through half words in a tinny voice: "What I don't understand is why you've been treating me so horribly—worse than I would treat a dog."

"We don't hate you," Aisha responded. "We actually like that you're a nice girl with much to offer. What we hate is what you represent. The North comes to the South and sends a young white woman without asking us what *we* want, without seeing if we already *have* the skills we need. And this from an organization that says it wants to promote solidarity. We've seen this too many times before. Africa will never change if it's always like this."

I agreed that the organization should have negotiated with the African women first in order to be effective. At the same time, I insisted, there was no excuse for the way I'd been treated in Abidjan. I'd come with the best of intentions and was ready to listen and to work hard. None of the women had explained their positions to me. They seemed to see the world as an unbridgeable divide between North and South, and we had never broken the logjam.

As I spoke, I could feel something shifting inside me. An African friend once told me that to be successful on her continent, I should learn to be a bird on the outside and a tiger within. Finally, I could feel the stirrings of the cat. I was leaving behind the little girl who wanted to please, recognizing that if I were to be effective, I would have to stand on my own two feet and be myself. I was finished with being pushed around just for being young, white, and American, just as these women, so regal and dressed in glorious colors that only a blind person could miss, were sick of being invisible because they were black Africans. I had left a banking career to come here and be useful, and if I couldn't contribute, then I would leave.

I finally understood: In order to contribute to Africa, I would have to know myself better and be clearer about my goals. I would have to be ready to take Africa on its own terms, not mine, and to learn my limits and present myself not as a do-gooder with a big heart, but as someone with something to give *and* gain by being there. Compassion wasn't enough.

I think that was the moment when humility in its truest form—rather than an easy but false humbleness—began to creep in. Until then, I'd been too vested in knowing the answers and in being right. For the first time in my life, being right had nothing to do with being successful or effective. I also began to be more honest about what was happening around me—I couldn't stand all talk without action, and too many expatriates and elite Africans seemed to revel in it. I wanted to work directly with poor women themselves.

I wasn't ready to return to New York. I felt unable to face my boss at Chase and tell him I'd failed unequivocally, and yet the thought of staying another night in Abidjan was out of the question—at least if I could help it. I knew I would return to Africa but not to Côte d'Ivoire, at least not anytime soon.

MY FAMILY WAS LIVING in Germany, where my father worked with the army. I'd already planned to go home for Christmas anyway to see them and my boyfriend, but I would need to find the extra money to fly a little earlier. With less than $1,000 to my name, I spent another $400 on a ticket at the youth rate and caught the evening flight to Paris, taking my suitcases and leaving everything else I owned in boxes at the Hilton.

In Paris, I awoke to 2 feet of snow. The airlines had gone on strike and the only viable means of transport to my family in Heidelberg was via train. Still dressed in my cotton skirt and short-sleeved blouse, I headed off with only a lightweight sweater in my suitcase and was reminded of the many immigrants who had come ill prepared to new lands. Upon leaving Abidjan, I had just been too numb to consider anything but getting on the plane, as exhausted as I'd ever been.

At my family's home in Heidelberg, I tried softening the story for my parents, who had feared my move to Africa in the first place. But I couldn't hide the jaundiced skin hanging on my now much thinner frame. My mother suggested, or rather insisted, that I stay a few weeks in Germany, then return to New York to a career where I could prosper. We got into one of the only major arguments of our lives.

I reminded her that she and my father had encouraged their children to fly as high as we could, and this was my way of doing it. She responded that she feared losing me, had seen evidence to corroborate her concern, and knew how little communication would be possible once I went back.

"I hear that," I said, "but at the same time, you and I both know I won't be able to face myself if I don't go back to Africa and do something positive. So far, I've done nothing but fail there."

"But what will you do now?" she asked. "Everything was vague the first time you decided to go," she said. "What is different about this time? Will you have a real job description?"

I told her I'd figure it out once I returned to Kenya, where the organization's East Africa office was located. I liked the director, and it would be an easier way to find something for which I might be of use either there in Kenya or in a neighboring country. I had a long call with the president of the global organization in New York City and the regional director in Nairobi and asked if I could return to work in Kenya, at least for a limited amount of time. But this time I had two conditions: I wanted to work on tangible projects with concrete outcomes, and I would only work with women's groups who invited me to assist them.

Happily (at least for me), I found a position that fit exactly that description. To their credit, once the decision was made, my parents were only supportive. At the airport, my father told me he was proud of what I was trying to do, and my mother nodded, hugging me tightly and reminding me to be careful. "You are no good to anyone if you get really sick or, God forbid, something worse happens to you."

I always wished my parents would visit East Africa so they could see the work for themselves. I knew that if they went, they'd realize how little there was to fear and how much there was to love. But with four kids still living at home, long trips to Africa were out of the question for them. I promised to call at least once a month and write more frequently.

Because of my student ticket, I had to fly back to Côte d'Ivoire for a day and then return to Kenya via Nigeria. Since I couldn't afford to pay the extra fee to bring my boxes on the flight, I left them at the Hilton.

After landing safely in Nairobi, I was ready to go—again.

When I showed up to work at the familiar office, Marcelina ran to hug me. "Jambo, Jacqueleeen," she called. "You have come back to Maz. We will do all sort of good things now."

Seeing just one familiar, radiant face was enough to make me feel I'd come home. The organization's regional director helped me reach out to women's groups in East Africa, and in my first month back, in early 1987, I was asked to do my first piece of real work.

A fledgling women's microfinance organization was hoping to turn a corner in its professional development. After lending to women in Nairobi in both the slums and the city center, the organization's director wanted to know the status of the loan portfolio and how it might strengthen operations. The executive director and I met in her office on the second floor of a nondescript building in Nairobi. She told me she felt proud of what the organization had accomplished and also worried that its systems needed strengthening. I suggested we begin by doing a baseline study of where the organization stood, a sort of diagnostic of both strengths and weaknesses so that it had a chance of real growth in the future. We agreed I'd start working on analyzing the loan portfolio the next day.

I closed the door as I walked into the dingy hall outside the office and let out a little cheer. I had been asked to do something constructive and necessary. I was on my way.

With a pencil, a calculator, and a big green ledger, I examined every loan the organization had ever made and scrutinized every number. Long into the nights, I worked to unravel which borrowers were making payments, which were behind, which loans should have been written off. The process could not have been more tedious, but I worked feverishly with a renewed sense of purpose.

After hundreds of hours of work, I was finally finished. With a deep sense of accomplishment, I made the last entry. I had reorganized and restructured the microfinance bank's entire management information system by hand after piecing together fragments from different books and accounts. The books I received were in such deplorable condition that any half-decent accounting firm auditing it would have recommended shutting down the operation, but I was hoping to give the group a new start.

After scheduling a meeting with the director, I walked into her office with an air of professionalism and optimism.

I started with the positive: "Your organization is incredibly important to women in Kenya, already reaching hundreds in the slums. This is an exciting time for development and for women, and I'm proud to be working with you."

She smiled. I took a deep breath.

I told her that I'd balanced all of the financial records and completed an accounting of every loan. Then I presented her with a system in great order that would allow for stronger management over time.

She was still smiling.

"At the same time," I continued, "this diagnostic, if you will, revealed some problems to be addressed. Over 60 percent of the portfolio is in serious arrears. I'd suggest you write off 20 percent completely, put 20 percent on a watch list, and expend a lot of effort on the healthiest 20 percent of your problem loans. Of this group, the majority of borrowers are related to your board members in some way, so this is a problem you'll need to address, as well. The good news is that the organization is young and can do something now to stem the problems and turn operations around to become a great organization." I smiled weakly, trying to look positive and upbeat.

Her smile morphed into a straight line. I felt my heart rate pick up and I continued, this time at a quicker pace. "Don't worry," I said. "I have a plan for sorting this out. The first step in solving any problem is to identify and name it."

She looked at me and stared. Now it was her turn to take a deep breath.

After a long, palpable silence, she thanked me for being so helpful and diligent. She needed to reflect on the findings, she said. She wanted to study the report.

"Then we'll have a conversation about what to do," she added. "Why don't we plan to meet with everyone next week?" One of her colleagues walked into the room and she spoke to her for a long time in Swahili, her face guarded and stern. I knew I had done something wrong again.

Somehow, I'd returned to the same bad dream, playing the same role in a different scene.

I waited for a week with no word. Nervously, I met with the director and asked whether she'd had time to think about my report.

"I've been meaning to talk to you," she muttered, not looking at my face. "Your very good report has been lost. We can't find it anywhere. I'm so sorry after all that work you did."

In that precomputer age, I had written everything by hand except for my typed summary, which was worthless without the backup data. It had all been destroyed.

My heart dropped and I fought to hold back the tears, gripping my chair with both hands as I listened to her. "We can start over," she said in a calm voice, "but we think you will help more doing other things. Why don't we wait another week, see if we find it, and revisit our next project?"

I didn't say a word, couldn't really, at least not without betraying how much it hurt. That night as I lay in bed, I wondered why the executive director hadn't just told me I wasn't needed. I ached down to my bones.

"Maybe they didn't really want to change," I thought to myself.

Or maybe I'd been too direct, too bright and sunny for my own good. Maybe the executive director was sick of smart foreigners who thought they had all the answers. The fact remained that the organization's operations were disastrous. But again, my ability to solve the problem did little to help if the women themselves didn't want to implement a solution.

The next morning I awoke to the sounds of a Kenyan dawn. The noise was so extraordinary that I laughed aloud, thinking it was easier for me to sleep through the sounds of the New York City streets than the waking of life in this country, where birds call loudly to one another, monkeys fly from tree to tree, insects buzz amid the dewy grasses, and flowers blow perfumed kisses to the bees. The cacophony told of a wild party of seduction and courtship, of lovemaking and nourishment—a feast for the senses. The sheer beauty and sensuality of Kenya dampened the hurt of a second failure, at least for this morning.

By midday, numbness was setting in again: I felt helpless, unable to make things work. I thought I'd learned humility and this time had really felt I was bringing my skill set to the table in a way that could be useful. But the director of the organization had rejected all that I'd done. I had been unable to communicate my honest desire to help fix a broken system without judgment; or maybe the Kenyan director herself just hadn't wanted to see what needed mending. In that way, she wasn't very different from complacent bankers I'd encountered elsewhere.

I wanted to help, but that didn't matter to anyone but me. Finally, I began to see that I should have been clearer about having a mandate first and gotten real buy-in, not just a perfunctory agreement, and then brought the right people along throughout the process so there were no surprises. The question was one of leadership, of having the patience and skills to bring people with me—and I had yet to learn that fully.

I also began to reflect on how to build accountability into nonprofit organizations. Donors could convince themselves to give to nonperforming organizations based on hearing a few good stories. The world needed something better than that.

I never worked with the organization again, but about a year later, I heard through the grapevine that the microfinance institution was in serious financial trouble. A year after that, a group of Kenyan women, including several of the board members, came to its rescue, working closely with foundations, restructuring the board, and putting the organization back on its feet—through the power of local ownership.

Twenty years later, I met with one of those women, who told me the organization now serves more than 100,000 women across Kenya and is one of the most highly regarded institutions for the poor in the country. Back in 1987, I couldn't help but feel devastated. Now I understand that it can take years for a new kind of organization to get on its feet and a few years after that for it to walk. The key is to find local leaders who own the dream and will make it happen.

ABOUT A MONTH LATER after I'd done the project with the Kenyan organization, Veronique, the woman I had met at the conference for women and credit, walked into my office in Nairobi. She hadn't called in advance, but had simply shown up.

"I am in Nairobi for meetings and hoped you would be here," she said. "In Rwanda, we have been talking about you and hoping you might help us to study whether it makes sense to start a credit program for women and how we could move forward if we decided to do so."

I didn't hesitate. Though I wasn't exactly sure what she wanted me to do, the invitation was clear. Already, our interaction felt different, unclouded and concrete. I felt a surge of gratitude and a chance to prove myself. I told her I'd be there that same month.

She promised to send me the terms by which I could be hired. When I asked how long I would need to stay, she looked at me, drew a breath, and said, "Three weeks."

It sounded like heaven.

For the next week, I could barely sleep, but I managed to read a bit about Rwanda, pack a small bag, and get myself to the airport. I knew I would not be returning to Nairobi for a while, though I kept my apartment there. I was determined to stay in Rwanda until I had made something happen.

CHAPTER 3

CONTEXT MATTERS

"Hope is a path on the mountainside. At first there is no path.
But then there are people passing that way. And there is a path."

—LU XUN

The 2-hour flight from Nairobi to Kigali begins over the wide-open expanse of the Kenyan savanna and ends among the mountains of Rwanda. I stared out of the plane's window, enraptured by Africa's shifting landscape, repeating the capital city's simple, lyrical, and lovely name to myself: Kigali, Ki-ga-li. It rolled off my tongue like the hills that surround it. Kigali—it could be a woman's name. I liked the sound of it.

We flew through a full blue-gray sky hovering over a tremendous charcoal river that coiled through undulating hills like a giant cobra in the grass. The view was breathtaking. Every inch of land was cultivated in neat squares of banana, sorghum, maize, coffee, and tea patched together by red dirt roads, like an enormous quilt in shades of green draped over the land.

We landed at Kigali's sleepy airport, which had one main terminal shaped like a square crown of pale yellow pillars bent and reaching outward, topped with a flat burnt-sienna roof. Scores of people stood on the observation deck, waving eagerly at the arriving passengers. In fact, the plane had so few people on it that I'm sure there were more waiting than coming. I looked up to see who might be standing there, though I knew I wouldn't recognize a soul.

With so few of us disembarking, it took only about 5 minutes to reach the baggage belt, where a tall driver named Boniface in a blue United Nations (UN) uniform was waiting to take me to the UNICEF office. He was dark-skinned, with a broad nose and a wide, pockmarked, happy face that was at once boyish and manly. He spoke French with a heavy, lilting, singsong African accent that lifted the end of nearly every phrase.

"What do you know about Rwanda?" he asked. Before I could answer, he jumped in: "You should try to visit the mountain gorillas, the national park, and the beautiful lake region."

"What about work?" I smiled.

"Oh, yes, you can work, too," he answered.

I laughed. "This could be a very good life—work during the weeks and explore the country on weekends!"

"*Mais, bien sûr,*" he said with a wide grin. "Rwandans don't go to those places because they are so expensive. But I can take you, a foreigner."

On the 15-minute drive to town in the white, UN-issued four-wheel-drive vehicle with the familiar pale blue UNICEF logo on the side, I saw flowers blooming everywhere, and the main road was smooth and clean, though I could see red dirt streets and paths running across the hillsides of the city like the loose weaving of a child's pot holder. Square little houses in Candy Land colors—bright pinks and blues and yellows—sat back from the roads, each with its own little garden. Billboards for condoms and soap, for car repair and face bleaching creams stood alongside the road, advertising goods the poor could spend money on to become whiter and more Western. And this was a country *without* television. In 1987, the consumer culture hadn't even begun to penetrate it.

We dipped into an industrial area filled with trucks and cement factories and then climbed a hill toward town, where the world turned suddenly, shockingly greener. Bright red flame trees, purple jacaranda, yellow angels' trumpets exploded in a profusion of colors. The sweet smell of frangipani wafted through the air, and the hips of women with baskets and bananas on their heads swayed to and fro. The streets were lush and redolent with flora and birds swooping through green canopies: a pocket of paradise.

Once we got into central Kigali, we drove up the long hill past an imposing church to the main roundabout, where the post office stood next to three small banks, all native to Rwanda. I was struck immediately by how clean and organized the city was. A big, yellow hospital, the parliament building, and an entire row of international aid organizations—the United States Agency for International Development, the United Nations Development Program, the World Bank—lined the main avenue. Kigali stood apart from other African capitals in its quaintness. With a population of just about a quarter million then, it lacked the grandeur and ostentation of Abidjan, the urban intensity of Nairobi, and the feeling of destruction in bombed-out Kampala.

On the side roads were embassies hidden behind brick walls and metal gates, including those of Germany, Belgium, France, Russia, China, the United States. You could discern the colonial history of this country in the names of the nations represented. Though Rwanda has no substantial natural resources or port access, it is a helicopter flight away from the Democratic Republic of the Congo (then Zaire), one of the world's most resource-rich countries, with reserves of plutonium and uranium. In the chess game of the cold war, Rwanda had thus occupied a privileged position with superpowers that wouldn't otherwise have noticed its existence.

We drove up a dirt road to the UNICEF office, a white, two-story building with arched rooftops behind a metal gate. Next door, a schoolyard filled the air with noises from uniformed schoolchildren, the girls in bright blue skirts and the boys in khaki shorts and short-sleeved shirts. A shirtless boy by the roadside in ragged shorts herded a half dozen longhorn cattle. We were driving behind a white Mercedes, the first of many we saw on the roads, standard issue for government officials and distinguished diplomats. For most people, walking seemed to be the primary mode of transportation. The roadsides were packed with women carrying their wares on their heads, schoolgirls holding hands, men walking arm in arm. I liked the sleepy, easy feeling of the place.

On my first afternoon in the office, Boniface explained the UNICEF system for employees: "Everyone without a car—in other words, most Rwandans—is picked up by UNICEF's vans in order to arrive at work before the starting time of 7:30 a.m. There is a 2-hour break for lunch, when everyone is transported to and from their neighborhoods to eat at home, and then the vans drive everyone a fourth time at the end of the day—back to their neighborhoods once work ends at half past five."

It seemed like a lot of driving, but I had already observed that there were few restaurants and no fast-food shops. Public transportation didn't serve certain areas, and all but the very elite lacked private vehicles. Getting workers back and forth was therefore an essential priority.

Boniface walked me upstairs to meet the director of UNICEF's Rwanda office, Bilge Ogun Bassani, a powerful, elegantly dressed Turkish woman with a dazzling smile and a solid handshake. We discussed the job I was there to undertake: determining whether a credit system for women was feasible and, if so, helping to design a financial institution for women. UNI-CEF would pick up most costs and provide me with an office and drivers.

Bilge was a trailblazer in that she understood that the power of an institution like UNICEF could provide legitimacy to a new effort while also giving me as a "consultant" all the flexibility I needed to be entre-preneurial.

"I want to do something for the women here," she said. "Women are too often neglected, and yet it is through them that we can best reach the children." She also understood women's need to earn income if they are to make more and better decisions. I liked her.

Bilge directed me downstairs to my new desk, and though I was again in a new place, for the first time in Africa, I began believing that somehow—maybe—I'd finally found a home.

After introducing myself to the colorful, quirky, international staff in the office, I called Veronique, the woman who had invited me to Rwanda in the first place. After a quick hello and how do you do, she breathlessly began listing people I should meet for my study. My French had improved, but still I understood only about half of what she was saying. The difference this time was that instead of feeling intimidated, I felt a yearning to be better, and an ease in asking for clarification when I needed it. We were off to a good beginning.

I've always started new undertakings with a delicious sense of excite-ment. The terms of my contract were simply to determine whether some kind of financial institution for women was needed and feasible. To me, the question seemed superfluous. This was a country where women comprised half the population, yet had no access to banking facilities. Of course a financial institution focused on poor women was needed. The real question was what it would take to make the institution real. My plan was to talk to as many people as I could, learn as much as possible, and then just start building. The work would teach us what was feasible and what was not. Of course, I didn't tell anyone this was my ultimate plan; it didn't make any sense to get everyone's hopes up and not follow through with action.

First step: endless phone calls and meetings. Veronique recommended key people to meet in the economic sector as well as the country's only three women parliamentarians, Prudence, Constance, and Agnes, whose last names I couldn't pronounce.

As I sat at my desk dialing the phone and speaking my still-middling French to assistants all over Kigali, one of UNICEF's expatriates invited me to a dinner that evening at the home of a French couple in town. In Kigali's tiny expatriate community, newcomers were always welcome for a change of pace. I accepted gladly in a spirit of having another adventure.

Given the humble character of Kigali itself as well as the simple exteriors of its houses, I was surprised by the mix of luxury and sophistication I saw at the dinner party. The walls and floors of the impeccably decorated house were covered with Persian rugs and African tapestries. One woman wore a blue taffeta skirt; and all came dressed as if they were dining at an upscale restaurant. The hostess served French food and wine while the dinner guests, mostly Europeans, debated global politics and complained about Ronald Reagan, America, and everything Rwandan.

Intrigued by the women in evening attire, I asked the colleague who'd invited me to the party who they were.

"Most are married to aid workers or UN civil servants," she told me. "Even those who want to work often can't get visas. Though some do significant work as volunteers, other women languish at the country club, wishing they were anywhere but here."

She added mischievously, "And their boredom does wonders for the state of extramarital affairs."

A Belgian man with thick blond hair, deep blue eyes, and a rugged appearance that betrayed a hard-earned weariness took it upon himself to give me a primer on the country. "In Rwanda," he said, "there is a great sense of order and discipline. This country is called the pearl of Africa for a reason. She is the land of a thousand hills—so beautiful and green, and you can get a lot done here, too. The people, they follow rules. You know, the masses were yoked thrice—by the feudals, the colonialists, and the Catholics. It is a lot, but you can see development projects work better here than anywhere else on the continent. It is almost *too* easy, in fact. But be careful, because with all of this discipline and progress comes a lot of deception."

I would reflect on those words for decades to come.

As the evening wore on, the wine flowed along with stories of Rwandan mishaps having mostly to do with hired maids and cooks. I heard the story of a housekeeper who was asked to whitewash the rims of a car's tires and ended up whitewashing the entire Mercedes, and one about the gardener who found a snake outside and put it in the expatriate's hamper for safekeeping. I found the stories about "these people" demeaning and tiring and later fell asleep thinking about the paradoxes of a physically spectacular country having a soul punctured by the competing forces of racism, colonialism, development, and geographic isolation.

The landlocked country seemed to cut people off from new ideas, so that conversations centered on the mundane, despite some of the extraordinary work people were doing. I pondered the strangeness of expatriate life, realizing that none of us at the party understood much at all about Rwanda or Rwandans, though we were the ones called "experts." I knew that this was just a single snapshot from a single night, but the bored facades of too many of the people at the dinner depressed me.

I awoke early the next morning thinking about what had bothered me most about the evening. Some of the expatriates had put low-income Rwandans in another category altogether—a box marked "other" for people who couldn't save themselves for trying. Yet we were supposed to be here to create real opportunities that would only work if we believed in the people we were serving. I decided to avoid the cynics and the "careerists" and promised myself that I wouldn't remain an expatriate for too long without rerooting myself in my own country. A creeping cynicism seemed inevitable in anyone who is always a visitor rather than someone with no choice but to live with the consequences of what he or she does. I also began to understand why I was so attracted to the notion of giving women access to loans, besides believing in it as an issue of justice. By lending women money instead of giving handouts, we would signal our high expectations for them and give them the chance to do something for their own lives rather than waiting for the "experts" to give them things they might or might not need.

I was changing. Though I'd been uncomfortable about focusing on women when I was first given the opportunity to come to Africa, I'd begun to see that if you support a woman, you support a family. I'd also learned that I definitely didn't like the word "expert" when it came to development. I still don't.

The question for me now was whether Rwanda was ready for microcredit—were there enough people and institutions to support the idea? I also questioned whether the Grameen Bank model would work in Rwanda. Bangladesh had something this country didn't: a history of trading and a feeling of solidarity among the people, especially since nationalism had taken root because of the war with Pakistan. Everything I read discussed how Rwanda operated as a feudal economy composed mostly of farmers living off the land. Some low-income people had started bartering for needed goods and services, but except for the Muslim population concentrated in Kigali, this was not known as a country of traders. I made a long list of questions to ask people and readied myself to present them first to my new partner in the study, Veronique.

Boniface picked me up to drive me to the Ministry of Family and Social Affairs, where we walked down a dark corridor and looked for Veronique in every room. I heard her rich voice before I saw her. As in every other office, Veronique's space was furnished with two desks, both constructed of dark wood, both covered with piles of papers and books, some yellowed, apparently from remaining in the same place for years.

Standing next to Veronique in the dark and dingy office was a shy, unassuming woman wearing a long skirt and flat black shoes. She was just a few inches over 5 feet tall, with a broad face and skin the color of coffee beans. She had large brown eyes that drooped at the sides, projecting a crinkly empathy further emphasized by a gap-toothed smile. Her hair was combed back into a loose crown. Her only adornments were a wedding band and a tiny gold cross on a chain around her neck.

She introduced herself shyly: "*Amakuru,* Jacqueline. My name is Honorata."

"*Bonjour.*"

Veronique, already a teacher to me, gave me a gentle shove and laughed. "Now you say '*Imeza.*' When someone says '*Amakuru,*' you answer '*Imeza.*' It is only polite."

"What does it mean?" I asked.

She laughed and hit me on the back. "So many questions already!" she said, adding, "It's very simple. *Amakuru* means 'What news?' A sort of 'How are you doing?' When you say *imeza,* you are answering back that it is just okay."

"What if it is more than okay?" I teased.

She laughed and shook her head and I knew we would be friends. I reached over to shake Honorata's hand, and she surprised me by clapping her right hand over my left shoulder and her left on my right elbow while leaning her face to the right of mine. My body naturally did the opposite, mirroring her. Then we switched. It was an awkward gesture at first, but a more intimate way of greeting—a double hug rather than a handshake.

Throughout the exchange, Honorata laughed quietly, covering her mouth with her hand. She wasn't showy in any way and seemed genuine in her desire to help women change their lives. Though Veronique was the more effusive communicator about our project, it turned out to be

Honorata who knew which people we needed to meet, made the right calls, and set up my schedule. She also accompanied me to meetings while offering a running oral history of her country.

Veronique and Honorata were bemused when I said I wanted to meet tomato sellers, business owners, and priests as well as their list of government ministers, NGO directors, and U.N. aid workers. These were the women we would ultimately be serving, so why wouldn't we start there and assess their needs? They finally agreed, and Honorata added that we should speak with some of the women's groups she knew, as well.

The early days of the project were now filled with meetings, informal conversations, and just watching the way the world worked for women in Kigali. We would ask government ministers and development workers about their economic aid programs for women and found a number of grant-based programs. Several officials told us how they intended to reach millions with programs to give women maize mills and other "labor-saving devices." I would think of a photo I once saw of a rural man riding a donkey as his wife walked alongside, carrying a load of wood on her head. "Labor-saving devices for whom?" I would ask. "And how do we know they are the right ones?"

Ultimately, most agreed that an experiment in providing credit to women made great sense. We sat for hours inside each of three commercial banks; not a single low-income woman walked through their doors. In the Kigali market, women told us they paid up to 10 percent interest daily to moneylenders so that they could run their businesses. Clearly, we were onto something.

Where individual opinions differed was in whether we should charge interest to the women, an ongoing debate in microfinance programs the world over at the time. Many people we met at international agencies felt it was unjust or plain usurious to be charging interest to some of the poorest people in society.

"How can you justify making money off the backs of the poor themselves?" one woman asked.

Though we explained over and over that the organization was a nonprofit and would not cover the costs of lending, our arguments often fell on deaf ears.

"These women have no collateral," one minister told us. "How will you know they will repay?"

"With your grants, you know they will *not* repay, so this is, to start, a bonus," we said. "Furthermore, everything we're seeing from other programs in the world indicates that poor women do, in fact, repay."

When we returned to the market and spoke to the women *themselves,* there was great excitement about a program that would lend to them at fair interest rates (we didn't know what it was yet, but we knew it would be much lower than what they were currently paying). We would help them with skills and connect them with other women. Ultimately, it was these women we listened to most carefully.

After a few days, Honorata, Veronique, and I had had enough. Two reasons poor women needed this program were because they *didn't* have collateral and because they had extremely low income levels. The women themselves certainly wanted access to credit. There would always be naysayers, we told ourselves; in fact, it was this spirit that ultimately inspired the organization's name, *Duterimbere,* which means to go forward with enthusiasm. Besides, by this time a formidable group of "founders," was emerging, powerful women in Kigali who stood behind the idea of a credit institution for women and were willing to work to make it real. Though we had yet to work out the details, our momentum was building.

Still, we had to revisit the question of whether or not to charge interest, even with some members of Duterimbere's founding group. At a meeting with several of the women, I was asked to explain again why we wanted to make money from poor women.

"We will *not* make money," I repeated, "at least not in the short term, though we could grow and sustain ourselves if we truly built an institution that covered costs in the long-term. Think of charging fair interest as practice for the women to interact with the formal economy. It will help them build real businesses—and they *want* the option to borrow! Don't you think the poor women are capable of success?"

"Of course they're capable," one woman shot back.

"Then let's give them a chance to prove to us—and to themselves—just how capable they are. In time, they'll be able to borrow larger amounts of money. They'll have a track record for the first time in their lives."

Against local conventional wisdom, our founders' group bet on the strength of the women and the belief that ultimately they belonged in the formal economy. We decided to charge interest at near-commercial bank rates.

The organization was beginning to take shape, but the most important work was establishing the political goodwill to give the institution grounding. Our biggest asset in getting started was the commitment of the three most powerful women in government. Prudence, Agnes, and

Constance, the only three female parliamentarians in the country, had emerged from the first generation of women given a chance to succeed in a society where modern political leadership was in its infancy in 1987.

Rwanda had been independent for less than 30 years, and women still had many fewer rights than men. Though they were a tiny minority in the 60-person Rwandan Parliament, these three strong, visionary, capable individuals were paving the way for generations of Rwandan girls and women.

Of the three, Prudence seemed the most grounded, dynamic, and authoritative. She came to every meeting prepared with facts, always knowing the various players involved in any decision we needed to make. She reminded us that opening banks to women would be threatening to the status quo, so we should remember to tread lightly, but with savvy.

"I dream of a day," she told me, "when women will have more power, when they will be afforded the respect that men receive. And you know, I can see it coming," she said, always with a twinkle in her eye.

I adored her.

Prudence delighted in visiting the rural areas with me, always wearing long dresses on her sturdy frame, carrying herself with a regal air that was never at odds with her kind nature. Her soft, melodic voice narrated local stories peppered with colloquialisms that gave the poorest women of the hillsides permission to have a sense of hope. Though I understood barely a word of her speeches because she always spoke in Kinyarwanda, I loved watching her in action, feeling the confidence she exuded and the sense of warmth and comfort she imparted to the women around her.

Prudence and Rwanda's then president, Juvénal Habyarimana, both hailed from the north of the country, so she had some access to high circles. She was also aware of the power of her feminine wiles and unafraid to use them. "To get a man to trust you," she once advised me, her black eyes sparkling behind thick-framed glasses, "wipe off a bit of imaginary dust from the shoulder of his jacket. It will communicate that you notice and that you care—and might slightly disarm him, which can be a good thing, yes?"

If Prudence was the visionary spokeswoman, Constance was the workhorse—a nun with circular, wire-rimmed glasses sitting on round cheeks, always dressed in her brown habit, deeply committed to serving the poor through action, not just prayer. Although she served in Parliament, she spent at least part of her days working more actively with the church and the women's groups she loved. Once when I needed to discuss our new organization's operational structure with her, she told me to come to her parish. She was busy doing something that she wanted me to see.

Boniface drove me to the outskirts of Kigali, where we saw the brick church standing tall amid fields of sorghum and sunflowers. We parked the car and I walked instinctively toward the sunflowers, looking for my favorite parliamentarian in a nun's habit. She walked with a jump in her step, waving her hand back and forth like a fan the way the children did, her bespectacled face beaming.

"Those sunflowers are no competition for the brilliance of your smile," I called out.

Constance laughed. "Oh no, oh no! I am just so happy today. Just you come and look at these sunflowers," she called. "They are magnificent, yes?"

"Yes," I laughed with her. "They are wonderful! But what are you doing here?"

Constance didn't respond, but pulled me by the hand so that we skipped like schoolgirls past the fields, where I had to tell her again how beautiful the sunflowers were, and then inside the barn, where boys were riding stationary bikes to fuel a rudimentary contraption that pressed sunflower seeds into oil.

"Good exercise, yes?" Constance grinned.

"Constance! Is this your business?"

"Not my business," she said. "But you know I am supporting women's income-generating projects through the church. It is my real passion and the reason I am so supportive of our work to create a microfinance institution for women in this country. Here these women are growing sunflowers and then they are pressing the seeds into oil so they can sell it. Maybe it will be a model for what our organization supports, don't you think?"

"It seems interesting," I said. "But I don't understand any of it. Does the church own the land? Do the women share the profits or do they at least earn a wage? Do you know what kind of price you can earn from just selling the sunflower seeds? And then again, do you know the price you will get from the sunflower oil?"

Constance looked crestfallen. "We don't have the answers. But look at the women working, and the boys, too. You see, they need jobs and now they are doing something for the community."

"Constance," I said as I smiled and put my arm around her. "I'm not saying this isn't a worthwhile project. I just want to understand how the numbers work a little bit better to make sure that, first, the women and boys really can expect to be paid and, second, that it is a project that can last more than one season without the donor's support. That's why loans are so important. If you depend on grants each year, then the sunflower project will only work if the donors keep giving. If we can make this profitable somehow, then the project can continue whether or not anyone wants to give you money."

"That would be a good thing," Constance said. "I may not have much of a head for business, but I like to see people working."

I told her I'd take a look at the economics involved in growing sunflowers and pressing the seeds into oil to determine if the project could grow strong enough to justify a loan. I'd seen too many well-intentioned projects like this one fail, in part because the donors weren't interested in seeing it become sustainable. They would insist on doing projects that had little to do with making a business work. But I was still hopeful.

Constance was right: She had no real head for business, but her heart was made of gold, and her spiritual commitment to seeing God in work and not just prayer was one I deeply admired. But running a business requires a tough side, too. It turned out that the idea for the sunflower project came from a Canadian donor, and Constance was happy just to try it with his money. When we looked at the economics of her small field against the price of sunflower oil, it quickly became clear that this couldn't be more than a charity project unless we expanded the land significantly.

"Unless the donor is willing to pay a large amount every year, this project won't succeed for very long right now," I told her.

"But God will provide," she said.

"Ah, that is a different story," I said.

In the end, Constance decided she wanted more for her people as well. The sunflower project, she concluded, was indeed a lovely way to teach women how to grow and process the seeds, but it wouldn't succeed in the long term. It also wouldn't fit the criteria for our new organization, for we were going to concentrate on small businesses that could be run by and for Rwandans and could make a long-term difference in people's lives.

And we would make loans, not grants. "It doesn't feel as good as grants," Constance told me, "but the women will learn more and grow stronger." From then on, Constance became a great storyteller for our new organization, helping wealthy and poor alike understand the power of giving each individual the tools of credit so she would have the potential to change her own life. "We are not handing out gifts," she would say, "but are bringing forth the gifts inside the people themselves."

Agnes, the third parliamentarian, was the true politician of the trium-virate. Not one to be seen with her hands dirty, she would nonetheless often travel to the rural areas to give speeches and what she called *animation*—talks of encouragement. She was always kind and extremely disciplined in her commitment to the organization, but she struck me as someone who loved the trappings of her office—the title, the pageantry, the feeling of holding an audience in her thrall as she spoke. Her desire to raise women's economic and social statuses was authentic, but vanity and a focus on the self were equally parts of her.

The leader, the dreamer, and the politician: These three women gave political heft, visibility, and heart to our new organization. UNICEF's backing bolstered our credibility as well, and there were a lot of other individual supporters. Notable among them was Annie Mugwaneza, a white Belgian woman with straight red hair in a pageboy cut that framed her freckled face. Annie never wore a trace of makeup on her heavily lidded eyes fringed with blonde lashes, and her daily uniform was a blue cotton skirt and either a white, button-down blouse with a Peter Pan collar or a T-shirt, everything as plain and understated as she was.

Annie Mugwaneza, born Annie Roland, had lived in Rwanda nearly 20 years by the time I met her. She had come to the country as a missionary and then fallen in love with a tall, handsome Rwandan named Jean Mugwaneza. After the two decided to marry, Annie never left. Marrying a Rwandan meant that if she ever left him, she would have no right under Rwandan law to raise their children outside the country without her husband's permission. Legally, the children were the father's property. I never asked Annie how much she'd thought about the future when she married Jean. She always seemed to enjoy her life and was fully committed to Rwanda.

Annie had several sons, which gave her some measure of stature in a society where boys are the preferred gender. She was a good mother, a good wife, and someone who could be outspoken while working on behalf of all women, not just the privileged ones. This little band of women led our charge as we lined up potential funders and gained commitments from various agencies to help with business planning and training. We created bylaws and drew up a work plan for the next 6 months. I had already extended my stay, and UNICEF agreed to cover my additional expenses. I moved from UNICEF's guesthouse to a rented room in a Canadian aid worker's airy home that featured a zebra skin on the wall, a garden out back, and the occasional friendly snake that made its way inside.

I continued to learn about business as usual in the development world. Once, as part of a "social mobilization" effort, UNICEF hired an expensive Italian designer to create a poster campaign aimed at convincing women to vaccinate their children. The posters were gorgeous photographs of women and children with simple messages written in Kinyarwanda about the importance of vaccinating every child. They were perfect, except for the fact that the extremely low female literacy rate in Rwanda made it likely that words written even in Kinyarwanda would have little impact. Much better would have been pictures that told stories—or even better, messages integrated into songs that could have been sung by the women and passed from one to another as they walked the hillsides. Just seeing this process, though, helped me to think differently about how to design future messages and programs, how to move away from our own view of how things should be done and observe how people live and communicate with one another.

My learning curve could not have been steeper, but I was coming to relish this new country, feeling like an explorer on weekends, surrounded by eclectic friends who were adventurers living life to the hilt. Most were young and, unlike the ones I'd met at that first dinner, all were hopeful and hardworking, a mix of North Americans, Italians, French, and one outlandish Zairean musician named Leonel who wrote a song called "Fucking Cozy Kigali." We'd all dance to it and other music at Cosmos nightclub, a dark, cramped box of a place in Nyamirambo.

At Chez Lando, a local hangout, we ate shish kebabs and grilled bananas and washed down our meals with Rwandan beer. During lunch breaks, I would run up and down the hills of Kigali with children scampering behind me laughing and shouting, *"Muzungu, muzungu,"* or "white person." The European expatriates thought I was insane for running in the midday sun to the tunes on a Walkman, but they chalked it up to my being American.

I was living in borrowed houses as I'd kept my inexpensive one-bedroom flat in Nairobi. Since I'd originally come to Kigali for just a 3-week feasibility study, my plans to stay always hinged on the next phase of work: *I'll do this for another 6 months until things are stable* was my mantra. Envisioning only a short tenure, I tended to stay with friends in their homes or rent big, empty houses by myself.

With neither a telephone nor a television, I did a lot of reading: Nadine Gordimer and J. M. Coetzee, Chinua Achebe and Ngugi wa Thiong'o. I fell in love with African writers, captivated by the starkness of their words and the richness of their worlds. On weekends, my friends and I would pile into jeeps and drive for hours. It was nothing to drive 7 hours one-way early Saturday morning to visit the green, lush hills of Massissi in Zaire and then turn around on Sunday night and drive back home. We would go windsurfing and fishing in gorgeous Lake Kivu and drive through Akagera National Park, which was largely destroyed during the genocide in 1994. We made our way to Bujumbura, the capital of Burundi, and would wander through the streets and eat tiny fried fish and French fries on the shores of the lake. For elites, Rwanda offered great adventures in some of the world's most beautiful settings.

But Rwanda is a place of highs and lows: The juxtaposition of some of the most wonderful experiences of my life with the everyday realities in Kigali created, at times, a jarring sense of schizophrenia. Starting anything new is an all-encompassing proposition, and typically I worked 16-hour days. Doing this in a different language, in a place far from home, where navigating even simple things could thwart the best intentions challenged me to my bones. There were plenty of nights when the sheer injustice of the world in which I lived would come crashing down. With no means of communication other than letters, a sense of isolation would envelop me, and there were nights that ended in tears of tiredness and sadness for a world that didn't seem to want to see the possibilities right there in front of it. In those times, I would turn to music. Peter Gabriel, Joni Mitchell, Carole King, and Cat Stevens began to feel like good friends on lonely nights.

Mornings were better. I started most days with a run as dawn was breaking and returned exhilarated. When all was said and done, the Rwandan women and I were making real progress. There was great excitement in the capital that a new institution for women was being created by locals, not just by expatriates. Within months, we'd registered the organization, signed off on the bylaws, created a board, and raised local money. We were funded and ready to go.

The founding members gathered one evening to announce the registration of Duterimbere at the Women's Network office, where about 40 women filled the sparsely furnished room to the bursting point. The air was crackling with electricity, and again I had the sense that history was being made—but this time, I was part of it. After Prudence introduced me, I spoke in French with resolve and tremendous excitement, and they craned their necks toward me and applauded throughout my speech. I felt intoxicated by the sheer joy of that first step.

After the meeting, Prudence, wearing a black and red dress, her hair smoothed back elegantly, whispered in her girlish giggle that she thought most of the women had probably understood only half of what I was saying. "Sometimes your French is so funny," she said, adding that at least everyone had felt my passion completely, and it was that, not my facility with language, that they had applauded.

Embarrassed that my French was still so clumsy, I apologized profusely. She smiled, put her hands on my shoulders, and looked me in the eye.

"You should never worry about such small things," she counseled. "Language has very little to do with the words you say and everything with how you say them. Everyone understands what you are doing, even if the words sometimes don't follow."

Then she added, "And just so you know, we also like very much how you dance, for you listen to your own rhythm there, too."

Despite my having given a speech that few could understand, we launched what would become one of the largest lenders to the Rwandan poor. We had yet to make a loan, but we had a governing structure, money, contacts, and an amazing amount of heart—and we were a local organization created by and for Rwandan women.

After assisting Duterimbere to get on its feet, I couldn't leave until I helped it at least learn to walk. I extended my contract again and returned to Nairobi for a week or so to pick up a few pieces of clothing and favorite things. I *did* know we had no choice in Rwanda but to succeed.

We asked the Rwandan women to contribute some of their own money, despite being told by "the experts," who were far better at theory than practice, that women were too poor to give anything. Though the women didn't have much, nearly everyone we met donated what they could, helping to build a real partnership with local participation.

The members of the founding group put their reputations, their time, and whatever money they could find on the line. After we raised money locally, UNICEF provided our first grant of $50,000. Bilge Ogun Bassani also supported us by giving us a temporary office, drivers when we needed them, a stamp of legitimacy, and my salary, too. I learned the importance of giving different kinds of people seats at the table early in order to bring new ideas to reality.

Now all we had to do was determine how to make loans—and how to get the money back. It sounded so simple.

CHAPTER 4

BASKET ECONOMICS AND POLITICAL REALITIES

"If you don't like the way the world is, you change it.
You have an obligation to change it. You just do it one step at a time."

—MARIAN WRIGHT EDELMAN

Before we began lending money, our little group met for the first time as a board, though it was unlike any board meeting I'd imagined. Honorata picked me up on a Saturday afternoon and we drove together to Veronique's home, to find her wearing a white cotton dressing gown and a full cast on her left leg. Her hair was standing straight on end, and her eyes looked sunken, as if she hadn't slept in weeks, a likely situation given the crying baby she was rocking in her arms. "Meet your newest Rwandan daughter," she said to me, smiling as she put the tiny girl in my arms and turned around to hobble to the couch.

Rumor had it that Veronique's husband had pushed her, causing her to fall down a hill and break her leg. I couldn't imagine this powerful woman allowing herself to be bullied by anyone, especially not when she had a tiny baby in her care. But I remember when she told me that only when women control money will they have the power to walk away from being hurt. We were having lunch together, and she talked for a long time about the horrors of domestic violence. "Here, the courts protect the husbands," she said. "In some ways, beating your wife is expected as part of family unity, and you know they always go after the feisty ones."

I'd never met a Rwandan woman feistier than Veronique herself, though she had been subdued on that day when sharing stories about women who were the most unsafe in the shelter of their own homes.

That afternoon at her house, as we waited for the others to arrive,

Veronique was her old self, waving her hands as she dreamed aloud about what we could accomplish together. We spoke about *umuganda,* or community work, that was performed each Saturday morning by everyone in the country, a sort of pulling together to meet Rwanda's needs. In many ways, *umuganda* was classically Rwandan—highly organized work that everyone was expected to do. In Rwanda, government projects work in large part because the country is so small and organized. When government has a plan to enforce, it has only to pass it on to the country's 14 prefects, who communicate it to the *bourgmestres,* or local mayors. For *umuganda,* a community might be told one week to hoe a field; another, to plant trees—all under the supervision of a local official.

People from the expatriate community are often invited to join. Once, I hoed a field of potatoes with a small group of women, lifting the hoe's wooden handle over my head and then pounding it into the ground over and over again. Though the dirt smelled sweet and the air fresh, it was backbreaking work that lasted for hours. The next day, I could barely stand up straight. My hands were covered with blisters, and every muscle in my body ached.

Veronique laughed when I told this story. "You are still soft," she offered, "not like Rwandan women."

And then she added, "You know, *umuganda* is also a way for the government to ensure that everyone is where he or she is supposed to be." I didn't have time to dig deeper into the meaning of her words, but I began to notice that people did indeed seem to keep a close eye on one another in this country.

The others arrived and took their seats around a wooden coffee table in Veronique's government-issued house. Prudence and Agnes looked regal and serious in their long white dresses. Honorata and Annie wore full navy skirts and white T-shirts, and Constance, her brown nun's habit. Prudence had brought with her a wonderful French Canadian woman named Ginette who had recently left a successful corporate career and marriage of more than a decade to seek an entirely new life. She understood how to build operations and systems and she loved management. I knew myself well enough already to know that I could inspire people and help create a dream, but I needed the assistance of a professional manager to build an organization that could sustain our collective vision.

Once we were all settled, I looked around the room and thought of the life I'd left behind, where women wore "power suits" to work and little black dresses to evening cocktail parties. I remember mornings when, leather briefcase in hand, I had felt a heady rush just walking into Chase Manhattan Bank's massive marble lobby of the bank. And a big part of me missed the 22nd floor at the bank, where I had a specific role and a desk in a skyscraper on Wall Street that was filled with colleagues who understood me and I, them. Now I was in a Rwandan's living room talking to women in long dresses in a country with which I was still unfamiliar. I didn't fathom then that *most* big dreams originate in someone's living room with a small group of people, regardless of where they come from or how they are dressed.

Our meeting began on a formal note as Prudence, our first board chair, called us to order. Veronique, who was always less serious, sat poised at one end of her couch, her wide foot perched on the skinny wooden table, giving her breast to her daughter and wildly waving her hands as she told another story. Yellow sunlight poured through the windows, bouncing off the clean white walls of the tiny house.

We moved through our agenda: confirming that we would name the organization Duterimbere, because of our own commitment to going forth enthusiastically; officially hiring Ginette; and discussing an action plan. The board designated that Agnes would serve as the organization's first executive director. I thought the appointment was odd since she was a parliamentarian, but Prudence explained that many high-ranking officials held other jobs, as well.

We all agreed that Agnes would be perfect for the position. She had the necessary status as well as the inclination to do the work. We knew she would give it her all to make Duterimbere succeed and so the board unanimously made her the organization's first executive director. As for staff, Prudence mentioned that she wanted us to meet a young protégée of hers named Liliane, who had recently graduated from university and could be a powerful ally to Ginette as she put operations in order.

The next week, Ginette and I met Liliane at one of the local restaurants in town. I liked her from the moment we met. The other women referred to her as "the blue one" because her skin was so dark, it was bluer than black. She wore her hair cut close to her head so that her dark eyes and smile dominated her face. Liliane exuded a youthful innocence, though her serious air gave both Ginette and me confidence.

"I graduated from the University of Butare," she told us, "and want to work on women's economic development. I learn very fast and work even harder."

Ginette explained that Liliane would spend time working directly with the women in the market, helping them with business planning and ensuring that loans were made and repaid in a timely manner.

"Prudence told me this is a very big position," Liliane responded, "but I've worked toward this and will not let the women down. I can promise you that. I won't disappoint Prudence, either. She's such a big woman and she's put herself behind me, I know that."

We did hire her, and Liliane and Ginette ended up becoming a formidable team. In the next few weeks, we located a light and airy office to rent above a tailor shop in the middle of town. Its interior walls were painted pale blue, with big windows in both the front and the back. An external staircase ran up to the office, but the stairs were so small and rickety that almost daily I ended up tripping over a few stairs in my long cotton skirts. And, somehow, I never learned to take the stairs differently.

While setting up our office, we met a kind, talented Zairean artist named Dieu Donné who designed a logo for us depicting women dressed in red and green marching, fists clenched and bodies leaning forward with enthusiasm, toward a rural bank. Prudence teased that the women were walking more like me than like so many of the low-income rural women, who held themselves more demurely. But everyone else seemed to like it and the logo stayed, for this was to be an organization of aspiration.

In those early days, we spent a lot of time in Kigali's markets talking and listening to the women, this time to understand better why they would want to borrow money. Most were interested in expanding their tiny businesses. "I pay too much to the moneylender," a tomato vendor told Liliane. "I could borrow at a low interest rate; I could sell more and take more money home to my family." Another wanted to borrow enough to buy a goat with the hope that the animal would reproduce and she could earn even more money.

Some of the women had outsized dreams. One of our first potential borrowers wanted to start a bookstore, explaining that she'd had the idea because there were too few books in Rwanda.

"True," we responded to her, "but what qualifies you for this business? Do you know how to run a store? What do you know about selling books?"

She quietly admitted that she wasn't really qualified. "I am illiterate. But I would like to learn to read, and I want my children to have books."

She didn't get the loan, but her spirit was emblematic of what we were looking for.

I loved spending time in the Kigali marketplace—the bargaining, the camaraderie, and the constant chatter of vendors and customers. I loved the way barrels of dried beans stood together like stout men at a beer fest; the beautiful red tomatoes piled in pyramids; the bright yellows, greens, and pinks of so many different types of bananas; sunny oranges, blushing mangos, and pale fennel and leeks. I loved the smells of the fruits and flowers and the feel of rice when I ran it through my fingers.

What I didn't like was that it was impossible to find locally grown coffee. Despite Rwanda's reputation for producing some of the best coffee on earth, locals had to settle for tins of Nescafé instant coffee. And it peeved me that men sold high-margin products like fish and powdered milk while women were consigned to tomatoes and onions, items guaranteed *not* to make money. I wanted to see at least some women breaking these local economic barriers.

As we spent more time in the market, we began to see an entire ecosystem unfold. Of course, the moneylenders were there, providing cash at the astonishing rate of 10 percent per day. Most people, strapped for cash, bought and sold a great deal of their goods on credit. Overall, money was scarce in the marketplace. However, the women still managed to save. Just as I would see in Kenya and other African countries, the Rwandan market women had created a traditional system of saving and lending among themselves.

Known as merry-go-rounds, or *tontines,* these small groups of a half dozen or so women would come together on a regular basis, weekly or monthly. Each would contribute about $1 each time the group met. At the meeting, one member would be given the total amount collected to use for whatever she required. As the women became more successful, they would sometimes contribute more than a dollar; and sometimes the group as a whole would put the extra money aside for group savings.

We understood from the merry-go-rounds that women were capable of saving and borrowing and we started lending small amounts, mostly to women selling fruits and vegetables in the market. They would borrow something like $30 and then repay us in monthly installments. The women liked having a passbook where everything was written down, and most of them repaid their loans in a timely manner.

We still were feeling as if we were just getting started when several international donors approached us to see how they could support us as well. The attention—and money—was exciting. But we were still getting our feet wet and didn't know exactly what we were doing. The real problem with the money from such donors was that it usually came with strings attached—they wanted us to carry out *their* projects and typically wanted the money spent within a year, something I didn't think we could promise.

A woman from a high-profile development agency once came to our office and offered us $100,000 to do nutrition workshops for women in rural areas. She looked very professional in a cotton suit with her hair swept up.

"I've heard you do very good work and I saw Agnes give an excellent speech recently," she told Agnes, Ginette, and me.

"We're just getting started," I told her. She went on to explain the importance of doing nutrition workshops in rural areas so women would know how to better feed their families. I didn't see the link with our stated mission, which was to lend with the aim of boosting business development to improve women's economic conditions.

"Healthier women will make better borrowers," she told us.

While I agreed absolutely, I knew we didn't have a team in place to start conducting nutrition workshops when we were just beginning to build our lending business. "Nutrition isn't part of our mission," I explained. "We are singularly focused on providing women with microloans."

Simultaneously, Agnes jumped in, saying, "You are right about the needs of women in rural areas and we would be well placed to support them. We would love to partner with you."

I wasn't amused. I didn't want the organization distracted from its mission. At the same time, I understood that Duterimbere ultimately needed to be a Rwandan organization in every sense—and that meant its decisions needed to be made by the Rwandan women themselves. If, for example, Agnes and Prudence were set on an idea, even after a fierce argument (and there were a few), we would do it. After all, they were the ones who would have to face the long-term consequences.

Agnes agreed with me that taking on a nutrition project risked a loss of focus, but she still thought it would be better for us to take on the project than to give it up.

"Teaching nutrition to women will help us find borrowers," she reasoned.

Prudence agreed with Agnes that the offer was too tempting to pass up, so Ginette began working with Liliane and Agnes to identify consultants who could help train women in basic nutrition. They carried this out over the course of a few months, all the time complaining that our real work—that of lending in the marketplace—was being neglected. Ultimately, while the attendees of their workshops said they enjoyed the lessons, it was never clear that any tangible changes resulted from our efforts.

Agnes was always inclined to say yes to the money when it came our way, and there were a lot of donors looking to give it, especially given Agnes's charm, flexibility, and abilities of persuasion. Liliane was less skilled at fund-raising, but more clearheaded, determined, and unimpressed by anything that distanced us from our core business of lending. I came to cherish her quick mind, her toughness, and her refusal to suffer fools. She expected excellence and pushed the women to be better than they thought they could be. And she had one of the greatest laughs on earth.

Sometime in our first year, we became concerned when a number of women fell behind in repaying their loans. Determined to discern what was happening, Liliane went to visit the home of a rice trader who claimed that her bag of rice had been stolen by thieves. As she listened to the woman explain why she couldn't make her payments, Liliane noticed an enormous sack in the back room, walked over to it, and discovered that it was filled with rice. The woman began waving her hands, offering excuses, but Liliane was no longer listening. She slowly and calmly explained that she appreciated the woman's good words, but the loan was due and had to be repaid. When the woman defiantly turned her back on her, an infuriated Liliane simply walked out.

An hour later, Liliane stormed into my office. "Jacqueleen," she cried, holding out her hands for emphasis, "I am too frustrated. We must do something about these overdue loans right away. The women have a responsibility. They have a contract with us. They know the terms of the loan. If they have a family crisis, that is one thing—they should let us know. But this isn't the case with that silly woman. She isn't paying because she thinks we don't really care whether she repays or not. And others are watching what we do about this. We have to show them that we care."

I thought a lot about Liliane's phrase: *"We have to show them that we care."* Indeed, several women initially saw no reason to repay. They knew the money was coming not from a neighbor but, in their eyes, from a big, obtuse agency filled with nameless rich people from across the planet who didn't think much of the poor anyway. Why should that institution really expect poor women to repay? And how much would it notice if they didn't?

Those early women borrowers were testing us, and their approach was rational. If we were the types who made excuses for them if they didn't pay so that they suffered no real consequences, then they would feel like fools if they *did* pay.

We have to show them that we care: This meant hanging in there with the tough questions and holding our clients accountable even if the rest of the world didn't.

Liliane and I got in the car, drove to the edge of town, and continued for another half hour down a muddy road to see the rice trader again. We arrived at her cracked-mud hut and the large woman wearing a white sleeveless top over a long violet skirt welcomed us with tea, declaring immediately how much she loved Duterimbere, showing no memory of the difficult conversation she'd had hours before with Liliane. We, on the other hand, were in no mood for tea and lies.

We asked about the big bag of rice in her home, and she told us it was her husband's military ration. Liliane wasn't interested in what the husband did. She saw that the woman was not in crisis and wanted to ensure that the woman understood that she had made a commitment and we expected her to fulfill it. Otherwise, the woman should not hope to borrow from us again.

She promised to do so and offered us more tea. We shared a quick cup, and Liliane began to trust that this time the woman might actually repay. As we walked back to our car, Liliane whispered, "She knows we are serious now. I think she respects that in us, for she sees herself as serious, too."

Before the week was over, the rice trader visited the office and repaid the loan in full to an again amiable Liliane. Over time, the rice trader would become one of the bank's best clients, taking on increasing loan amounts, repaying, and building her business to the point where she hired three others.

WHILE THE DUTERIMBERE TEAM worked on understanding how local businesses operated—and how to be simultaneously tough and compassionate—the parliamentarians were focusing on bigger policy issues. They were determined to change the Family Code in Rwanda's legal system. As in so many developing countries, the Family Code was established by government to cover issues such as the roles of women and children, domestic violence, marriage, and divorce. In the mid-1980s, Rwanda's Family Code was especially detrimental to women, who had few rights and were often bound by their husbands' permission. The parliamentarians believed this inequality was especially exacerbated by traditions regarding bride price.

Bride price is a long-held tradition whereby a hopeful groom provides a settlement to the father of the bride. In Rwanda, the bride price might be three cows, an enormous sum given how much people typically earned. For larger Tutsi families, cattle were part of their existing patrimony, but grooms from poorer families ended up paying off the price to their in-laws forever. Prudence, Agnes, and Constance flatly rejected the notion of bride price, as did most women they knew, believing that the tradition inherently created a system of indentured servitude. Women suffered, being treated as chattel while their husbands spent their lives "paying off" their fathers-in-law for what they legally owned.

The parliamentarians knew they couldn't abolish an age-old tradition without taking politics into consideration. They proposed not to abolish bride price, but to make it less financially onerous while honoring its symbolic value.

They went to Parliament with a proposal to reduce the expected bride price to three garden hoes, valued at about 1,000 Rwandan francs, or $10. When the measure passed, the women of Duterimbere celebrated the victory with Fantas, cake, and merriment.

The next morning we awoke to a new world. Instead of jubilation in the streets, rural women were up in arms: "Yesterday," they protested, "we were worth thousands upon thousands." Today we are worth only 1,000." The symbol of the hoes, the object with which they toiled daily, was seen as a further insult. Throughout the country, women were enraged. A number of parliamentarians visited Constance to reprimand her for pushing such bad policy, ignoring the fact that it had passed by a clear margin.

The next day, our beloved Constance was killed in a hit-and-run accident. Though "witnesses" said she'd been accidentally hit by a truck, people who knew her believed it was a deliberate murder meant to send a signal about pushing for "unreasonable" changes. We were in shock. Clearly, a majority of the 57 male parliamentarians had passed the resolution as well, but that didn't matter. Laying the blame at the dead nun's feet would enable everyone else to distance themselves.

The day I heard the news of Constance's death from Ginette may have been the day I really grew up. My time in Côte d'Ivoire had taught me about humility: I came to Rwanda ready to listen, but without a critical eye. I saw only good in Rwanda's community orientation, in the way families took care of one another, in the lack of corruption and the simplicity of life. Suddenly, our friend with the big heart was dead, and the power of community revealed itself in the price of an individual. Life was neither as easy nor as free as I had imagined.

Two men approached me in a restaurant one evening, rebuking me for "ruining their women." I had had nothing to do with the bride-price issue, hadn't participated in the discussions about it, didn't even know it was being planned. The female parliamentarians themselves were apparently out of touch with their own rural countrywomen—not unlike elites around the world today, who often don't really know the poor who elected them. Indeed, today's most privileged individuals are often more comfortable with elites from other countries than they are with their own less-privileged fellow citizens.

As we mourned Constance, whose commitment to the women of Rwanda had never faltered, life moved along as if nothing happened. I came to know death as a familiar visitor for the first time. Death in Africa is not hidden, but rather woven into the fabric of everyday life. Each week someone missed work to attend the funeral of a family member or friend. The work moved more slowly than I'd expected, but we were making progress.

Prudence and Agnes continued to make speeches about the need to improve women's economic conditions. Liliane and Ginette made more loans to women in the marketplace. Honorata busied herself working with women's groups and looking for potential new borrowers. I wrote a manual for how to build a lending agency like ours, using many of the materials I'd gathered during Chase Manhattan Bank's credit training program, a 10-month mini-MBA course used to teach each new lending officer the rules and practices of banking. Distilled to the basics, almost everything Chase had taught us about high finance was relevant for lending to the poor.

Though we often felt a bit battered, our dream was coming to fruition. In the process, new lessons flowed like the many little waterfalls ribboning down Rwanda's abundant hillsides.

One afternoon, Boniface and I drove to a marketplace about an hour outside Kigali. We arrived at around 5:00 p.m. after driving along red dirt roads lined with fragrant eucalyptus trees. Suddenly we came upon a huge blanket of color—a rural marketplace, where hundreds of vendors had gathered. Most were starting to leave on foot or to line up for buses to take them home. The sun would be setting in an hour, and the air had a chill in it. I felt the edge of loneliness that was a part of too many early evenings in Rwanda for me.

Maybe there was something about the sky; more likely, it was just being so far away from everything and everyone I knew. I missed my family. My monthly calls home—at $13 a minute—resulted in little more than frustration over the echo and clipped sentences. "How are you doing? Fine?" was the extent of the average conversation.

As Boniface and I walked together into the market, we happened upon two women sitting on their haunches, each in front of a single Rwandan basket, the kind retail stores like Bloomingdale's now call widows' baskets, and sell to raise money for genocide survivors. The baskets were identical, both beautiful and well made, though neither had a single differentiating characteristic.

"How much is the basket?" I asked the first woman.

"A thousand francs," she replied—$10 at the time.

"That is too expensive," I replied and gave her a knowing look.

Then I added, "The going rate for these baskets is closer to 600 francs ($6). I can't pay 1,000 ($10)."

She stared at me. Her friend said nothing.

I let a moment pass in silence, hoping they would jump in with entrepreneurial flair and start bargaining. They didn't.

"Can you give me a better price?" I asked.

No, she said. "The cost is 1,000 francs."

"How much is *your* basket?" I asked the other woman politely, trying to spur competition with the neighbor.

"A thousand Rwandan francs," she responded.

Remaining focused on the second woman, I said, "You know and I know that you have nearly doubled the price of the basket. I live near a store in the city that sells these exact baskets for 600 francs, not 1,000. I don't have to buy the basket today. But I like you, so I will pay you 800 francs for your basket."

"No," she said, eyes downcast. "The price is fixed. It must be 1,000 francs."

I felt frustration rising because they weren't playing my game. I was willing to pay a 30 percent premium to test the market. There were no other customers anywhere in sight, and yet neither woman showed an interest in bargaining. We talked for a long time, haggling over the price and making each other laugh when no one budged.

Finally, I summarized our situation: "Okay. You each have one basket to sell, and you refuse to compete against one another. I am willing to pay much more than anyone else today, so one of you could sell me the basket and then split the earnings. There are many solutions."

The women shook their heads in unison. Finally, the first woman looked into my eyes intently. "You see," she said, "I will not take a sale away from my sister. We will not change prices so that one of us gets the sale. And I cannot change the price because this basket is all I have to sell. I need to take the bus home and pay school fees for my children. I cannot bring home a basket but must be able to cover the costs. So I will sell the basket for the price I need."

Here was a new logic, one based on scarcity and hope, however unjustified. After all, I was still standing there and clearly wanted the basket. So as long as I was still in the game, there was a chance they would get their price.

Markets are about finding willing sellers and buyers. But we often don't know the incentives and constraints within which people are operating.

I tried to wait it out. Boniface and I threw glances back and forth. He obviously wanted me to go without buying the baskets because he didn't want me to look stupid, like a tourist.

I knew I would never really make my point, at least not that day. I knew that giving them the money would reinforce their strategy, but I also knew I couldn't come back each day to help strengthen their businesses. The women wanted to go home but would stay all night at the market if they had a chance of getting the extra RWF 400—probably more than a week of take-home pay. The RWF 400 or $4 would mean a lot more to them than it did to me. Given that I was neither teaching nor proving anything in this standoff, I gave each woman 1,000 francs.

Back in the car, Boniface told me that the women had taken me for a fool.

"Sometimes you have to be a fool, or else your heart can turn to stone," I muttered, not having a better answer.

"If I were coming back to that market, I wouldn't have done that," I shared my reasoning. "But we're not coming back, and if I didn't buy the baskets, they wouldn't have had the money to go home. Sometimes it's okay for all of us to win little victories in life. I can afford the loss of 400 francs—and," I grinned, "the loss of ego in front of you."

Boniface shook his head, unconvinced. "You paid too much for the baskets."

I looked at him. "My friend," I said, "you better just promise me not to tell a soul, or I will lose my reputation for toughness."

He laughed so hard, for so long, that he had to wipe away the tears. "I am telling everyone in Kigali. Or else you can give me 1,000 francs and I can give you a very nice basket that I buy for 600."

"Promise me . . . ," I laughed back.

He just shook his head, turned the key, and started driving.

Daily life revolved around money, from tiny amounts to more serious cash. In our first year of operation, Duterimbere's total budget was less than $50,000. In our second year, our budget quadrupled. After doing the nutrition workshops, Agnes and Prudence accepted money to do food-processing workshops and to expand into rural areas, though we were not ready. Our management processes were still too weak. Ginette feared the fattening budget, with neither enough managers nor robust systems to support it. We spoke to Prudence, who always listened, and we agreed to slow down operations until we could train more good people—a major task given that we now had branches in other parts of the country.

As often happens when nonprofit leaders become visible, Prudence and Agnes began attending international conferences to spread the word that Rwandan women were helping themselves through their entrepreneurial efforts. Liliane and Ginette stayed at home, trying to run the operations and teach women the basics of lending and business. Each day seemed to teach us more about what we didn't know than about what we did. But we were making progress.

For months, we worked with a woman to come to understand her maize-milling business and get her ready for a loan. She'd been borrowing from the moneylender at 10 percent daily to sell grain and wanted to upgrade her business and her life. Before the final signing of the loan documents, she told Liliane she first needed to talk to the minister of her Seventh-Day Adventist church.

The next day, the woman approached Liliane in tears. "Usury is forbidden in the church," she said, "and so I cannot accept the loan." No matter what Liliane said, the woman refused to acknowledge that she was paying more than five times as much to borrow money from the moneylenders and would never be able to run a sustainable business that way. The difference was simply that they didn't charge interest, but rather fees.

I went personally to see the woman's minister, trying to suppress my rage. No matter what I argued, he would not be moved. "You are trying to change our women," he finally told me, something I'd heard many times by then.

"I am working with Rwandan women who are trying to change the conditions in which they live," I answered.

"You cannot charge usurious rates" was his response.

I got nowhere. Working in Rwanda meant interacting with churches in some capacity. On one hand, they provided a great sense of hope and faith to people in need of a belief in a better future—even if it was in another life. On the other, because of the enormous power they yielded, some individual religious leaders could impose their own notions of what was right on others. Our focus became learning how to navigate political institutions and work with the best individuals inside of them, the churches included.

Other frustrations came from the good intentions of international agencies. One agency offered us the opportunity to send a group of rural women to India to learn about entrepreneurship and opportunities there.

"Rural women?" I asked. "Who thought of this one? Poor Rwandan women speak not a word of English, let alone French. They've not traveled more than 20 miles beyond their homes, and they want them to cross the Indian Ocean? And for what? Why not send the parliamentarians, who can represent Rwanda, interact with all kinds of Indians, and bring back lessons learned?"

But once again, the donors controlled the money and the idea.

Agnes and Prudence thought the trip would broaden the women's visions and bring recognition to Duterimbere internationally. I didn't think we'd done anything yet to deserve such recognition. The institution was less than 2 years old. We needed to focus on what we were doing, not send poor rural women around the world.

Liliane agreed with me. "These are women who have never been to the capital," she said. "And your Americans want to send them to India. Wouldn't the money be better spent building a school so that they could learn to read?"

I concurred, but we lost the argument. Liliane was designated the leader of the trip.

She returned a week after leaving, exhausted, and explained to Ginette and me, "We arrived in New Delhi to hot, suffocating air and too many people. The women couldn't understand English. Our translator would try to speak to me in French, and then I would translate to Kinyarwanda. It took a long time, and no one really ever understood what was happening.

We visited a group of farmers, and it was exciting to see interaction among the women, though again, no one understood what anyone else was saying. That night one of our women fell very sick. It turned out to be malaria. She hadn't wanted to tell anyone about it because she was afraid to ruin the trip. By the time we recognized the disease, she was too sick. We rushed her to the hospital, but after 2 days she died. The other women refused to do anything while they waited for her. They decided the trip had been cursed. I couldn't argue with so many crying women, so we came home."

We were stunned, even if there was a hint of "we told you so" in our minds. Ginette promised to meet with the women to talk about what had happened and to try to glean some lessons from the experience. She would first wait a few days so the women could at least recover slightly from the trauma.

Visibly shaken, Liliane told us over and over how sorry she was for not completing the trip, despite our attempts to tell her she'd done exactly the right thing. Still, she had loved meeting the Indian people and longed to travel to other places. She reached into her bag and gave each of us a necklace—a dainty one to suit Ginette's style and a big silver one that fit me perfectly. How Liliane had time to think about us in the midst of chaos was beyond me.

Everyday life got better. We hired more staff and made more loans. Almost everyone was repaying, and Duterimbere was becoming known across the country. Prudence, Agnes, and other founding board members worked long into the nights approving loan applications and reviewing progress. The level of seriousness—and of contribution—was thrilling. This was what I'd imagined development could be.

One of the lessons of start-ups, though, is that whenever you think things are going well, something happens to hand you back your humility. Given our rate of growth, Ginette had hired accountants to review our books and strengthen our financial systems. After about a week, the accountants walked into her office with serious faces, telling her they needed to talk privately.

There was a problem. In the next days, they discovered more than $3,000 in missing funds and a number of exaggerated and forged receipts. All signs pointed to Agnes.

Agnes had signing authority for all funds with the banks and was responsible for all expenses. When approached about the missing money, she seemed genuinely flabbergasted, and dismayed.

"How can I help find the criminal who did this?" she asked indignantly.

Prudence called an emergency board meeting, to which Agnes was not invited. That night nervous tension and anxiety crackled in the second-floor room. What would we say to the donors? Who would fund the organization again? Prudence reminded us that while these were difficult problems, none was more complex than dealing correctly with Agnes, who was one of the most respected women in the country.

With Prudence's leadership and, in essence, permission, we decided that we would never know who actually stole the money, but that Agnes, as director, must be held accountable, at least internally. We would tell the outside world that she was leaving because her duties as parliamentarian and legal expert had become too onerous for her to also run the growing organization. Prudence was asked to give her the news.

The next afternoon, Prudence asked for her resignation. Agnes was indignant. As director, she could use the money as she saw fit, she claimed. Prudence suggested that the work was too burdensome for a parliamentarian; this became the official story. A piece of ice formed between Prudence and Agnes that would never melt.

In the year after Agnes resigned, she and I remained on good terms. We both pretended that nothing had ever happened. She was still an advocate for women and remained friendly with most of the leaders at the helm of Duterimbere. I was slightly stunned by the fact that we'd lost two of the three parliamentarians who had first established the organization, one to a probable murder and the other to corruption. But I didn't spend a lot of time thinking about it. I was much too busy getting on with getting on.

CHAPTER 5

THE BLUE BAKERY

"Poverty won't allow him to lift up his head;
dignity won't allow him to bow it down."

—MADAGASY PROVERB

In meeting women in and around the markets of Kigali, we rarely found a business that employed more than one woman and maybe one or two of her youngsters. I wanted to know what it would take to build a business that actually *created jobs for* poor people. There had to be something more than selling tomatoes or rice or baskets; besides, I wanted to see for myself what it would take to make a business work in Rwanda. I started asking around to see if anyone could point me to a business with more than a few workers.

Honorata, the shy woman who worked with Veronique, told me about a project she'd helped create for single mothers in Nyamirambo, the popular section of Kigali where lower-income people lived. When Prudence overheard us, she whispered in my ear that the women were prostitutes. I shrugged but didn't really pay attention, as it seemed to me the word was used too easily in Rwanda. Women who danced late at the same nightclubs I did could easily be labeled wanton or worse. Besides, I was eager to visit any legitimate business with potential for real growth.

Boniface drove us through the wealthy neighborhood of Kiyovu, down Avenue Paul VI, and into Nyamirambo. The day was hot; the air, heavy; the streets were jammed with cars crawling along, manuevering around potholes. Women walked hand in hand carrying enormous bundles on their heads. Small shops stood one after another, almost always doubling as homes. Kiosks, tailors, hair salons, pharmacies, stores that played videos at night were painted blue, green, yellow, orange, though the paint had worn off over the years and the colors had faded. The unpaved side roads were filled with old auto parts and the burned-out bodies of ancient vehicles. At the top of the hill stood a large mosque painted white with stripes of bright green. It reminded me of a wedding cake, a small oasis rising out of its chaotic surroundings.

The "kiosk Allah"—a little shop selling sundries—and an Islamic school were located next to the mosque, where the streets divided. Nyamirambo had a sizable Muslim population for a country that was mostly Catholic at the time. Turning right, we passed a tailor shop, a clothing boutique, and a shoe repair store, in front of which stood a 3-foot-long wingtip oxford shoe on a tall stick. Two doors down stood our destination: a singularly unimpressive gray cement building that housed Project AAEFR (Association Africaine pour des Entreprises Féminins du Rwanda).

"I've worked with them for years," Honorata told me. "The women have such good intentions, and you will like them, I am sure."

All I could hear was my mother telling me that the path to hell is *paved* with good intentions. Her moral philosophy was that we show the world who we are through our actions, not merely through words or intentions. The detritus, disasters, and despair unwittingly created by well-intentioned people and institutions across Africa were evidence that my mother was right.

The group known as the Femmes Seules (or single women, code for unwed mothers) was one of many women's groups organized in part by Honorata and Veronique's Ministry for Family and Social Affairs. The women, among the city's poorest, would gather for training and some form of income generation. This particular group focused on a "baking project," which consisted of making and then selling a few goods in town and sewing dresses and crafts on order. In a moment, it was clear to me that "income generation" was a misnomer. Only one woman was sewing at all; the rest were simply sitting quietly.

There were about 20 of them in the cramped front room, all identically dressed in green gingham short-sleeved smocks, sitting on two long wooden benches in front of a pine counter with empty shelves behind it. There were no baked goods to be seen and no sign advertised what the group did.

"How long have they been waiting for us?" I whispered to Honorata.

"I don't know," she responded, "but they are used to waiting for visitors."

I hated that dynamic: powerless women just sitting, waiting all day if a donor was expected to visit, hoping someone might come in the door with help but feeling powerless to do anything for themselves.

I looked around at the women appreciatively. Bowing my head slightly, I said hello: "*Amakuru.*"

Faces lit up, and one woman held her hand across an otherwise unfettered smile. In unison, the women responded "*Imeza,*" meaning "fine." When one or two began talking to me in Kinyarwanda, I looked around awkwardly at Honorata and felt great relief when she began to translate. Any small effort to communicate on my part elicited gracious appreciation. Kinyarwanda is complex and difficult, and has what seems like four or five syllables in every word. The women applauded when I used some Swahili, for at least most of the Muslim women spoke that language. Still, I knew my African-language skills were on a child's level at best.

A solid, affable-looking woman named Prisca, also dressed in the green checkered uniform, stood in front of the group. With smiling eyes, a square jaw, and a wide, open face, she reminded me of my great-aunts who were built like tree trunks, with strong hands that knew hard work and sweat. She took my hand.

"Welcome," she said. "We're happy you've come to visit." She was hoping I would bring resources, preferably money, but her warmth was genuine.

While Prisca and I spoke French, the women stared. In Rwanda, children of the elites were taught French from a young age, but the poor learned only Kinyarwanda in primary school. Most of these women had spent only a year or two in school at most and couldn't speak a word of French. They seemed to range in age from 18 to their late twenties and carried themselves with an air of innocence and simplicity, wearing not a speck of makeup, jewelry, nail polish, or revealing clothing. Most women wore flip-flops, and their dresses could have passed for prison attire.

I thought of the word *prostitute* and the distancing power of language. Women with no money and few options are too easily categorized as throwaways. The poorest women in Africa often raise children while their husbands work in other places—if they even have husbands—and their poverty sometimes causes them to sleep with a landlord when they can't afford the rent. It is an act driven not by commerce but by the need for survival in a cruel market. Whether or not any of the women in this project ever did this was not a concern of mine. I was infuriated by the license people felt to brand women who, though incredibly disadvantaged, shared the dreams of everyone else.

After I introduced myself, the women shyly revealed their names:

Marie-Rose, Gaudence, Josepha, Immaculata, Consolata—names that reminded me of doilies and lace, not business. There was gentleness in the way each responded, and I wanted to find some way to be of service.

I could see that the sewing project was going nowhere, especially with the country's burgeoning secondhand clothing business. I asked Prisca to help me understand the baked goods project. First, she gave me a tour of the little two-room building where the project was housed. In the back room, an electric oven stood alone, flanked only by a table and a waffle iron. Outside, several pots filled with samosas shimmying in oil sat on handmade stoves. The women were preparing a snack for us, though we'd come with no money and no promises.

I asked Prisca how the project operated. "It's simple," she said. "Each morning, several women come very early to prepare the day's selection. It is always the same, but the people like that."

I would come to know that selection better than I ever wanted to: beignets (fried lumps of dough), *batonnets* (the same dough molded into sticks and fried), samosas, tiny waffles, and hot tea with milk and sugar. The women would take the goods to the government offices in the middle of the morning and sell them for 10 francs each. They'd then come back with whatever cash they'd earned and give it to Prisca, saving whatever food wasn't sold for the next day.

In concept, I liked the idea. I knew from my own experience at UNICEF that people would get very hungry by 10:30 or 11:00 in the morning because everyone arrived at work at 7:30 and didn't have a break until lunchtime. There were no little stores selling snack foods on the corners, and people rarely brought treats from home. The problem with the "project mentality" was that the quality of the goods was mediocre, and there didn't seem to be a system for deliveries.

"How can I be of help?" I asked.

Prisca answered, "The women are too poor. They earn too little money. They work every day, but the project is losing money every week."

Honorata nodded in agreement.

"How much do the women earn?" I asked.

"Fifty francs a day," Prisca responded—50¢. "And most are raising multiple children."

"How much do you lose?"

Prisca took out the big green ledger in which she carefully recorded every franc spent, earned, and paid to the women. On average, the project was losing about $650 a month.

"Who covers the losses?" I asked.

"Two charities," Prisca said. "But I don't know how long they will renew our funding."

"They shouldn't renew it," I wanted to say but held my tongue. Six hundred and fifty dollars a month in charity to keep 20 women earning 50¢ a day. You could triple their incomes if you just gave them the money. It was a perfect illustration of why traditional charity too often fails: In this case, well-intentioned people gave poor women something "nice" to do, such as making cookies or crafts, and subsidized the project until there was no more money left, then moved on to a new idea. This is a no-fail way to keep already poor people mired in poverty.

I wondered aloud why the charities didn't get tired of keeping the enterprise going just to employ a group of women for so little income. How would this survive in the long term? How would *the women* ever really change their circumstances?

Prisca shrugged. "People get by."

"Prisca, that's not enough," I said.

"No," she said, visibly embarrassed, "it isn't."

I was foolish to start with criticism. This is where so many Westerners fail: After a quick appraisal, we're ready to tell people in low-income communities not only what's wrong with what they're doing, but also just how to fix it.

I apologized and tried again: "Could you be selling more? Could you cut costs?"

They already had, Prisca explained. "It is easier to find more people to buy than to cut costs." She looked at me as if the ball was now in my court.

I thought for a moment. "I'll make a deal with you," I said slowly. "If we drop the charity and run this as a business, I'll help make it work." I held out my hand. "Are you okay with this?"

Prisca lifted her left eyebrow in surprise. When she took my hand, she emphatically responded "*Sana,*" meaning "very much" in Swahili.

Our goals would be those of any business: to increase sales and cut costs. We'd start tomorrow, and we'd turn this project into a real enterprise with profits and losses.

As Honorata and I climbed into the jeep, I looked at her and laughed. "Who would have thought that I, who cannot cook to save my life, would end up helping a group of women with a bakery in Nyamirambo? Honorata, do you think the women will be up to the task of running this as a business instead of a charity project? Do you think I'll be able to teach them to sell? I mean, the women themselves hardly said a word, mostly looking at the floor while I spoke. I don't think this is going to be easy."

She looked at me with an impish smile. "Maybe the good Lord wants to teach you something, too."

I started early the next morning. The women greeted me warmly, smiling broadly. Without a common language, we communicated through gestures and sprinkled words of French or Swahili. While the women prepared for the morning, I reviewed the books more thoroughly than I had the previous afternoon. The bakery had a long way to go, but the feeling of starting something that might change people's lives invigorated me. The world had written off this little group, yet they had a chance to do something important for themselves, and in doing so, maybe they would change perceptions of what the poorest women are capable of accomplishing.

Because we started with 20 women, it made sense to expand our revenues quickly to cover costs. Rather than convince our few current customers to buy more doughnuts each day, we needed to increase the number of people we served. And at that time in Kigali, the only way I could think of achieving this was to go door-to-door, targeting agencies and institutions with enough employees to make it worth our while to visit.

I asked Prisca to translate for me: "Who will volunteer to come with me and speak with ambassadors and agency directors in town to see if they will offer our bakery services to their employees?" Twenty faces all turned downward.

"Don't worry," I said. "I'll do the talking, but you need to learn to market, and it will be fun."

No movement.

Consolata, a tall, thin woman whose long face reminded me of a Giacometti painting despite the wide gap between her teeth, made the mistake of glancing up before the others did. I chose her to be my partner. The other women laughed and clapped to think of their shy friend knocking on office doors in Kigali.

Consolata was an elegant woman of few words who always wore a jean jacket over her gingham dress. She sat next to me in the backseat of the UNICEF jeep as Boniface chatted in French up front. Consolata could only understand when I stopped him to ask him to translate.

"What do you normally say to people in the offices when you want to sell to them?" I asked her.

"Normally, I don't say anything," she nearly whispered. Boniface had to ask her to repeat herself before he could translate. "I just walk through the government agencies and everyone knows what I'm carrying, so they call me over." Honorata had convinced the entire Ministry of Family and Social Affairs to allow the women to sell, and it was the project's biggest client.

We discussed what it takes to find a new customer—how to establish a relationship, build credibility right up front, and provide the potential customer with a sample of the goods. Though Consolata looked at me like I was crazy, she listened to every word.

We visited five embassies and most of the UN agencies that first long day. Though Consolata said little, we made progress. After the French Embassy agreed to invite the women to their offices the next morning, I gave her a strong hug and, after a moment of shock, she laughed and hugged me back. We arrived at the project in Nyamirambo as the sun was setting, exhausted, both of us content. We had doubled the number of customers—and we had gone well beyond the Rwandan government departments to supply UN agencies and a number of embassies, too. We were in business.

The next morning, I arose earlier than usual to jog through the misty, leafy suburb of Kiyovu to Nyamirambo, where the world was waking. The equatorial sun had barely risen. Women with baskets of bananas on their heads with their small children beside them walked like shadows in the soft morning light. It took less than half an hour to arrive at the project, where I found the women already hard at work, squatting on their heels, cooking doughnuts in a traditional woklike pot over an open fire while hurling gossip back and forth, producing an enchanting melody to accompany the crackle of hot oil shimmying as the lumps of dough hit the pan.

By 8:00 a.m., others began arriving to clean, help with cooking, and then organize the freshly made goods into bright orange plastic buckets. Each woman was responsible for taking what she could sell and returning the leftovers. I watched Josepha and the others choose their selections, the orange buckets a lovely contrast to their green gingham dresses. They would pick up a thermos of tea as well, walk into the street, and disappear into a crowded white minibus, juggling their wares on their laps as best they could. For at least some, the new day took courage, for they were going to embassies and other places where they'd never been before.

Sales jumped in the first week, but not as much as they should have. Something was wrong with our inventory accounting. We just didn't make enough money at the end of the day in relation to what had been prepared in the morning. When the women returned their buckets and gave us the cash they'd earned, Prisca and I couldn't account for more than a third of the goods produced. My heart sank with the knowledge that the women were stealing. We were putting so much goodwill and trust into this—into *them*. Didn't they owe us some level of appreciation or accountability?

Apparently not from their perspective. For example, one woman had told us she'd sold 10 products, but by our calculations, she had taken 23. She was either eating a lot of greasy doughnuts herself or selling them and keeping the money. I was crushed; Prisca was more sanguine, reminding me that Consolata, Gaudence, and a number of other women were being completely honest.

I tried not to take it personally, though I knew the women were testing my mettle. We couldn't count on their being honest out of appreciation alone—they'd seen too many like me come and go. The bigger question was how to fix the immediate problem and then create the right incentives for the business to sustain itself long after I'd left.

The existing bookkeeping system had been built entirely on trust and lacked any checks and balances for accountability. No one had noted how many goods each woman took in the morning, making it impossible to calculate whether they were returning the right combination of cash and unsold goods in the afternoon. As it turned out, some of the women were simply keeping the money they collected, not thinking about the consequences. I realized that some women didn't take the system seriously because they didn't see *us* taking it seriously.

I had seen this dynamic play out already with some of the borrowers at Duterimbere. The women were testing us, and this time I knew what we had to do in order to show them that we cared.

Prisca and I stayed up late crafting a simple system that would ensure accountability and reward individual behavior as well as group success. In the morning, we delivered a stern talk about high expectations and how we were all in this together. If there were profits, everyone would share in them. If there were losses, everyone's pay would be reduced, accordingly. The women would be paid a base wage and then earn a commission on total individual sales. The success of this venture would become the responsibility of the women themselves.

I was becoming clearer in setting expectations; more importantly, the women began treating me with a greater degree of respect. Human beings establish rules of interaction early in almost all relationships, and we still had work to do in breaking the charitable project mentality and turning this into a business.

Every Friday we gathered as a group in the front room of the project's building for a combination of Business 101 and a pep talk. Often I would ask the women to role-play with me. One week, I volunteered Gaudence, the gloomiest of the group, to be the saleswoman. Gaudence had close-cropped hair and the droopiest eyes I'd ever seen. Making her smile became one of my goals. While I didn't exactly see her as the group's natural extrovert, no one else came to mind, either.

"Okay," I said in French, always with Prisca translating for me. "I'm from the neighborhood and I smell samosas cooking, so I come inside. What do you do?"

Gaudence looked down, holding her hands behind her back. She stood still and said nothing.

I took a deep breath.

"Let's talk about eye contact," I continued. After discussing the basics of making customers feel welcome, I tried role-playing again and got little response. Gaudence was miserable. The women howled with laughter.

I decided to try again with someone else. "Consolata, I'm sitting next to you on the minibus, feeling hungry. Can you sell me something before I get off the bus?"

When Prisca translated, the room erupted with giggles that flowed like just-opened champagne.

Consolata just shook her head and mumbled.

Prisca smiled her oh-poor-you-who-have-so-much-to-learn smile.

"Why?" I asked.

Prisca didn't wait for the women to respond. "Because women do not just ask strangers to buy things on buses," she said with an air of exasperation.

"Why not?"

The women burst out laughing all over again. They tried to be formal, but this was too much fun—for them.

Prisca explained, "Because it is not polite."

Not polite: a perfect euphemism for "it is not done here." In other words, women who saw themselves on the lowest rung of society's ladder would never have the confidence to interrupt someone on a bus to try to sell him something. It just wasn't done here, and the women knew it. Though I understood the custom, I wanted to push the issue to see if I could instill greater confidence in these women who had such potential for growth.

We returned to our class on customer relations and building a market where everyone knew our goods and wanted to buy from us. The more animated I became, the harder the women laughed.

Seeing that I was not attuned to the women, Prisca said kindly, softly,

"Jacqueline, you are so American. Here, women won't look someone in the eye, won't talk to someone they don't know. You have to accept it, for that is how things are done."

"I know that, Prisca, I really do," I said, exasperated. "I just want to give the women a fighting chance. I have never unquestioningly accepted the status quo, so why should we do that here in Rwanda, where change can be a good thing? It isn't like I'm asking the women to do something wrong. I'm just trying to nudge them a bit to think about how we might turn our project into a real bakery, with real incomes for all of them. That means getting a little bit uncomfortable, but we don't have to break all sorts of customs."

"I understand you," Prisca said, "but change is slow here. You have to give the women time."

"Measuring success through our profits can be a great incentive for change, Prisca," I said.

She just looked at me and shook her head kindly.

"Okay, just watch this," I said. Grabbing an orange bucket filled with little doughnuts and waffles and samosas, I marched up the stairs to the sunlit street. Standing out front, I talked to the people passing by and in no time sold 10 doughnuts, more than some women had sold all day. Then I turned around with a flourish, marched into the room, and took a bow.

The women clapped and chortled, waving their hands in the air. In contrast, Prisca held her face in her hands and shook her head again. "Jacqueline, no one will say no to a tall American girl selling them things on the streets of Nyamirambo!"

Finally conceding defeat, I decided to save lesson two for another day.

But I would not acquiesce. To try and increase sales, I ran competitions for the women to see who could sell the most (no one would participate). I held training sessions on how to treat customers (the response was tepid at best). I continued the pep talks every Friday and reminded the women that we were going to create a real bakery and not just a project, that we would bring quality snacks to people all over Kigali. Prisca would translate and the women would smile patiently, and though I wasn't always sure they understood what I was saying, sales began to improve. Finally, something was working.

Within several months, the project was profitable. The women were coming to work on time and, though they still weren't enthusiastic sales-people, they were becoming known around Kigali for their bright orange buckets and affordable snacks. More and more institutions signed up for deliveries, and the women began to see—for the first time in their lives—a real correlation between the effort they put into their work and the income they earned. They began to believe the organization could succeed and that they themselves would play a key part in that success.

Still, for every two steps forward, there was often one back. One afternoon, I received a call from a friend who had expected the women to deliver an order of goods for a party; nothing had arrived. I called Prisca. She informed me that none of the women on duty had shown up. This was in the age before cell phones, so it took a while to track down Consolata, Josepha, and the others. Finally, we learned they'd all gone to the funeral of a friend, thinking the order for baked goods could wait.

I drove to the bakery project with Boniface to find Prisca and a few of the women she'd tracked down in the neighborhood working feverishly to fill the order. We were nearly 2 hours late to the party, but my friend at least pretended to understand. Still, I was livid and Prisca was embarrassed. The next morning we asked the women who had attended the funeral what had happened. They answered very matter-of-factly that their friend had died and the lady with the party would have to wait.

That Friday, we called a meeting. The women gathered on the benches and sat silently, most just staring ahead. We talked about promises made and the importance of promises kept. "We're not telling you not to go to the funeral," Prisca told the women, "but there are enough of us here that you can find a replacement for yourself if for some reason you can't work. Remember this is *your* business."

The women were only beginning to internalize that the success of the project was really up to them. For it to succeed, everyone had to see it as a full-fledged enterprise. We had enough customers to turn a profit, and it had become time to claim ourselves to be a legitimate business. Though I'd told the women this on my very first visit, it was several months before they began to believe it.

I shared with Prisca an idea I had to turn the little house in Nyamirambo into a real bakery from which we could sell our goods directly to neighborhood customers. Townspeople already referred to the project as a bakery, but it didn't have a main store, a place where people could drop in to buy our goods. The women would still go into town to offices each morning with their buckets, but once we had an actual store, we could increase sales, build our brand, and begin to expand into other product lines. Prisca loved the idea.

The first step was to give our building a fresh coat of paint. The exterior had been painted a dull gray stucco; the interior beige walls were smudged and scratched. Everything needed sprucing up. Consciously trying to learn to listen and not just hand out my own ideas, I offered to pay for the paint and other materials, but insisted that the women choose the color themselves.

When they would not offer an opinion on the color, I resisted making my own suggestions, knowing the women would try to please me instead of saying what they really felt. I told them repeatedly that this was *their* bakery, on *their* street, in *their* country, but my words seemed to land on deaf ears.

"What do *you* think?" they would ask.

One week, 2 weeks, 3 weeks passed. Each week, I asked the same question. Each week, I got nowhere.

Finally, at the end of the third week, I gave up, unable to take the waiting anymore. "What about blue?" I asked.

"Blue, blue, we love blue. Let's do it blue."

At the only paint store in town, I purchased a bright blue paint, picked up blue-checkered cloth for curtains, and found several big pieces of plywood to make into signs. The women sewed perfect curtains, and I spent an entire night painting signs to hang inside and outside the bakery so that we would have an identity as the blue bakery of Nyamirambo. The signs were written in French for prestige, though most people in Nyamirambo could understand only Kinyarwanda, and many couldn't read. Status counted for a lot.

When painting day arrived, everyone turned out to help. My friend Charles, a tall, lanky, 25-year-old French Canadian who worked for the United Nations Development Program, arrived dressed in his signature wrinkled oxford shirt and khakis. The women warmed to him the minute he turned on the music and Aretha Franklin's rhythmic melodies and golden voice filled the streets. Together, we looked at the color in the paint cans—it was a pure blue, bright and straightforward, and everyone liked it.

The original idea was to paint the interior walls bright white and use the blue for trim, both inside and out. But this approach was not as satisfying as painting a wall blue like a morning sky. We even painted some of the windows blue. The women danced, laughed, and painted the world. Gaudence's short hair became speckled with blue paint. Parts of the sidewalk out front were painted bright blue, and little blue freckles appeared on the face of the gray stucco walls outside. Above us, the clear sky felt like a giant crystal dome, and a gentle breeze seemed to tinkle blessings upon this forgotten corner of the world.

A neighborhood crowd gathered to watch the phenomenon of women wielding blue paintbrushes, refusing to acquiesce to little boys begging for turns to paint. Onlookers munched on waffles and people danced in the street. When Aretha shouted "R-E-S-P-E-C-T," hips and paintbrushes moved to the rhythm. Even Gaudence was smiling.

After more than 8 straight hours of painting, we were finished. I joined the women outside in the street to look at what we'd accomplished. We were hot and hungry and covered in blue. For a minute we didn't say a word.

It was so beautiful.

The color was perfect, I said. Most of the heads around me nodded in agreement—except for that of Gaudence.

I looked at her as she sucked in her breath. "What?" I asked with my eyes.

She whispered to Prisca, who shook her head slowly.

"What?" I asked again, one eyebrow raised.

"She thinks it is very nice," Prisca translated, "but you know, Jacqueline, our color is green."

Gaudence had been the only one courageous enough to tell the truth about the paint color, but she'd waited until it was too late. We all agreed that the color of the bakery would have to be blue—but the women would continue wearing their green gingham uniforms for contrast.

I walked home alone from Nyamirambo that evening, covered in paint, feeling tired, elated, and also perplexed that I'd tried so hard to listen and still ended up choosing the wrong color. On one hand, I hadn't wanted to wait for months until the women made a decision. On the other, I began to understand that I could have listened better, for listening is not just having the patience to wait, it is also learning how to ask the questions themselves. People who've always been dependent on others for some kind of charity or goodwill often have a hard time saying what they really want because usually no one asks them. And if they are asked, the poor often think no one really wants to hear the truth. I had to admit to myself that I was still building trust.

The reality of our beautiful new bakery didn't stop the setbacks, of course. One morning I walked into the offices at UNICEF and was told by a frantic Damescene, the office assistant, that half of Kigali had called. "It seems that everyone in the city is suffering from eating the baked goods," he said.

"What do you mean by 'suffering'?" I asked.

He looked at the floor in embarrassment. "You know," he said gently, "maybe they are having pains in their stomach, and many are going home sick."

Feeling like Typhoid Mary, I called all of the embassies and government offices to apologize and promised to take care of the problem. Boniface and I drove quickly to the bakery and approached the women cooking in back.

"Everyone is sick with the runs," I said. "Did you do anything differently?" They shook their heads.

I asked to see what they were preparing. The smell was stale, sour, and rancid.

"When did you last change the cooking oil?" I asked.

"Oh, never," Josepha answered gleefully. "We have been adding just a little more each day. We are keeping costs low so that we can have high sales and more profit."

Next lesson: quality control.

Despite the bumps in the road, within a few months we had cornered the snack market in Kigali, expanding beyond our repertoire of fried dough in a variety of shapes to making cassava chips and banana chips (thinly sliced, fried in oil, dusted with salt and chili powder, then placed in plastic bags) and peanut butter. When we purchased plastic containers from the local honey factory for the latter, I began dreaming about starting a factory to create hundreds, if not thousands, of jobs, for I'd witnessed the difference the bakery had made in those 20 women's lives. Few investors or donors were prepared to invest in Africa, yet I was seeing tremendous potential for change. I told myself that at some point in my life, I would come back with more experience to start a factory or do something more directly focused on large-scale private enterprise that created new jobs.

But for the moment, my life when I wasn't working with Duterimbere was focused on ensuring the bakery was a success. The cassava and banana chips turned out to be favorites with the locals. We sold our spicy chips to most of the retail stores, and people would drop by the bakery in Nyamirambo to pick up packets, as well. I still did too much of the marketing, but in time the women gained the confidence to venture into stores to replenish orders. Sometimes, a few of the women and I would walk through little shops in town just to point proudly to our products on the shelves. Together we had created a new product that hadn't existed before—and people liked it! Nothing could be more satisfying.

Within 8 months or so, the women were earning $2 a day—four times more than when we started together, and much more than most earned in Kigali; and in some weeks, they earned more than $3. Few people earned that kind of money in Rwanda, certainly not women. For the first time, their incomes allowed them to decide when to say yes and when to say no. Money is freedom and confidence and choice. And choice is dignity. The solidarity of the bakery also gave them a sense of belonging that made them even stronger.

Once the bakery cornered the market for snack foods, we decided to focus on bread. The bread in Kigali was generally atrocious. The United States and a number of countries in Europe were dumping surplus wheat grown by heavily subsidized farmers on countries like Rwanda, so that rich and poor alike had little choice but to buy bleached white, weevil-ridden flour. A few stores in town made their own bread, but it was often stale. At the same time, sorghum fields abounded in the areas around Kigali, and the price for it was low—possibly the key to creating a rich grain bread.

Prisca and I discussed the value of bringing nutritious bread to the market, especially for low-income women who would benefit from the lower cost. An Italian woman gave her a recipe, and she experimented until she'd baked a delicious whole-grain bread. We tried selling it in Nyamirambo, but quickly met with failure. Poor urban Rwandans preferred the white bread, not because it tasted better but because it was a symbol of luxury, of something imported. It didn't matter that it was more expensive—in fact, the higher price made the imported bread even more desirable.

Despite the many experiments, the failures, and the setbacks, the little bakery continued to flourish under Prisca's leadership, and she created at least one place in Nyamirambo that operated on its own merit, covering its costs with the products it sold and teaching the women that they could control their own lives. It operated for a long time after I left—until the genocide destroyed so much of what was beautiful.

The story of the bakery was one of the human transformation that comes with being seen, being held accountable, succeeding. I had the privilege of watching the women acquire a sense of dignity once they were given tools for self-sufficiency, and I learned that language is perhaps only half the equation in how people communicate with one another. I discovered the power of creating a business with real accountability. And I learned to be myself and to laugh at myself, to share in the women's successes, and, maybe most importantly, to listen with my heart and not just my head.

CHAPTER 6

DANCING IN THE DARK

"I have only one request. / I do not ask for money / Although I have need of it, /
I do not ask for meat . . . / I have only one request, /
All I ask is / That you remove / the roadblock / From my path."

—OKOT P'BITEK, "SONG OF AN AFRICAN WOMAN"

It was early 1988, and I was still spending most of my time in Kigali with Duterimbere and the blue bakery. Given my schedule, I had only my early morning runs for recreation as well as reflection. I have always cherished the dawn, especially in Africa. I love being part of a place's awakening—watching the sky glow brighter, listening to the birds and insects calling. In Kigali, thick fog floats across the dark green hills like a band of whipped cream until it burns away to unveil the bright blue sky. Canopied streets filled with bougainvillea and hibiscus heave their heavy scents, swirling perfume in the air.

One mild morning, despite the wake-up revelry, I could barely move a muscle. My joints ached, my head pounded, and nausea swirled. Dragging myself to the breakfast table, I described my symptoms to the houseguests, an Italian doctor and his wife, a nurse from Uganda. After glancing at one another, Margaret put her hand to my head and said simply, "Malaria."

They gave me quinine and I went back to bed, where I would stay for the next few days, moving in and out of raging fevers accompanied by wild, intense dreams and deep pains in my elbows and knees. One minute my body would be racked with chills and the next, feel like it was on fire. Almost everyone I'd known in Rwanda had had malaria and some, like the woman from Duterimbere, had died from it. I now understood how the African continent could lose so much work productivity due to this illness alone: Each year, about a quarter *billion* Africans contract cases of malaria.

My friends calmed me, fed me papaya, gave me medicine, and made me drink hot tea. There is a Kiswahili saying: "Medicine for heat is heat." Hot tea for hot days and for fevers, too. I stayed in bed, wondering how long it would take to feel my energy again, grateful that I usually lived with such good health.

The delirium and achiness lasted about a week, and I was eager to jump back into life. There was much to do with both the bank and the bakery, and I didn't want to waste any more time. Cesare, the doctor who had such a gentle manner, urged me to take a day or two more to rest, and it was on the last day at home that Prudence visited unannounced.

She walked into my room and teased, "Maybe this was the only way God could help you slow down and rest a bit."

"Not funny," I responded, assuring her that I had relaxed and was feeling refreshed and excited to get back into the thick of things again.

Prudence sighed. "Oh, my dearest. We love how hard you are pushing the work forward. At the same time, you might be going too quickly for where Rwanda is right now. We have to move at the right pace. Change is more gradual here, you see? And we need to bring all of the women with us and not run too far ahead of them.

"What makes it harder to keep up with you," she continued, "is that our lives have so many obligations attached to them. We have funerals and weddings and births and so many commitments, you see? If you don't slow down, I worry that Duterimbere will rely too much on you and not on Rwandan women themselves."

Her honesty caused my face to flush and my stomach to drop. I was stunned that the women didn't like my pace, for no one had said a word to that effect. In fact, just the opposite had seemed true. Each time we met another deadline, everyone would cheer and remind themselves that we were doing the impossible. Of course, I'd been driving hard, anxious that the institution might flounder without a sense of urgency.

I took a deep breath, trying hard to listen to what Prudence was saying, knowing she was probably right. Perhaps my pace had been more about my agenda than theirs.

"What would you suggest I do?" I asked her, somewhat defensively.

"We've been thinking about that and talking to Mary Racelis."

Mary, UNICEF's East Africa regional director, was a great community organizer and a friend.

"We all think that with your energy, you would be well placed to spend 2 months here in Rwanda and then go to a UNICEF office somewhere in East Africa for 2 months to work with women in slums or rural women as well on enterprise development. It will give you the chance to see so much in Africa and also to help us build something that will last."

Though it stung to be considered a puppy, all eager and bouncy, the thought of having a break from Rwanda every 2 months was appealing: There was something about Kigali itself that felt oppressive. I wasn't sure what kind of work would be waiting for me in other East African locations, but I loved exploring new places.

A week later, I left for Nairobi to spend a few days with Mary Racelis. Over a plate of eggs and toast, the diminutive Filipino woman put her hand on my shoulder and told me what a gift Prudence had given to me.

"Do you know how lucky you are that she trusts you enough to tell you the truth?" she asked. "Prudence wants you to succeed just as she wants Duterimbere to succeed. She's just letting you know the right way to do it, not because you were doing anything wrong, but because there is a way you could be doing things more effectively. By giving women work plans and leaving them on their own for 2 months and then coming back reenergized, you will be helping to build an institution brick by brick."

AT IT TURNED OUT, I loved my life in Nairobi. Though it was just a few hours away from Kigali by plane, I always felt like I was returning to a mini-Manhattan when I boarded the flight to Kenya. Whereas Kigali was a small town with just a few restaurants and crafts stores, Nairobi was a true city, with galleries and bookstores, movie theaters, and a big international community. I would meet friends to watch foreign films at the French Cultural Center, have sushi at one of the Japanese restaurants, or dance at the Carnivore Restaurant, where waiters walked from table to table with enormous skewers of hartebeest, crocodile, and eland.

Maybe most important to me, the modest third-floor walk-up apartment I'd rented when I first arrived in Nairobi was as close to a permanent home as I had during that period. It was a one-bedroom with indoor-outdoor carpeting, a tiny kitchen and living room, a bathroom with an enormous tub, and small balconies in back and front—not much to brag about, but it was mine and I loved it. I'd decorated the walls with tapestries from my travels, batiks from the local markets, and baskets galore and would fill the rooms with fresh flowers whenever I was in town.

The apartment's interior was as colorful as the people who lived and worked in the building, mostly young, newly middle-class Kenyans or refugees from Somalia and Ethiopia, all striving for better lives. Since none of us had a telephone, we would shout to one another from our balconies and simply knock on doors to drop by. It was like dormitory life, though my travels to Kigali and other African capitals meant I was rarely there.

Despite these absences, I employed a short, affable woman named Rebecca to come to the apartment twice a week to clean though, in truth, there was very little to do. Even if I wasn't around, she would check up on things and water plants. Whenever I was home, Rebecca would ask for an allowance for bread, sugar, tea, and milk so that she could snack while she worked. She seemed to go through huge quantities, but I didn't pay much attention.

While working one morning in Nairobi, I drove back to the apartment after realizing I'd forgotten an important document. Though Bilo, the usually dour morning guard wasn't at his station in front, I thought nothing of it. I ran up the stairs and swung open the door to find the entire staff from the building on break in my living room, all with teacups in their hands.

"Rebecca," I said, "is this how you use the tea and bread?"

"Oh, yes," Rebecca answered sheepishly, head down at first. Then she quickly looked up, eyes shining, "But they are appreciating it so much, isn't it!"

I just shook my head and announced that teatime was over. Once everyone left, Rebecca and I had a long talk about taking things for granted. She said she understood but a minute later asked if she might still invite workers for tea, because not every employer allowed it. I shook my head again, but from then on, we had a tea allowance as long as people stayed in the living room and she took responsibility for anything that was missing. Nothing ever was.

On weekends, I would sometimes take the overnight train to Mombasa, a sleepy port city on Kenya's coast. White-gloved porters would bring bedding and dinners of Indian curry, and I would read novels through the night as the train chugged across the savanna and on to the Indian Ocean. I loved the Arab-influenced architecture of Mombasa, the swaying palm trees in the sand, and the easy pace at which everyone walked. Muslim women covered in their chadors would squabble with one another, trading their wares, their bangles tinkling against pretty wrists. At night, friends would gather at the beach to sip cold beers and listen to locals and hippie tourists singing and strumming guitars.

Along with good friends, there was still time for romance, though I remained always more committed to my work than to permanent relationships. For most of the time I lived in East Africa, my Colombian American boyfriend, dark-eyed and curly haired, lived in Addis Ababa, and we would meet for adventures every month or so in locales from the far reaches of Ethiopia to the Kenyan savannas to the volcanoes of Rwanda, where we would watch the mountain gorillas and marvel that they were so like us. Whatever money either of us earned was spent on travel, and though our relationship didn't last, our romance energized me for the harder moments in daily life.

After we broke up, for a short while I dated a Swedish-born rhino tracker raised in Kenya, a tall and willowy blond man with a gentle personality and a deep love for Africa. Sometimes we'd meet right after work to drive through the Nairobi Game Park at the edge of town with a bottle of wine and a picnic as the sun was setting. On the savanna, we'd point in awe at the graceful silhouettes of acacia trees in the fading light, smell the dirt and wind and the coming rain, and then dance slowly outside the car, besotted with the endless swirl of orange and pink sky and the slow loping of the giraffes and antelopes near the water holes, feeling the sweet ache of being so fully alive.

My life in Nairobi, as in Rwanda, was one of extremes, moving from magical adventures to the realities of life for the very poor, sometimes within a single day. On the other side of the city's tracks, more than a million people lived in slums such as Mathare Valley, Kibera, Pumwani, and Soweto, in shantytown houses made of mud and corrugated metal sheets. There were no clear streets, just winding alleyways, open sewers, the smell of trash, and wandering children sniffing glue. Men skinned goats and hung meat in open-air markets that swirled with flies. That this world existed in such close proximity to the gorgeous tree-lined suburbs of Nairobi and its spacious national park made the desperation even crueler.

Despite horrendous material conditions, enormous strength emanated from those slums. I met many women who were raising five or six children on a dollar a day, mostly on their own, often working as maids in town or selling bunches of greens or tomatoes by the roadsides. Some made charcoal from ashes and mud, others sold water or made *changaa,* a lethal moonshine made from grains like maize and sorghum which they sold from *changaa* shacks that were easily recognizable because of the fancy cars parked outside, most of them belonging to Kenyan government officials. Though women typically lived in one-room boxes with dirt floors, their homes were usually immaculate, and the dishes and pots on hand were clean and neatly stacked.

Meanwhile, I found myself frustrated once again by development "experts" who looked in from the outside and suggested clever solutions that created a lot of noise, distorted markets, resulted in systemic corruption, and accomplished little. On the bright side, the international development field had recognized the importance of investing in women, for study after study demonstrated that, unlike men, women would spend any additional income on school fees or more food for their children. Bilge had said it when we first met in Rwanda: Help a woman and you help a family.

While the importance of women was clearly recognized by most aid agencies, the actual solutions were misguided, mostly because few of the experts at agencies tried putting themselves in the shoes of the women. One of the Kenyan government's programs focused on giving grants to women's groups so they could start and manage "income-generating projects." The idea was that women worked well in groups and could earn additional income by running a maize mill or a water kiosk, a poultry farm or a crafts project. Each group would be asked what it wanted to do and then given about $500 to implement its idea. The income from the group activity was intended to amplify what each woman was already earning from her own efforts.

Initially, the program looked like a great success. Grassroots projects sprang up among women's groups across Kenya. The donors would visit, say, a group of a dozen women who had built a chicken coop for a couple hundred chicks. The women would proudly present eggs that had recently been laid and talk about how they planned to sell them to the community. They would serve the donors Fantas and, often, cookies, and sometimes sing and dance, as well. The donors would leave feeling satisfied, happy that they were making such a difference.

In reality, most donors were doing little to change lives, and in some cases, they were making things worse for the women's groups—at least that was my growing impression. Too often, 6 months after receiving their grant, a project's chickens might all die from a flu for which the women lacked proper medicines. Sometimes neglect by individual group members would leave a project in decline. There seemed neither rhyme nor reason to the ways different groups took on their projects, and no one seemed to pay attention to the actual finances.

I raised my concerns one night over dinner with Mary Racelis, for she had witnessed firsthand the extraordinary resilience of people living in slums and approached low-income communities with great respect. I told her that I was concerned that the results of the women's projects, partly funded by UNICEF, might not be as rosy as the government officials were reporting. From fellow development workers, I'd heard that many projects had been abandoned by the women.

Mary offered me a short-term contract to review the programs, counseling me to spend my next 2 months away from Kigali in the slums of Nairobi, Mombasa on the coast, and Kisumu on Lake Victoria. At the end of the period, I would be expected to recommend changes to the program if they were needed. I knew Mary would take it seriously, and I didn't hesitate to say yes.

I've met amazing individuals such as Mary inside big institutions, though her leadership abilities were a cut above those of the others. She was unafraid to seek and speak the truth, and she let young people lead. A few days after my dinner with Mary, I met a woman from another international agency that also funded the women's groups, and I voiced the same concern about the effectiveness of the "income-generating programs."

"How do you define success?" I asked.

"We want to lift women out of poverty," she told me, leaning back on her wooden chair, her hair pulled back in a tight bun, her arms crossed in front of her dark blue jacket.

"Yes, I know," I acknowledged, "but how do you know when you've been successful?"

"You can see it with your own eyes."

"But how do you know what you are *seeing* without real measures of accountability? And how do you know when you've failed?" I asked.

Her cold blue eyes narrowed to slits. "We have no failures. Even if things don't work out, we learn from everything we do."

Her pat answer stopped me cold. "I agree," I said, "we should learn from failures, but we have to name them first, talk about them, *learn* from them."

"Of course," she answered flatly, but she wouldn't cite a single mistake. Her opaque circularity flummoxed me. I thanked her and walked out.

In reviewing the women's groups' programs, I worked with a Kenyan woman from the Department of Local Government named Mary Koinange. While the department was known equally for a shameful lack of urgency and a dearth of results in the slums, Mary herself was a stand-out. A lively woman of about 50 who wore prim, high-collared dresses and lace-up shoes, she shined with great spirit and a fierce sense of right and wrong. Mary shared countless stories of life before indepen-dence and walked with the air of someone who knew suffering and feared it might come again. My days were filled with her questions and frank philosophies about life.

"I want to be free like you," she once declared.

I told her she was.

She shook her head slowly. "African women," she stated, "are not free. Especially not poor ones. When we dance we can be free, but life for women is too hard."

The two of us began visiting women's groups across the country on a daily basis as part of our work for UNICEF. At the time, it was illegal in Kenya to hold a meeting of more than 10 people without reporting it to the government, which is why so many groups of women were officially registered. Everywhere we found women's groups who spoke proudly of what they did, and it was only when we pressed them for details that their stories began to unravel.

At one site near Kisumu, a sleepy town on the shores of Lake Victoria, the government had supplied a women's group with concrete for build-ing houses; however, when we arrived months later, we found that noth-ing but the foundations had been laid. There wasn't enough cement for complete houses and there was no money to continue construction. Mary nearly spat at the lost opportunity.

"Much poorer people in Nairobi's slums just start by building two rooms with whatever materials they can afford. Then the family rents one of the rooms and uses the income to help expand the house over time. I know families who have made a real business—big business—out of renting rooms. Why don't the agencies start by looking at how smart people already are instead of giving them things that will make them fail?" she groaned.

I sighed, looking at the slabs of cement on the ground—empty prom-ises for a better life symbolically strewn next door to the hastily erected shanties where the women were actually living.

The slums at the outskirts of central Nairobi were some of the tough-est places I'd ever been. Groups of boys sniffing glue were a common sight, and crime was rampant; open sewers ran along muddy, narrow pathways. Public services like piped water, electricity, and garbage col-lection missed the slums altogether, though the people who lived in those urban squatter settlements would get water usually by paying a lot more than their middle-class counterparts did to local entrepreneurs who knew how to break into mainline pipes. People survived through unyielding determination and focusing day-to-day.

It was in the slums of Nairobi that the development community nonetheless had great hopes for success due to the resourcefulness of the women, though we still found as many failures there as anywhere else. Some groups were given grants to construct legal "water kiosks," which consisted of a water pump in a little booth, where women could charge a reasonable price for water and then lock the kiosk at night to protect it from vandals.

The problem was that the pumps were often faulty, and the women were each expected to volunteer one day a week at the kiosk. They rarely showed up simply because they couldn't afford it. One group of four candidly told us it was easier earning income the way they'd always done it, whether by selling tomatoes or charcoal on the street. Besides, their water tap had broken one day, and they didn't have the money to repair it.

We saw countless examples of well-intentioned projects gone wrong: Hundreds of maize mills, an important labor-saving device, lay in disrepair because the locals weren't trained to fix them. Or the mills would lay idle because the village lacked access to the proper fuel to run them. Good-hearted people would build schools without thinking about the costs of hiring and supporting a teacher—not for months but for years— and the schools would stand empty. Women would be encouraged to make crafts though there was no market for them, and so we'd visit homes piled to the ceilings with unsold sisal baskets.

For 6 straight weeks, Mary and I would meet at 7:30 or 8:00 a.m. and drive till nightfall, going from group to group in my sky blue, 25-year-old Volkswagen Beetle, which lacked seat belts and headlights. Its wheels were out of alignment, and when it hit potholes, a daily occurrence, the steering wheel would shake violently, forcing me to wrestle with it until the wheels spun smoothly again. Starting the car required pushing it down a hill, jumping in, and then popping it into second gear. The car's quirks kept us laughing, but both Mary and I were suppressing a seething anger at the apathy and corruption of those with power and the crushing poverty that surrounded us.

"Is corruption a cause of poverty?" I asked Mary one afternoon. "Or is poverty a cause of corruption?"

"It is both, isn't it?" she answered sweetly.

I loved her calm manner, the way she would remind me that crime and poverty have been around since people started selling things to one another and that anger didn't help us in our work. "You must find a way to laugh whenever you can," she advised. "No one can hurt or kill when they are laughing."

"True," I said, "but we have to work on changing the whole game somehow, make corruption on all sides a source of greater shame—and reprimand those who are doing it." Mary, twice my age, smiled that I-wish-you-luck-I-really-do kind of smile I would come to know well.

Another challenge was eliciting truthful answers from women. "They've seen too many people like you come into their lives," Mary told me, "so why should they be honest with you? There might be some chance that you give them money if they answer your questions in the way you want to hear them."

What amazed me was how quickly the women learned the jargon of the development agencies and played it back to people like me. "How big is your market?" I would ask a group of women who were trying to sell their handicrafts.

"Big," they would answer.

"How big?"

"Oh, very big."

"And what did you use your grant for?" I would ask.

"For working capital," they would say, unable to explain what they meant. It wasn't that the women were hiding anything. Implicitly they seemed to understand the imbalance of power between us and used what they could to even the playing field.

I remember speaking to a group at the outer edge of a Nairobi slum about their goat-raising project, I was huddled in a hut in a light, cool rain, struggling with Swahili, stumbling over words, grateful that the women seemed to be listening, even if they looked confused. Finally, a brave woman asked me shyly whether I was talking about *buzi* (goats) or *busaa* (homemade beer). I laughed out loud, realizing I'd unintentionally been talking about the latter the entire time; the women chortled with me.

Thus began a conversation about the sale of *changaa,* or moonshine, one of the most profitable products the women could sell.

"Why can't we get a loan for our liquor business?" they asked. "The donors prefer giving us money to make baskets that no one wants," a woman joined in excitedly.

I responded that aid programs couldn't support something illegal. I had never tasted *changaa,* but I'd heard stories that in some villages its nickname had something to do with having your insides blown out and that people sometimes died from drinking from a bad batch. (As recently as 2005, the *New York Times* reported scores of deaths from people drinking the illegal brew, which has apparently become only more lethal over time.)

"But my best customers are government officials who drink all day," she responded. "And it is the only way I can earn enough money for my family to survive."

She had a point. Unless we could find something that could bring in a similar level of income, it was difficult to tell women they couldn't make the moonshine, especially when the "big fish" were their best customers.

Over our many visits, Mary and I came to understand the *real* process of government grant-making to women's groups. The local government department was divided into districts, each one run by a district officer, or DO, in charge of overseeing and supporting the residents in his or her area. Under the income-generating program, each DO was allocated grant money to disburse. Typically, the local DO would reach out to the women's groups in the district and ask for proposals for income-generating projects. Each group of 20 or so women would request $500 or $600 for their "projects." Once approved, the groups often would give the DOs kickbacks, or "fees," for their time and effort. Women told me it wasn't unusual for the "fee" to be 20 percent of the grant's total value. It didn't matter that the projects generated little, if any, income for the women involved.

Despite the failed systems, I saw great vitality and generosity in the individual women who survived whether or not they received donor support. The women would pool their money whenever a child was sick or a family member passed away. They helped one another laugh and sometimes just get by, which wasn't always easy.

One morning I walked past the corpse of a man who'd been "necklaced" the night before. Thugs had thrown a tire filled with gasoline around his neck and set it on fire. A group of men stood around the charred body, which smelled indescribably profane. When the body was removed, its image still remained scorched into the ground itself.

A few nights after the necklacing incident, I began writing our report for the Department of Local Government and UNICEF. A few nights later, I took a night off to go to the local cinema to see *Cry Freedom,* about the life of South African freedom fighter Stephen Biko, who understood that freedom is not just about political liberty, but also about economic independence and the power of choice. The women in the slums were operating under dependency, not freedom. If the donor community couldn't help these women liberate themselves, they needed to get out of their way.

ONE AFTERNOON, I REMAINED too late in Mathare Valley, one of Nairobi's most desperate slums, talking to a women's group until the darkening sky reminded me to leave. I crawled into my Volkswagen and sat for a minute, watching the slum dwellers run back and forth, setting up tables of dates and sweets and pitchers of water. It was the season of Ramadan. The neighborhood was coming to life again after the long, hot day as the Muslims got ready to break the fast and spend time with family. I was transfixed by the women's black veils flying, the children running, and a big purple cloud floating in the sky above. Day turns to night in an instant in Nairobi, especially when the rains come in one fell swoop.

With no warning, sheets of water began to fall, sending the women scurrying to their homes. As my car sank into the sludge, the wheels kept spinning but gained no traction. Tiny houses made of cardboard, mud, and coffee cans, with roofs of corrugated tin and plastic, seemed on the verge of floating away. Two girls wearing *kikois*—brightly colored cotton wraps serving as skirts—laughed as they carried huge woven baskets on their heads. The rain poured and poured, soaking the earth, turning dirt roads into rivers, and making it impossible to drive. Knowing it would be a dark, lonely return up the hill into town once the road was dry, I wanted to cry.

Suddenly there was a tapping on my window. I ignored it.

Tap tap tap again.

Standing outside was a slight, crooked woman with raisin eyes and a walnut face. She seemed to pay no mind to the storm swirling around her and motioned to me to come near, apparently offering the shelter of her little hut. I lowered my window, and though this was one of the most dangerous slums in the country, a place where I clearly didn't belong, there was something about her expression that made me trust her immediately.

"*Jambo,*" I sighed. "Hello. How are you?"

"*Nzuri sana,*" she answered in a scratchy voice. "*Habari gani?*" Very well, how are you?"

"I'm fine," I lied, irritated that we were exchanging pleasantries in the downpour.

She looked at me quizzically, then let a moment of silence hang as if she were contemplating my worth. Then that gravelly voice snapped, "*Kuja.*" Come.

Without another thought, I took her small, leathery hand and followed.

Awkwardly, we skipped across a muddy path toward a metal door. Opening it slowly, the old woman motioned me inside to a dark, chaotic room measuring perhaps 8 feet by 9, where 10 or so women were dancing to the beat of a single goatskin-covered drum played by a wizened old man seated in a corner. His skinny legs were crossed, his eyes half-closed. He appeared to be in a trance, lost in a world ruled by the primordial beat of the drum. I could feel the beat in my stomach and heart, so much so that I couldn't help swaying, moving slowly to the rhythm, feeling like I'd fallen into an alternative version of Alice's Wonderland.

Around me, the women glowed with unbridled, exuberant life. White teeth flashed joyful smiles. Muscular brown legs shook and glistened with sweat. Brightly colored cloths in turquoise, fuchsia, orange, and lime shimmied around thick waists. Bare feet pounded the dirt floor, dancing wildly.

The women danced in pairs, each one facing another, bent at the waist and touching only at the cheeks. They shook their shoulders and hips in a frenzied motion, ululating all the time. I joined the dancing, attaching myself first to one woman's cheek and then another, shaking, laughing, losing myself in the darkness, the noise, the heat. My face, wet with sweat and pressed against my counterpart's cheek, was the only part of myself held in relative stillness. The rest of my body felt electrified, hyperstimulated by the constant beat of the percussion, the staccato pounding of the rain on the tin roof, the eruption of passion permeating the air.

A lithe young woman flew out of the hut into the rain without a word and returned wearing a necklace of tin bottle caps that rattled like a snake when she shook. *Shshshsh tshsh tshsh tsh tsh tsh shshshsh tshsh tshshshs.* The necklace swished as the drum pounded. Sweating, breathing, undulating, shaking, shimmering, dancing in the darkness and heat. For a moment, all the frustration and rage inside me disappeared.

"Woo hooo," I yelped, and the women laughed and laughed.

This was the secret: Dance with the women, scream with joy, let sexuality be defined on your own terms without even touching one another. Be gorgeous, free, ecstatic. It was one of the most extraordinary moments of my life.

The fury inside the hut continued for perhaps another half hour, maybe more. But just as quickly as the room had exploded into motion, it fell completely quiet. The sky had turned dark blue. Steam from the mud floor swirled gently. I realized I'd not yet said a word. I felt a profound shyness overtake me and awkwardly introduced myself in Swahili, shaking each woman's hand, thanking them for the dance.

Walking out of the hut into the night felt like leaving a New York City bar in the middle of the afternoon. The evening was soft but accusing; the narrow paths and roadways, empty. I climbed back into my little car and sat for a moment. My body and my big white skirt were drenched as thoroughly as if I'd been walking in the rain. I yelped one final time in homage to these women who had found respite, a moment of relief. With that, my car jumped to life, and I flew up the hills and into town.

The next morning, I approached my friend Monika, an expert in all things Kenyan, to relate the previous night's adventure. I needed a reality check. Hesitating and stammering, I finally told her about the experience.

Laughing, she explained that I must have come across a group of women from the Kamba tribe, for they are known for their great love of percussion and dancing. "Kamba women learn from a young age to dance and not to fear being sensual," she said. "And you can see it when they move. Oh, how lucky you were!" she laughed.

For the next several weeks, I spent most days and nights completing my report, to be submitted to both the government and UNICEF. I focused on the good intentions as well as the few successes and tried to state unambiguously that the programs cost much more than they benefited people, but without alienating government officials to the point where they would disregard the report altogether. As Mary Koinange and I drove to the Department of Local Government to make our final presentation, I felt a great sense of anxiety. We arrived at the drab public sector building and went inside.

The deputy minister was waiting for us in his large office. He was beady-eyed and overweight and wore a black tie with white polka dots. Brown wingtips graced his feet, and on his pinkie, he wore a big gold ring. There were no papers on his desk and no phone, either, just a placard reading "Deputy Minister." We had sent him our report a week in advance, and I was surprised and pleased to find that he'd actually read it, even if he made it clear he hadn't liked the contents.

"The report is too pessimistic," he grumbled in a baritone voice. "Obviously, you didn't speak to the right people. I have seen miracles occur with those same women's groups." He ushered us out, passing us on to another official in a big, baggy suit, who drummed his fingers on his paper-cluttered desk in a dingy office. After a nearly identical conversation, we were shown to yet another tired official in another shabby office.

This one was lean and nervous and sat squeamishly in a wooden chair that seemed too large for him. "Yes, yes," he said finally, "lots of improvement needed, lots of work to do. But who will do it? Now you have told us what we are doing wrong; what will you do to make it right?"

I said I didn't think it was just up to us to make things right: The government had to decide that it wanted to see things done differently, as well.

I suggested that the aid money go directly to an NGO with the government's consent and that the NGO be held to strict accounting principles and regular reviews with a robust set of checks and balances.

"Yes, yes," he agreed, "checks and balances are very good. But government is the one who is accountable."

"To whom?" I asked. In fact, who was accountable anywhere in the system? If the donors had really examined those women's projects after a year, they would have seen how few successes there had been and might have already made the needed course corrections. They certainly could not have justified pouring millions more into the projects. It was too easy to be blindsided by the singing and smiles and the women's happy testimonials of the women.

If the women had been given the chance to *borrow* for a project they believed would generate income, they would have focused more seriously on the work. A market mechanism would have provided a better feedback loop for both women and donors. Instead, the system festered under low expectations and mediocre results.

The next week, I returned to Kigali, more sure of and humbled by the strength of individual women, more interested in market mechanisms, and certain that I'd become more savvy. But I was unprepared for my next adventure—being fleeced by a guy named Innocent.

CHAPTER 7

TRAVELING WITHOUT A ROAD MAP

You see, I want a lot / Perhaps I want everything: / the darkness that comes with every infinite fall and the shivering blaze of every step up.

—RAINER MARIA RILKE

Back in Kigali, I rented a two-bedroom house in Kiyovu, the city's most fashionable neighborhood, right behind one of its few skyscrapers, the National Bank of Rwanda, a tall, cream-colored edifice at the edge of a leafy residential block. Simply and starkly furnished, the house had concrete floors, a basic kitchen, a small living room, and two bathrooms. A pretty backyard garden filled with orange lilies, pink and purple cosmos, and yellow angels' trumpets made it feel like a castle to me.

After nearly 2 years of working in Rwanda, I'd finally found a rhythm, valuable friendships, and a sense of belonging. After a morning run, I would eat a quick breakfast of sliced mango and sweet little bananas, then either walk down the dirt road to UNICEF for meetings or wait for Boniface to pick me up and take me to Duterimbere or the bakery. I almost always worked late and would often have dinner with friends, usually at someone's home, or spend the night reading or writing letters.

Sometimes I'd go to a local restaurant, where you had to be prepared for a meal of tilapia, a white fish from Lake Kivu, regardless of what was on the menu. It always played out the same way: When we'd ask a waiter what was available, inevitably he'd say, "So many things. Tell me what you want."

And we would say, "Are you sure?"

And the waiter would nod.

Against all rationality, we'd ask for something like roast chicken or a club sandwich, and the waiter would tell us he was sorry, they were all out. Finally we'd give up and order grilled tilapia with rice. And the waiter would break into a wide grin for making us so happy.

In truth, tilapia is delicious, but too much of anything can be, well, too much.

After a while, other things in Rwanda also began to feel like too much. One day in the market, Boniface pointed to a middle-aged woman wearing a yellow dress and told me she was a spy. I nearly burst out laughing, but acknowledged to myself that we all talked in hushed voices about politics, even in our own homes. I just hadn't connected that habit to the fact that Rwanda had a sophisticated network of spies keeping tabs on people. Order and control trumped freedom every time.

"So, is she really a spy? You can swear by it?" I asked.

"I swear by it," Boniface answered. "I'm sorry it makes you sad, but it is just how life is here."

I looked at Boniface and thought about trust. *Trust*—it is such a simple word and so critical to the functioning of any good society. Where was trust in Rwanda? This was a country where there was almost no corruption, and I'd never once been asked for a bribe, but did they really trust one another? I knew the women in the market sold nearly everything on credit, so there was obviously trust within neighborhood circles; but it could easily have been shame or fear that led people to feel secure that eventually they'd be repaid. The lack of trust—and of personal freedom—was beginning to wear on me.

I didn't expect it to hit me at home, though. The house I'd rented came with a guard whose name was Innocent. A slight man, maybe 5 foot 8, he had a very boyish look—hair trimmed almost to his scalp, button-down shirts usually hanging over a pair of cotton pants and sandals. He must have been in his late twenties or early thirties, for he already had two school-age children. He was a likable enough person and told me he would also do gardening on weekends. The setup seemed ideal.

His job was simple: Each night, Innocent would sit by the locked gate in front of the house and ensure that no one but friends entered. Sometimes, coming home late, I would find him fast asleep, sitting on a wooden stool, his head resting against the gate itself, but for the most part, he took his job seriously and showed up on time, giving me a feeling of security.

Though he'd only worked for me for several months, I gave him a bit of extra money—about $100—to help cover school fees for his children. His monthly wage was only about $60, and I knew how long it would take to save $100. Sometimes I'd invite him to share lunch or dinner with me if I was home.

One Saturday afternoon, I left Innocent working in the garden while I went to play tennis with my friend Charles, who had helped paint the blue bakery. A graduate of Oxford and a diplomat's son, Charles wore tortoise-shell glasses, moved easily between French and English, and had the air of an intellectual. He also played mean games of tennis and squash and was constantly trying to convince me to join him, as there were few willing participants his age. I, on the other hand, was an atrocious player and had no interest in participating, especially not at the local country club.

The Cercle Sportif boasted not only well-kept tennis courts, but also a beautiful swimming pool and the country's only 17 horses. "I'll teach you," Charles insisted, "and the trainers at the club are fantastic."

"You know this will be a disaster," I laughed, but I finally agreed to join him for a lesson at least.

The day was perfect—a bright blue sky with white puffy clouds and neither the bite of heat nor the press of humidity in the air. We jumped into Charles's tan Renault and drove down the hill to the club.

The trainer was a handsome young Rwandan man who had learned to play tennis by working as a ball boy and then befriending one of the frequent players, who coached him to the point where few could beat him. As Charles ridiculed my feeble attempts at serving, I watched the trainer, impressed by the way he carried himself, his obvious discipline in learning the sport, his talk of starting his own business one day, his overall drive and ambition. I wondered what he would ultimately do with his life. Meanwhile, Charles watched, teasing me for being distracted.

"Okay, c'mon, one game together, then we'll go," Charles begged. After a so-called game, we decided to celebrate by going to the Mille Collines hotel for a "Four Seasons" pizza and beer, a typical Sunday afternoon activity for expatriates and Rwandan elites.

The Four Seasons pizza claimed to use four kinds of cheeses. "Charles," I said, "don't you find this rather dubious since there is only one kind of cheese in the marketplace?" It was a white cheese, not creamy, more like a Gouda, only sweeter. I always wondered why we couldn't find even more varieties—after all, Rwanda is famous for its cows.

"On the other hand," I told Charles, "too much choice is another problem altogether." He just shook his head, smiling.

"Wait till you go home and feel overwhelmed at the grocery store," I teased him. "You may miss our limited choices here."

As we sat in white plastic chairs under yellow umbrellas, watching children splash in the big blue pool after having just played tennis at the private club where we were coached by personal trainers, I reflected on the fact that I couldn't have afforded this lifestyle in my own country. It is said that three kinds of people come to Africa: missionaries, mercenaries, and misfits. Regardless of labels, there was something about being part of a tiny, privileged elite that ultimately wasn't good for anyone.

After finishing our beers, Charles reminded me that we'd been out for more than 3 hours and risked being late to an evening reception to which we'd both been invited. I gladly accepted his offer to drive me home and wait while I changed. At the house, I left Charles sitting on the standard-issue Rwandan couch reading a book while I went to my bedroom.

It took only a minute to discover that most of my clothes and jewelry—pretty much everything I had with me in Kigali at the time—were missing. I called out to Charles and showed him the nearly empty closet—no dresses, no skirts, no running shoes, and no watch.

"How did this happen?" I asked, my voice trembling.

"Maybe Innocent decided to wash everything?" Charles suggested. But the bakery had just earned $100 from a bake sale, and I had hidden the money in a box and put it at the back of the closet. That was gone, too. This was an inside job.

"Let's ask Innocent," I said sadly, appreciating that Charles never gave me a look that said, "I told you so," though I knew he was thinking I'd brought some of this on myself by treating the guard in such a familiar way.

I called out to Innocent, who walked into the room sheepishly.

"Innocent," I said, suddenly not amused by the irony of his name, "who did this? And where were you when it happened?"

"I was out back, Mademoiselle Jacqueline," he whimpered, a tear running down his face. "Those men must have been too quiet and too fast. Maybe they saw you leave and me go into the garden." His skinny body was bent, and he held his hands together in a pose that made me feel sorry for him.

"How could they make no noise?" I asked more aggressively. "How could you not have heard a sound?" I knew he must be lying. The house and garden were too small and too close together for robbers to have come into the house in broad daylight, found my bedroom, and taken everything in it without Innocent hearing something. Even if he had been in the garden, we always kept the front door locked, so a robber would have had to break into the place before stealing anything.

Innocent's demeanor reinforced his sense of shame. I wanted to hand the situation over to someone rather than have it be his word against mine. I couldn't go to the police, who were likely to throw Innocent in jail—and who knew what might happen then? My options were to ignore the incident, call the police, or be my own judge and jury. Though I disliked all three, options one and two were untenable.

Feeling sick to my stomach, unsure of what to do, I tried calling Innocent's bluff.

"Charles," I said, "will you go to the UNICEF office and call the police? Innocent and I will wait here so that they can explore and decide who did it."

"No, mademoiselle," Innocent cried. "We don't need the police. They will think it is me."

When I asked Charles again to call the police, Innocent lay prostrate on the floor, telling me he hadn't done anything wrong but giving no clue as to who might have been responsible for robbing the place.

I'd believed that if I was good to Innocent, he would be good to me. But who was I to think that reciprocity worked as a principle between a foreigner and a poor local? He knew I wasn't staying long and might have seen me as a silly young woman, anyway. I wondered if he'd ever trusted me for a minute.

I felt I had no choice but to fire Innocent. Charles agreed. It was likely that Innocent already had sold some things to people in the neighborhood, it would be dangerous to lose credibility, and I had lost my trust in him. I wanted to get my things back but knew the prospects were slim. Still, I told Innocent that I expected to see everything back in the house, regardless of whether he was working for me or not. He shed another tear and walked out the door. I never saw him again.

When I reported all this to Prudence at the office on Monday, she told me I had been right to fire Innocent, but that I'd made a big mistake by not informing the police. People would say I was too soft. "Here, reputation is everything, and you will be taken for a fool," she said. "In Rwanda, it is more important to be respected than liked—maybe everywhere, in fact."

"But the justice system is unfair, and conditions in the prison are atrocious," I protested. "I worried that his punishment would have been much worse than his crime."

She just shook her head.

A week or so after the incident, I spied my sneakers on the feet of a guard who worked at a nearby house.

"Hey," I said, smiling, but with an assertive tone, "those are my shoes! Where did you get them?"

"They are mine," he answered softly but equally assertively.

"They were taken from me," I said. "Stolen. They can't be yours."

He stared at me, unblinking. It was a passive-aggressive kind of stare that let me know nothing was happening with this conversation unless I made a concrete move.

"How much did you pay for them?" I asked, not as assertively this time but still with a smile. When he said nothing, I asked again.

He looked at me, softening his gaze. "How much will you give me?" he asked.

I sighed and offered him $15 for my running shoes, which were impossible to find in Rwanda even if they were already nearly a year old.

"Give me $20," he countered.

"Fifteen or nothing," I said and started to walk.

"Okay, fine," he said.

When I turned around, he said, "Give me $17."

That's where we settled.

I couldn't stop thinking about the incident, the lack of a formal justice system that I could trust, whether I had been weak or strong (and according to whose values?), and whether or not Innocent was getting on with things. Certainly, he was a lot more financially stable with the additional $100 from the bake sale, and who knows what he gained from selling my things. But would he ever trust anyone fully? Would his children?

An incident in the following weeks convinced me, at least, that I'd made the right call by not going to the police. While walking to work in the morning, I came upon a group of people standing around a dying man lying flat on the ground, covered in dust and blood and feebly moving his head back and forth as if to protest, but saying not a word. The dozen people standing around, including three or four children, were kicking him and throwing rocks on his body in an almost resigned, passive manner.

I asked a young girl who looked on from a distance what had happened.

"He tried to rob one of the houses on the hill," she told me. "But the guards heard him and sent the signal for other guards to come and help. They hit this man with their machetes, but he didn't die yet. The people, they are waiting for him to die."

In Rwanda, when guards called for help, it was expected that everyone nearby would join in. Not coming signaled that you were somehow complicit in the crime. Frantically, I ran to UNICEF and called the police, but it took hours for them to retrieve the man, who was no doubt dead by then, having been convicted and punished on the spot by the neighbors. Damascene, the office's assistant, confirmed the man's death.

I asked if any charges had been made against his killers.

"Oh, no," the very sweet and soft-spoken man answered me. "The man who died was a bad man. He was robbing a house. The people were just punishing him for his crime."

I was shocked less by the inhumanity I saw than by the black-and-white approach to judging and punishing his crime. There was no question here of innocent until proven guilty. The guy was presumably caught in the act, and a harsh, cruel form of justice was meted out on the spot. Children saw their parents accepting and participating in the accused's fate, and no one seemed to consider whether he might just have been in the wrong place at the wrong time.

The big question for me was how to strike a balance between the quest for order—clearly a priority in this country—with the human craving for freedom. It was this lack of freedom and of trust that permeated most parts of life in Rwanda in the 1980s. Though I couldn't put my finger on it at the time, it was this shadow that would come to haunt the country and then feed the flames of genocide only a few years later.

During that same period, Charles told me that the handsome young tennis pro I'd met had left Kigali and was dying of AIDS. "They said he has malaria," Charles explained, "but everyone always says it is malaria. He must already have been sick when you played with him."

In the late 1980s, fully one-third of all adults in Kigali were HIV positive—one in three. But no one talked about it. The deaths of people I knew, the silence about the disease, and the callous qualities of Rwandan society were causing a growing weariness in me.

I STILL ENJOYED MY days and felt deeply for many people in Kigali, but it was time for me to go home at least for a while. I had spent more than 2 years living in Africa and, despite a rocky start, had helped build what I believed would become an important local institution in Rwanda. I loved the group of founding partners. They did the work, owned the institution, and would carry it forward. Prudence, Ginette, and Liliane were a powerful triumvirate. The future looked bright. The bakery, too, was thriving. My work was done.

I shared my thoughts with my friend Dan; we were completing a study of microcredit and what it meant for a family's ability to buy food. Dan was becoming known for his work on "household food security." He'd recently been in Malawi, a country that had exported maize while the poorest among its population, including refugees from nearby Mozambique, nearly starved. Dan wanted to know what we could do to ensure that families could take care of themselves.

We had long talks about the complexity of food aid and about how the United States and Europe protected their farmers so that during times of crisis, the only food distributed was food grown with tremendous subsidies in the United States and Europe. How could we convince bigger institutions that a better way of keeping people fed might be to give them the tools to feed themselves? What would it take to move food away from a charity mentality to one that empowered the farmers in Africa themselves?

I knew I wanted to get smarter and find a way to do more. Dan listened to me as I shared my thoughts about what I might do after Rwanda—go to school or start a business that employed low-income people. He suggested that we put that conversation on pause and stop for just a moment to celebrate what we'd accomplished in Rwanda and the rich life we had here, despite the difficult parts.

He proposed that we cook a fancy dinner, wear nice clothing since I'd just restocked my empty closet with a few dresses made by a tailor in Nyamirambo, and drink champagne.

We walked into AliRwanda, a luxury store for expatriates that featured a wide selection of goods at exorbitant prices, and headed straight for the seafood counter, buying two frozen lobsters flown in from overseas. Tilapia wouldn't do it tonight. Croissants and crackers, nuts and olives also found their way into our basket. There was a small but high-quality wine section, with wines from France and Italy and Chile. We were in heaven.

When Dan reached for two bottles of Moët champagne and put them in our basket, I cringed, not daring to ask the price.

The cashier, a large woman with thick forearms and a blue scarf around her head, stared at me intensely with her enormous eyes. Mine glanced downward in a rush of shame as I acknowledged to myself that I'd momentarily shifted into a New York way of being, where buying expensive food for wonderful meals was part of what it meant to be part of city life. The woman's look, though, was enough to bring me back to the local context: At $60 each, two bottles of champagne cost more than many Rwandans earned in a year at the time.

"Please remove the bottles from the bill," I told the cashier.

Looking at Dan, I added, "This is just too much, Dan." Though the food wasn't inexpensive either, in my mind the champagne tipped us over to the truly decadent.

Gently, Dan put his hand on my arm. "We said we were having a feast with champagne. You love champagne. And this is a first. Let's just have fun tonight."

He moved the bottles back toward the woman.

I shifted them the other way.

"I'm not sure I even want the champagne, Dan," I said. "I feel a little ashamed by it. I just don't know if it is right to be doing this while we're living here."

Dan looked at me. "I know it doesn't make a lot of sense on one level. We're working with the really poor, and you and I couldn't be more privileged in relative terms. But don't pretend to be someone you aren't. If you were at home, you'd celebrate with champagne. If you want to remain happy and alive in this work, you need to reconcile this part of who you are and understand the inconsistencies with the work you do and how it all fits into your whole way of being."

I looked at my lovely friend. As a young man, he'd lost his brother and had already endured great sadness in his life. His commitment to social change had never wavered. Maybe he knew something I didn't.

"Besides," Dan added, a devilish look in his eye, "our other choice is the Algerian red antifreeze we normally try to convince ourselves is drinkable wine. You decide."

I laughed out loud. We bought the champagne. On the drive to his house, we talked about choices and how they would just get more complex as we grew older. We lived with enormous privilege in all aspects of our lives. We had drunk fine wine at the French embassy's parties and already had traveled the world. Most precious of all were our passports that would allow us to leave the country whenever we wanted and our sense of empowerment that led us to believe we could accomplish the impossible. The challenge wasn't whether to buy a couple of bottles of champagne; it was instead not to take our privilege for granted and to use it in a way that served the world and our highest purpose.

Later I set a little table with a colorful cloth outside in the garden while Dan created a true feast on the tiny kitchen stove. The sky dressed in its finest for us, a blaze of crystal lights creating a heavenly chandelier. We put candles on the table and all around the ground and delighted in the thick, sweet nocturnal fragrance of frangipani. Mozart filled the air while we toasted to life and its contradictions, to doing what we could on Earth, and to avoiding complacency at all costs. Later we danced to reggae music as the meanness of small-town life melted away.

The next morning, on a long run, I thought about what made Duterimbere successful and what I wanted to do next in my life. I decided to apply to business school. When we ran Duterimbere like a business, though we raised charitable money, we succeeded. When we acted more like a typical nonprofit, neither holding ourselves to our mission nor measuring results, we usually failed. I wanted a better understanding of management and how to build businesses. This was what was missing when it came to the poor. In Rwanda, individuals got rich by going into government, not by taking an entrepreneurial risk (of course, there were always a few exceptions). I'd seen the incredible potential of the poorest people—the poorest *women*, who just needed a chance, not a handout.

Of course, applying to a US business school from a country like Rwanda in the 1980s was no simple matter. Just getting the physical application took weeks. Asking people to write recommendations meant sending letters and then waiting and hoping they would arrive or making expensive phone calls. Luckily, Prudence agreed to write one for me. Then there was the question of the GMATs, the entrance exam for business school. Since I'd missed the date for the exam in Nairobi, I decided to go to the next closest place, New Delhi. It would be a chance for adventure, as well.

Having prepared neither for the exam nor for India, I flew to Nairobi and then took the overnight flight to Delhi. The city's tangy, spicy smell enchanted me the moment I stepped off the plane. I was overwhelmed with color, beauty, sensuality, and scent. Even in the airport, the women sparkled like jewels, draped in fuchsia, lime, bright red, and yellow: I was going to like it here.

How you see where you are always depends on where you've been. In Delhi, I stayed at the YMCA, a clean place with $20 rooms clustered around a flower-filled courtyard. There I met an American couple who did nothing but complain. They found the heat oppressive, the city dirty, the people untrustworthy, the food too spicy. My experience couldn't have been more different. I would spend hours in textile stores, listening

to proud tailors talk about different weaves. I found an incredible spirit
of generosity and thrived in the chaos of the markets. And I felt intoxicated just by breathing in the colors and silks, the jewelry and makeup
on the women, the multitude of spices in the food. How could so much
variety and exuberance exist in one place?

I traveled to Agra to visit the monumental Taj Mahal, which inspired
me to sit and stare for hours, wondering about the Mughal civilization
that had constructed this masterpiece more than 300 years earlier. The
beauty of the marble walls and feminine domes, the Byzantine patterns
of lapis and ruby and other gemstones inlaid into the walls, the changing
color of the mausoleum against the setting sun—all of it astonished me.
I couldn't help but think of this accomplishment being achieved at a time
when the United States was in its infancy and compare it as well to what
had gone on in Rwanda at the time. What kinds of monuments and symbols would Central Africa create? Perhaps they wouldn't be physical
structures, but rather human achievements of the heart and mind.

I spent a few weeks journeying across Rajasthan by train, second
class, no air-conditioning. Despite the heat, I was mesmerized by this
land of exotic cities like Jaipur, blushing pink from the palace walls,
where elephants rambled through the streets and even poorer women
wore the most fabulous jewelry I'd ever seen.

The train broke down in Jodhpur, a smaller city west of Jaipur. I left
the train station with my backpack and found myself wandering through
the Brahmin part of town, a collection of little concrete houses painted in
traditional violet-blue. I'd wanted to travel all the way to Jaisalmer and
join a camel safari in the desert for a day or so, but when I returned to the
station in the late afternoon, I learned that there would be no service for
a day or two.

At a local guesthouse, I fell into a conversation with the innkeeper and
related my frustration at being stranded in Jodhpur despite my plans to
continue onward to Jaisalmer. He suggested I hire his friend to take me
through the desert on his motorcycle to the place where the safaris started.
He seemed like a good, honest man, and so I agreed, though it would take
more than a day to get there and another full day at least to return.

My guide's name was Chowdhury. He was a stocky man with a fringe of
black hair that nearly reached his dark eyes and a neatly trimmed but abundant handlebar mustache, necessarily wide to span his large face. A jocular
sort, he commented on everything, including the women walking with big
pots of water on their heads. "Here water is life, you know," he said.

I told him water was life everywhere, thinking of Mary Koinange in Nairobi's slums.

"But it must be women's work to carry the water," he added. "I think they have stronger necks in proportion to their size."

"Nice excuse," I teased, deciding not to start our trip with a political argument, for I wanted to savor the beauty of the drive. We passed tiny villages and emerald rice fields and saw every imaginable vehicle on the road: carts drawn by donkeys and oxen, huge trucks, white Ambassador automobiles, and colorful rickshaws. Finally, we reached the desert and continued to drive until the sun was setting. Our destination was the small home of a family who would allow us to sleep beneath the stars in their courtyard.

Spotting a man holding a camel on a leash at the side of the road, my guide stopped the motorcycle. "Let's go on a short ride now as the sun is setting," he suggested.

If only to get a rest from the back of the motorcycle, I agreed, and off we went. As the camel lumbered easily through the sand, I felt sublimely lost in the vastness of the desert with its beautiful patterns and dunes, so different from the terrain of East Africa.

After about a half hour, the camel came to a halt at Chowdhury's command. We sat on the ground, and Chowdhury offered me a drink of water as we listened to the sounds of the desert. Suddenly, he said, "Jacqueline, can I ask you something?"

"Sure," I said, "what is it?"

"Will you write your name in the sand?"

I smiled and carefully wrote my name.

"Now write my name in the sand." And he slowly spelled his name for me: C-H-O-W-D-H-U-R-Y.

Then he scooped up the two names and dumped the sand into his pocket.

"In Rajasthan, we have a tradition," he explained. "First, the woman writes her name in the sand; then she writes the man's name in the sand. And then the man scoops up both names and puts them in his pocket. And then they make love."

I looked around: emptiness in every direction. "I am an idiot," I thought to myself. "A complete idiot."

"Chowdhury, that is a nice tradition for you, but it is not *my* tradition." I told him I wanted to go back to Jodhpur immediately, that I didn't want to stay with the family anymore. He just shook his head without any real protest, and we got back on the camel and then onto the motorcycle and drove through the night until we reached the guesthouse, stopping intermittently for tea.

The night ride home was not the smartest approach to driving. Trucks with no lights barreled down the highway, and we swerved around huge oxen that would appear from nowhere in the motorcycle's headlight. We arrived at the guesthouse, covered in dirt and exhausted, after having sung nearly every traveling song we knew just to stay awake.

For the umpteenth time, I reminded myself that traveling as a single woman is not the same as traveling as a man. I was no longer an innocent abroad, but I still plunged into adventures, only rarely considering the consequences to myself and having neither time nor inclination for a great deal of reflection. I was out to change the world, to know it and to love it for all its exquisite beauty and perfection as well as for its flaws.

After a few weeks of wandering India and doing little studying, it was time to take the GMAT in New Delhi. I found myself in an early morning queue outside the American Embassy with hundreds of young, dapper Indian men and one or two other women.

We waited in the scorching sun from 7:00 a.m. until almost 11:00 a.m. with neither food nor coffee until a middle-aged Indian woman with a notebook finally appeared to inform us that 100 more people than expected had shown up. We would have to wait a few more hours for them to collect additional exams. Perhaps, she asked sweetly, some applicants could come back another day?

I told her I was living in Rwanda and had come to India just to take the exam. She said I would take it that day, but it might require a wait. Two hours later, I finally found myself in the Center for the Blind, ill equipped for us, with tiny sightless children wandering in and out of the room, sometimes bumping into our desks while we scrambled to fill out the test, all the while sweating in the monsoon heat, doing our best to ignore our hunger or thirst.

Halfway through the exam, a women's club opened its weekend celebration with music blaring from a loudspeaker outside. I couldn't help but laugh and put the entire exam into the context of where I was and what I was trying to do with my life.

Stanford was my only choice for business school because of its stellar reputation and its public management program. If my application was rejected, I reasoned, I would pursue another path. I returned to Kigali thinking about Africa's relationship to the rest of the world, its connection to India, and how I wanted to be a part of all of it somehow. I knew I needed time and additional experiences, and after being in Africa for more than 2 years, I started readying myself to go home.

BEFORE LEAVING, I DECIDED to climb Mount Nyiragongo, one of Central Africa's tallest volcanoes at 3,470 meters (11,385 feet), standing above Goma across the border in Zaire, about a 4-hour drive from Kigali. I loved hiking and climbing, as did my Canadian friend Charles. We'd already been teased for being the two North Americans who exercised in the midday sun when everyone else was taking a proper siesta.

One Friday we left work and took off for Goma in Charles's little Renault, driving through the streets of Kigali past markets teeming with fish vendors and young children in bare feet, ripped jeans, and T-shirts donated by US volunteer agencies. There was a tragic irony to young kids in rags wearing T-shirts boasting of the prowess of the Harvard rugby team or Princeton crew. Boys rode by on ancient Raleighs, carrying passengers, with cardboard signs saying "Taxi" hanging from their seats.

Listening to Bob Marley and Cat Stevens, we wound around small mountains covered with patchwork fields of maize and bananas. Longhorn cows loped alongside the cars on the road, followed inevitably by young boys with spindly legs who pushed and prodded the huge beasts. As we neared Gisenyi and, thus, Lake Kivu, though we'd seen it countless times, its sheer size and beauty left us in awe. Old, white colonial houses across the lake in Goma sat on manicured lawns along its shores, and sun-scorched fishermen stood and pushed their dugout wooden boats along the blue water with long poles, waiting for the evening catch. Tranquil ripples floated from the water's edge, and the evening sun sent soft beams of light pirouetting across the lake.

Close to the Zaire border, we drove faster so as not to miss the checkpoint's official closing. Crossing into Rwanda was effortless and efficient, but getting past the Zairians always required a negotiation. After arguing with the customs officials and refusing to pay a bribe, but finally getting clearance to pass, we were stopped by the guards again. They wanted us to take them to get a beer nearby. Two soldiers jumped into the backseat of the car, one of them holding an AK-47 across his lap. They directed us to a tiny shack where the beers were cold and the peanuts salty. We ended up sharing a beer while the soldiers insisted on telling us jokes and thanking us repeatedly, disregarding the fact that we'd not really had much choice in the matter.

A half hour later, we were on our way again. On the dark road, we passed a boy in shiny red pants and a bright yellow shirt strutting along-side women dressed in rainbow colors with babies on their backs. The very wind seemed to sing. In crossing that border, I felt like we'd left Kansas and arrived in Oz, where life was lived in Technicolor.

The car crawled through craters like an army tank on uncharted ter-rain, but within minutes we were in Goma, a sleepy town known to us mostly for its dance clubs. From the veranda of our hotel, we could see the black, stark lines of the volcanoes through the mist, and just outside in the darkness, we made out the shiny polyester colors of more boys on their way to dance. Knock-kneed baby goats scampered alongside tiny children walking with their mothers in the dark.

We dined in our hotel and then found a dance joint, a hot, dark little box of a place teeming with people, the scents of sweet, smoky sweat and perfume mixing with liquor and cigarettes. Women in tight satin dresses moved their hips provocatively as a DJ with a too-cool voice peppered his African-French with English and Swahili slang while spinning Madonna, Bob Marley, and African music. We danced and danced until 4:00 a.m. and decided that we would wait until Sunday to climb the volcano. The next day would be devoted just to seeing the countryside.

I went to bed thinking of the tragedy in Zaire. Mobutu Sese Seko had been president since 1965 and was reputed to have a $5 billion personal bank account in Switzerland, thanks in large part to aid money from the United States, France, and Belgium especially. The corruption and mis-management of his country had led to pervasive poverty, chaos, and a lack of education. I remember once meeting a little boy who asked me to take him home with me because I was a rich woman.

"How do you know I am rich?" I asked him.

"Ah, madame, because you are American."

"But I'm not rich," I said. "Just being American doesn't mean I'm rich. There are all kinds of people, rich and poor, there."

"In Zaire, we are all very poor," the little boy responded.

"Your president isn't poor. He's very rich," I teased.

"Ah, but madame, you see? He is the president!" he said with finality and assurance.

Morning came quickly, and I was grateful for having an easy day before our big climb, though we knew our decision to delay till Sunday would put pressure on us to get across the border before it closed at nightfall. After a breakfast of mangoes and bananas with a cup of strong coffee, we drove along the river past tiny villages of thatched-roof huts surrounded by aloe plants and bright red hibiscus. The sense of freedom compelled us to whoop and laugh aloud. Little could we imagine then that Goma would become the epicenter of the Rwandan refugee crisis after the genocide. It would get hit again when the volcano we were to climb, Nyiragongo, erupted in 2002, destroying nearly half the town and leaving half a million people homeless. But back then it was a simple place with few rules and beauty all around it—the right prescription for giving us a feeling of freedom often missing in Rwanda.

Driving across the country, we passed wide, open fields, gigantic blue lakes, and little villages of round, thatched huts made of sticks and mud. Women sat together drying peanuts in the sun as children ran to the side of the road to wave at us and yell "Hello, hello" in their sweet, singsong voices. We came upon a game park and spent hours amazed by the giraffes and antelopes, buffalos and monkeys, and the vast expanse of nature. After a couple of beers in the reserve's lodge, we finally realized how late it was. Night had fallen, and we still had a 4-hour drive back to our hotel in Goma.

Charles's car pushed along dirt roads in the blackness, the Renault's headlights illuminating skinny eucalyptus trees whose shadows looked like haunted dancers. We barely spoke, each of us watching for trucks flying at us or bandits roaming. Suddenly, into the glare of the headlights charged a roaring elephant, raising its giant trunk before charging across the road in front of us. Charles slammed on the brakes and the car swerved to miss the animal. Our hearts pounded as we watched the single, angry male continue on his rampage.

When we finally reached Goma, it was nearly midnight. The hotel dining room was closed. There was only one place to find food: the dance club. Off we went, eating fish and fries, unable to stop dancing again until 3:00 a.m.

The sky at dawn was nothing like it had been the day before. Heavy clouds portended storms, and the air was thick with moisture. We were exhausted, lacked proper clothing and gear for a climb, and couldn't find anything for breakfast because it was so early on Sunday morning. "Are we crazy enough to climb that huge volcano and come all the way back?" Charles teased. Knowing the answer, he added, "Just promise we'll take it easy."

Nyiragongo is just 8 or 10 miles from Goma, so we reached it quickly and found our guide, Alphonse, at a designated spot on the road. He was a short, athletic man with blue-black skin and a scowl on his face wearing army camouflage fatigues and a matching cap, with an AK-47 slung over his shoulder. I never saw him smile. It was clear that this guy wasn't going to lead us on any sort of carefree climb.

Alphonse asked us if we were strong and could keep up a good pace.

Charles responded, "It's no problem. We're in great shape. She runs and I play tennis every day."

I knew that was the wrong answer.

Alphonse didn't say a word. He just put us in our place with his one-man boot camp. With alacrity and drive, our taciturn guide stepped a full meter at a time at a pace that forced me into a full run. Though I could barely breathe, I was enthralled by the scenery: patches of bamboo and different varieties of hardy flowers in yellows and oranges. A thick canopy of trees covered the trail for at least a third of the climb.

As we reached the second and third stages of our 5-hour ascent, the air became much colder. My soaking-wet tank top and shorts were hardly adequate for these conditions. We trudged onward through more high-altitude vegetation, still dense and speckled with purple and yellow flowers. Toward the top, the terrain became rocky and bare—we were climbing on black and gray volcanic rock, slowly placing one foot in front of the other. I couldn't stop shivering from the cold and berated myself for not having paid heed when I noticed that Alphonse was wearing an army green sweater, a cap, long pants, and boots for this journey.

But the summit made it worth the work. The crater of the volcano was enormous, all rock in different shades of grays and browns and blacks with steam pushing through its cracks. It wouldn't erupt for another 14 years, but when it did, it would change the face of the area surrounding it.

To celebrate our ascent, the three of us shared the only food in our possession: a piece of Belgian chocolate and two hard-boiled eggs. Our single bottle of water was long gone.

And our adventure was just beginning. Within minutes, the gray sky turned bright white, throwing hail the size of golf balls at our heads. I began shivering uncontrollably. Our only recourse was to run down the mountain, trying unsuccessfully not to fall, sliding and ripping our shorts on the volcano's sharp surfaces.

Finally, we were back below the tree line, but torrents of water came in heavy sheets, transforming our path into a river with thigh-high muddy water. Still we walked, holding one another's hands so as not to fall. As we neared the bottom third, the rain finally slowed, but we ran into a blockade of branches and trees that had fallen across the path, creating an 8- or 9-foot wall that looked impossible to move.

Looking like drowned rats, we stood and stared, not knowing whether to laugh or cry. The thought of standing even for a minute without moving forward felt unbearable to me. I threw myself into the branches, only to collapse and scrape my legs from top to bottom. Finally, helplessly, we made our way over, breaking branches and falling, but somehow getting to the other side—and then we were home free. Nearly 9 hours after starting, we reached the road, a little worse for wear but happy to stand on flat land.

It was after 5:00, and we had to be at the Zaire border crossing by 6:15 or 6:30 to ensure that we'd reach the Rwandan side by 7:00 p.m., when the border closed. But we were ravenously hungry, and I was shivering uncontrollably. When Alphonse put the back of his hand to my forehead, his first warm gesture of the day, he said I had hypothermia and insisted on taking me to a place he knew where they would give me soup.

Though I had a difficult time even holding the spoon, the soup was the best I'd ever tasted.

We thanked Alphonse, jumped in the car, and sped for the border, making it through with no time to spare. Hit by altitude sickness, I threw up all the way back to Kigali. The next day, we could barely walk. But I recovered, and both of us were euphoric about what we had done, even if the volcano had humbled us to our cores.

I came to Africa similarly unprepared, with no road map, no tools, insufficient gear, and no protective layering. The mountain beat me up, tested me, and tested me some more. And after nearly killing Charles and me, it sent us a blue sky with a gorgeous sun shining on our faces, followed by the kindness of strangers.

Like the volcano, Africa can stun you in an instant. It can throw floods and drought and disease at you, sometimes all at the same time. In the next moment, it will tease you with its magnificent beauty, so even if you don't forget, you can find a way to forgive. Ultimately, it keeps you coming back for more.

CHAPTER 8

A NEW LEARNING CURVE

"We are made wise not by the recollection of our past,
but by the responsibility for our future."

—GEORGE BERNARD SHAW

The holiday season in Kigali made me long for family and snow, Christmas trees and caroling. The December I knew I was leaving felt different—bittersweet. I knew how much I would miss the beauty of Rwanda, the women with whom I worked, great adventures, and the simplicity of life in general.

My friend Ginette and I hosted a holiday party for all of our friends. We taped snowmen we'd made from butcher paper on her wall, which was papered with a tropical scene from floor to ceiling—a popular decorating approach at the time. We baked cookies and made punch with vodka and passion fruit juice. Friends and colleagues came decked out in their finest and danced. Boniface, the driver, was hardly recognizable without his blue UNICEF uniform. Dieu Donné, the artist who had designed our logo, danced the entire night, dressed in Zairian attire. Prudence and Liliane were there, too, and would have danced all night had I not broken several of my fingers.

I was leading a group of children in a line dance of sorts, trying to translate the words to Simon and Garfunkel's "Cecilia" and looking over my shoulder as I sang. When I noticed a number of the kids widening their eyes, it was too late: I was already tumbling off a little bridge that stood about 5 feet over a makeshift canal in front of the house. I landed smack on the back of my hand and knew I'd broken bones the minute I landed. Ginette called her next-door neighbor, a doctor, to see if he could help. Arriving quickly, he held my hand in his, forcefully yanking one of my fingers and sending a shock of pain through my body. When I yelped and pulled **back** my hand, the doctor told me that I must be "a very delicate woman."

"You are not like Rwandan women, who are so strong," he said. "They don't even make noise during childbirth."

I stared icily at him.

He pulled a second finger, I thought I was going to vomit. "Please," I whispered, "it must be broken."

As if he hadn't heard me, he pulled my middle finger. This time, on cue, I threw up. Finally, he suggested I see someone in the morning.

With one day left in the country, I found myself in the Kigali hospital, waiting among patients suffering from AIDS and malaria. After the doctor x-rayed my hand, he showed me the three bones with neat breaks right through the fingers. He then created a humongous cast that stretched from my fingers to my shoulder and charged me a total of $2 for the service.

That evening, the women of Duterimbere held a going-away party for me. Wearing a maroon dress, Prudence presented me with a gold fertility necklace and a blessing that I would bear many children. The rest of the women gave me a beautiful quilt sewn with bright-colored renditions of my favorite scenes in Rwanda. In the center was Duterimbere's logo and along the sides were scenes from the blue bakery, children learning to read, the rolling mountains of Rwanda, the marketplace, and even a group of prisoners dressed in pink—in recognition that I thought it so strange that the government had decided on pale pink to dress those who had committed crimes.

"We've done something wonderful together," Prudence said to the whole group. "We've built an institution that will show Rwanda and the world what women are capable of accomplishing. This country will grow stronger because of this work and because of women's solidarity."

For a moment, I wanted to cancel my trip home to the United States and stay to see these dreams completely realized, though I knew that in reality this would take decades. A big part of me didn't believe I was leaving Rwanda, leaving Africa, anyway. Ginette told me that I might as well count on not leaving it for long, for it was clear the continent had gotten under my skin. I shook my head and said it would be *at least* a few years before I returned.

I found myself quietly weeping on the flight back home and thought of my younger self crying on the plane when I had first come to Africa. The places I'd been had changed me more than I'd impacted them, but

I'd also seen what a small group of people could do to change the world. I wouldn't have given up the experience for anything.

BACK HOME IN VIRGINIA, in January I learned I'd been accepted at Stanford's Graduate School of Business and had 9 months before classes began. Though being with my family was divine, "home" felt foreign to me—my interest in African politics was shared by few, and I would watch the eyes of friends glaze over as I told too many stories about the people I'd known there and the places I'd encountered.

I began searching for a short-term consultancy, something that would take me back to Africa. Through a number of connections, I secured a contract at the World Bank to focus on agriculture, women, and West Africa. Within weeks I was assigned to a project in Gambia, an anglophone country located in francophone West Africa. The nation is a sliver of an isthmus right in the middle of Senegal, along the strategically important Gambia River, a stark indication of how the colonial carving of territory in Africa had given no thought to what might make sense for the Africans who lived there.

My mission was to work with Gambia's Department of Agriculture on a $15 million soft-loan package from the World Bank. Highly paid consultants had been working for months with the Gambian government to craft the proposal, but despite hundreds of thousands of dollars in fees paid, neither the Gambian government nor the Bank itself thought the final product was adequate. I was asked to review and complete the proposal to the satisfaction of both the Gambian government and the World Bank. Having seen Duterimbere run for more than 2 years for a fraction of what was paid to the bank's consultants made me resolve to do things differently, but I wasn't sure where to begin.

The consultancy started in the plush offices of the Bank in its Washington, DC, headquarters. I loved seeing people from all corners of the globe walking the halls—learned men and women, all focused on helping the developing world. I knew the Bank's shortcomings—its top-down approach and need to lend directly to governments, which had led to too many failed projects—but I also could see the potential of a powerful institution with the sole mission of supporting countries that had significant development needs.

Since my task was to revise a proposal for women agriculturalists in Gambia, I started by researching everything I could find on what the Bank had done previously in that country, especially with regard to women farmers. One project stopped me in my tracks: The Bank had spent more than $20 million over the course of more than a decade to implement an irrigation project for rice production. Early memos discussed how investment in an irrigation technology would greatly enhance productivity for the country's major food crop, rice, thus enhancing child nutrition as well as increasing farmers' overall income levels. The idea made good sense. Despite Gambia's being a coastal country, irrigation was needed for better production, and early cost-benefit analyses showed a likelihood of raising yields tenfold or more.

I could understand how experts initially might have determined this a sound proposal, but many years of investing in the irrigation program had yielded nothing but disastrous results. Rice production had actually declined, and the health of women and children in the area had only worsened; indeed, early death rates among children had *risen*. Despite the logic of irrigating land to improve agricultural productivity, tens of millions of dollars had been spent with little to show for it.

The story of what happened is textbook for traditional aid and how not to do it. Imagine the 1970s, when this project started. Well-intentioned agronomists and engineers from the World Bank arrived in Gambia, ready to help set up sophisticated irrigation systems that would improve food production. These men (most of the World Bank staff were men at the time) would interact with the government, which would identify farmers to work on the project. The project's farmers were typically men, though in Gambia women were responsible for growing rice while men cultivated the country's major cash crop, peanuts. So why focus on men? Because irrigation used technology, which was considered a man's domain.

The farmers laid the irrigation pipes and worked the land, ignoring their own fields, and rice production actually declined over time—not because irrigation wasn't needed, but because it was managed by individuals having experience neither with rice nor with the new technology. What is surprising is not the poor results, but that so little was done to address the project's problems for so many years.

Reading the proposal I was to work on did little to make me feel better: The money was mostly designated for giveaway programs that I thought would undoubtedly fail. For instance, $1 million had been allocated to purchase maize mills to reduce women's labor. Traditionally, West African women worked for hours milling maize by hand. By reducing this grueling work, women would have time for other things, including earning income. In theory, it made sense to provide technologies to reduce labor needs, but theory isn't enough. I'd already seen dozens of well-intentioned programs exactly like this fail miserably.

Typically, aid workers would help install the mills, and local communities would operate them until, inevitably the mills would break down. Few people knew how to repair them, so the mills would sit broken and useless. Other villages suffered a lack of diesel to fuel the mills. On top of these problems, the Japanese government had just donated thousands of maize mills to women's groups and villages across the country. The notion that the Bank's new initiative might provide thousands more mills seemed absurd.

Of all the initiatives in the document, one stood out: an experiment to more effectively sell fertilizer on credit to women farmers. I'd seen the importance of household food security in Kenya and Rwanda; individual farming families needed the tools to feed themselves through farming or earn enough income to buy food. The Green Revolution in India had demonstrated how better inputs—seeds and fertilizers—could improve agricultural production dramatically, but these options were rarely made available to smallholder farmers. The idea of combining access to credit with an input that could improve farmers' productivity was powerful.

I still had a lot of questions about the proposal, but I knew the next step was to go to Gambia and see for myself. In truth, I had missed Africa and was excited to be returning only months after I'd left Rwanda.

The nearly empty jet flew over the West African coastline and landed in Gambia's sleepy capital, Banjul, in a cloud of dust. All I could see were flatlands to my left and right and, in front of me, a tiny airport with a single terminal. A wave of thick, hot air hit my face the second I walked onto the tarmac, reminding me immediately of how much this tropical, flat part of Africa differed from the mountains of Rwanda and the dry savannas of Kenya.

A friendly taxi driver took me to the Bungalow Beach Hotel, a lovely place situated right by the palm-fringed ocean. The main house was painted white, and I had my own little apartment near the water, making it necessary to walk through beautiful tropical gardens to reach my room. A small restaurant under a thatched roof stood beside the swimming pool, and the hotel grounds were filled with beautiful, colorful birds. Outside my window was a tree full of yellow weaverbirds singing playfully and building their nests. I felt free again the minute I arrived.

I met my teammate a few days later; Duncan was a tall, slender engineer with dark hair and glasses. He always wore short-sleeved shirts with pencils in his front pocket and carried an enormous briefcase. Seated by the pool, we discussed our "mission" to craft a realistic proposal for the World Bank's $15 million soft loan to Gambia. I'd been appointed leader of the mission and shared my concerns about the task we'd been given and the work that had already been done. I didn't like the lack of accountability and felt that another $15 million loan, even with no interest, would do no favors for this country unless we were confident of seeing real changes in productivity.

Duncan agreed, and we discussed how we would approach the next weeks of work. We'd speak with everyone we could find, go out to the rural areas, meet farmers, consult with the government ministers, and be as fair and as thoughtful as we could. We were committed to doing the right thing for the Gambian people. That was our deal.

We spent a week or so in Banjul, located on an island at the mouth of the Gambia River and connected to the mainland by a bridge. The city's streets were always full of traders hawking their wares in front of two-story buildings with arched passageways that reminded me of some of Bombay's commercial streets. Women sold colorful batik fabrics and gold and silver jewelry, baskets, and vegetables, often under makeshift tents that shielded them from the hot sun. But for all of the petty trading, agriculture was what sustained the majority of people in the country.

As Duncan and I were leaving the capital to visit rural farms, we passed a row of eight women sitting by the roadside, selling oysters in the hot sun. They'd gathered them in the mangroves, a jumble of roots and plants along the banks of the Gambia River that created enormous swamps that held not only debris, but fresh oysters, too.

"One *dalasi* for a lid of delicious oysters," a skinny woman yelled at our car, her face breaking into a vivacious smile. Now I was *definitely* back in Africa, where, despite the crushing poverty that faces the majority of people, there is a sense of boundless enthusiasm that never fails to infuse me with energy.

In one of the villages, we met Haddy, an unforgettable, irrepressible fertilizer retailer probably in her forties, who knew the local farmers and understood the psychology of selling. Her massive body was draped in a deep purple, flowing robe, and her hands were adorned with huge silver and gold rings. She sat regally on an overstuffed bag of fertilizer and was filled with the confidence that comes from knowing more than everyone else about something—or at least *believing* you do. After 19 years of hard work, Haddy had built an irrefutably successful business. In one day, I learned more from this impressive saleswoman than I had in months of listening to experts in offices.

I suggested that my colleagues at the Bank wanted her opinion on their proposal to provide loans for inputs like fertilizer through large development and commercial banks.

"Nonsense!" Haddy explained. "First, we are living too far away from the banks, and second, we don't trust them. Further, most banks don't want to deal with farmers like us. They just want the big ones. The small farmers come to a retailer like me and borrow the money they need to plant and fertilize the harvest. You see, they have no cash and so they rely on credit until the harvest comes, and then they pay back."

"But how can you count on farmers repaying?" I asked.

"Because this is a small area and we know everyone. If I had more cash myself, then I could lend even more to the farmers. My credit to you would be strong. So you see? You have to bet only on Haddy, and I will take the responsibility for making sure the others repay me so that I can repay you."

"How do we know you are a fair seller?" I asked.

"You must ask the farmers and see what they say," she responded. "I want to help change my country. And I will serve it better than those big banks."

I didn't doubt her. And at least this was a starting point.

This idea made sense because it relied on the strength of the local people rather than on the largesse of foreign consultants who would never have to reach into their own pockets. Here was a chance to build on something that was already working. After speaking with other farmers and local distributors, we wrote up our proposal and readied ourselves to present it to the project coordinating committee of the Department of Agriculture. We proposed developing local credit and distribution systems to address the problems of local farmers. The idea was simple—and we believed it could work.

Down an open-air hallway, we met the woman who headed the committee in her stark white office. Draped in an enormous dress of screaming yellow and defensive blue, she sat behind a wooden desk, her eyes shaded by a pair of mirrored aviator sunglasses. She made me think of a vulture who considered us a mere distraction from the more political pursuits of her day.

Before I could get through my opening statement, the chairperson cut us off.

"Why would you establish a private retail network for women?" she asked curtly. "You will miss the women who are among the poorest of the poor."

I explained that we were attempting to promote the private sector in a way that reached poor farmers. If we could find a way to help the market actually work for poor farmers, then they could make their own investments in things like fertilizers and seeds and repay when the harvest came in. They wouldn't be waiting for an agency to give them things. I talked about needing a mind-set beyond charity to reach poor farmers: The farmers themselves were market driven and deserved solutions that could help them sustain themselves for years.

The woman missed the point of whether we would work through local distributors or develop banks altogether. She didn't believe in lending to the poor at all. We were back at square one. "You aren't helping the poorest farmers by giving loans to women already in business. They cannot be so poor if they have businesses."

I tried to explain that supporting women already in business could actually be good for many people. Besides, I told her, the businesswomen we were talking about were not wealthy by any means.

"The *poor* need our help, not businesswomen. Poor women farmers cannot afford to repay your loans. It is only when they get more money that they will be richer."

You couldn't argue with the latter part of her sentence, but I didn't know how to get out of the circular logic: Whatever I said fell on deaf ears.

"Just look at the track record of these giveaway programs," I protested. "Broken mills, lower production levels of rice *after 20 years* of work and money. This can't be right," I continued, maybe with too much self-righteousness, for I could feel my growing anger. "The only way this will work for the farmers is if they own it themselves, if they can see their own lives getting better because of their efforts and ability to control their own futures and not have to wait around for the government."

"You don't know this country," she reprimanded me.

"No," I agreed, "I don't, though I have been listening to farmers."

"Well, it is most clear that you don't know Gambia," she said and shut her book. The meeting was over.

We had an ally in the Department of Agriculture, and we continued to push for the fertilizer program. We also tried reducing the $15 million proposal to a $1 million grant that would be an experiment in building a self-sustained fertilizer distribution system, but it was ultimately rejected. Too much money and time had gone into crafting the larger proposal, and a smaller one couldn't be justified, apparently. I never saw the final loan document, but I believe that many of the original initiatives were reinstated, though no one could explain to me how they had a chance of success.

Although my experience at the World Bank was a frustrating one, I was glad to have had it, to have met a number of extraordinary individuals, and to have gained a better understanding of how incentives to move money out the door can lead to initiatives that can be damaging to local economies. And it reaffirmed my belief in creating structures with the right incentives for success and in finding real business leaders like Haddy and giving them the tools to serve their fellow citizens. I left eager to learn better management skills at Stanford, for I was certain that understanding business was fundamental to building systems for change.

After a solo drive across the United States, I found myself walking through the halls of Stanford's Graduate School of Business, feeling as if I'd landed in another universe entirely. Kigali made Palo Alto feel like a loaf of Wonder Bread. At the same time, I suddenly found myself with people who spoke my language, came to meetings on time, and made things happen. I loved the ease of it all and had never felt more privileged in my entire life.

Still, I longed for the colors of Africa, the smells of cooking over an open fire early in the morning, the sight of the purple rain marching across the land. I missed the simple way that people embraced one another; the way they asked about your family, your day, your health before discussing business; the way children waved their hands back and forth, like little Japanese fans aflutter. I missed bargaining for everything. I missed the optimism and resiliency of so many Africans I knew. I missed finding beauty in everyday things. I even missed the rotten roads in Rwanda, as my friend Ginette had predicted as she drove me to the airport in Kigali on bumpy, muddy streets full of potholes.

Most of all, I missed feeling useful.

"I'm supposed to be an anthropologist, so what am I doing studying vector analysis and the Black-Scholes theory?" I asked a friend.

He reminded me that I'd come to learn the skills I needed to change the world—at least that was my mantra. The developing world needed management skills. It needed people who knew how to start and build companies, not just people with good intentions. It was growing clear to me that those who sought power and money made the rules; yet power alone could corrupt and corrode. "Power without love," Martin Luther King Jr. said in one of his last speeches, "is reckless and abusive," and, he continued, "love without power is sentimental and anemic."

The world needed both—I had seen this over and over in my time abroad. I wanted to gain the confidence—and skills—to make that fusion work.

The question was how to put the combination of power and love into action. My professors and fellow students were comfortable speaking about power and money. Love and dignity, on the other hand, were words people were often embarrassed to say out loud, or so it felt. There had to be a way to combine the power, rigor, and discipline of the marketplace with the compassion I'd seen in so many of the programs aimed at the very poor. Capitalism's future, it seemed to me then—and much more so now—rests on how much creativity and room for inclusion it can tolerate.

Before each semester at Stanford, professors give a preview of their upcoming classes to aid students in course selection. At one session, a tall, graceful elderly man in a gray suit and a fedora stood up to speak. He looked like he had been an athlete in his youth. His figure was lithe, his step easy. He carried a sense of gravitas that made it impossible not to listen to what he had to say.

"Why do civilizations rise and fall?" he asked, moving his hand in an elegant arc above his head, and then paused.

I thought of the Taj Mahal, of the contrasts I'd seen in different countries. I wanted to talk to him about them.

"Why do some people stop growing at age 30, just going from work to the couch and television, when others stay vibrant, curious, almost childlike, into their eighties and nineties?"

He paused again, and I was hooked; I felt he was speaking to me directly. Though I had no idea who this man was, I knew that he was going to play a role in my life.

That afternoon, I went to the professors' offices and found his name on the door: Professor Emeritus John Gardner. I knocked and heard a voice tell me to come in. John was sitting at his desk, hat off, jacket still on, reading a paper he put aside when he saw me. I stammered through my introduction and explained to him why what he had said had resonated so clearly with me. He'd been talking about the kind of person I wanted to be. I was craving more discussion about just those issues and, well, might he ever have the time to talk to me about some of them?

The room was quiet, and he stared at me with the kindest eyes I'd ever seen. "My dear," he said, "of course, we can talk. Sit down. But first I have to ask you if you knew you were wearing two different earrings?"

I told him I did, that I thought it made people think for a moment, and that might be a good thing—didn't he think so?

He laughed, and I sat down. We didn't stop talking until he died more than a dozen years later.

It was only after my first meeting with John that I learned he'd been secretary of health, education, and welfare under Lyndon Johnson. After resigning from the Johnson administration as one of the most powerful government officials in the country, he founded a grassroots citizens' organization, Common Cause, at age 56. John Gardner understood what self-renewal was all about—he lived it.

He also founded the Independent Sector as an umbrella group for nonprofit organizations; the White House Fellows to promote leadership in the young in Washington, DC; and the National Civic League to encourage citizen participation. Everything John did was about releasing human energies at all levels of society. His greatness came not from any title, but from the way he lived his life, with a rare combination of vision and drive, humility and grace.

John never stopped learning. I have a vivid image of him standing at the front of the class with pen in hand as he took notes each week on what the 10 people in the seminar had to say. That practice certainly made me pay more attention and listen carefully. If he were writing down what my class-mates were saying, then there was probably wisdom in it for me, as well. John spoke about the civil rights movement in the United States, about how social movements need both insiders and outsiders to make change hap-pen, about how important it is to learn to talk to one another across lines of difference—ethnic lines, religious lines, class lines, ideological lines.

After classes, I would sit in his office for hours. I did independent stud-ies with him as well, learning about leadership and starting organizations not for personal profit, but to benefit a greater community. He always had time to talk, whether it was about major social movements or the impor-tance of living with integrity, of treating everyone with the respect they deserve. And he taught just by being who he was. I would sometimes see him on campus, talking with a former secretary of state. John would call me over and give me a hug, even if I tried to walk by without him notic-ing, not wanting to interrupt his important matters. As he once said of a friend of his, John made the world better just by being in it.

Our most frequent topic of conversation had to do with community, what it meant, how to foster and build it. John believed humans thrive in relationship to each other and that communities in which each indi-vidual feels a sense of belonging and of accountability are key to our individual and societal success.

When I was considering what to do after business school, my choices were to accept a fellowship at the Rockefeller Foundation to explore enterprise-development strategies for low-income communities in the United States or to move to Czechoslovakia to work on a fund that would build small enterprises in that newly freed country just one year after the fall of the Berlin Wall. With my tendency toward wanderlust, I leaned toward working in a new land during a historic moment.

John felt I should instead accept the fellowship with the Rockefeller Foundation. "It will give you an important vantage point on what philanthropy is, both domestically and internationally," he said. "And you already have worked in a developing country building enterprises. Life at your age should be about putting new and different tools in your toolbox. You already understand that communities today transcend geography and that you belong to multiple ones—Stanford, women, the community that cares for Africa. But to be truly effective, especially internationally, you must root yourself more strongly in your home's own soil. It is time for you to know this country, as well. Only by knowing ourselves can we truly understand others—and knowing from where you come is an important part of knowing who you are."

"Surely there are enough people interested in this country," I told him. "My contribution will come from focusing globally."

He shook his head. "You should focus on being more interested than interesting"—something I'd heard him say countless times. "What happens overseas is profoundly influenced by what happens here, especially now. And the reverse is true, as well."

Following John's advice, I accepted the Warren Weaver Fellowship at the Rockefeller Foundation and spent a life-changing year looking at microenterprise and small and medium enterprise efforts in the United States, and comparing them to what was happening in Bangladesh and India in the realm of microfinance. It was a year of sitting on factory floors in the Midwest, visiting Indian reservations in South Dakota, and talking to ex-prisoners working on an organic farm outside San Francisco. The same themes continued to emerge: Business was a powerful way to bring discipline and rigor to solutions that could lead to a greater feeling of independence and choice among people too often treated as invisible. And John was right: It didn't matter if the people lived in Bangladesh or Bangor, Maine. Everyone wanted the same things. And low-income people the world over were challenged by many similar constraints.

At the Rockefeller Foundation, I met another mentor, its charismatic president, Peter Goldmark. He provoked me to ask the big questions about what could be, pushing me to look decades ahead instead of at what was immediately in front of us—specifically, to envision how philanthropy should evolve. Already in the early 1990s, Peter felt we faced a number of ultimatums—big, looming crises that we could avert only through tremendous innovation and collective action. He urged greater focus on the environment, specifically energy. He feared the proliferation of nuclear weapons. He provided support to building deeper understanding of the Muslim world. He was a true visionary who believed deeply in our ability to solve even the toughest problems and felt that greater innovation in private philanthropy could help lead the way to public solutions.

When my Warren Weaver Fellowship with the foundation ended, Peter urged me to accept a job I'd been offered to help a new, anonymous trust give away $100 million in grants in New York City over a 2-year period. It seemed like a dream job to me. People worked their entire lives to give away so much money, and here I had the chance to be part of something that could be profoundly influential.

But I learned quickly that giving away money effectively can be much more difficult than making it, especially when decisions are made by a committee and not an individual. Moreover, philanthropy can appeal to people who want to be loved more than they want to make a difference. While the former is not all that difficult, the latter can take a lifetime to achieve.

I also discovered within 3 months that the most powerful person on the board was much more interested in the being-loved part of philanthropy. It wasn't that the money wasn't put to good use—it was given to a number of solid institutions in the city. But to me it felt like the organization was losing an opportunity for real leadership in New York. Through John Gardner and Peter Goldmark, I'd seen how philanthropy could effect systemic change, and I wanted to be a part of that change. Both men had also taught me to dare to dream big—and the experience with the anonymous trust taught me that large sums of money don't always translate into big dreams or big results.

I told Peter that I was leaving the philanthropic sector to start a for-profit business that employed low-income people. Philanthropy, I told him, was too frustrating a sector for me because there was so little accountability.

Peter wouldn't hear of it. "If you think philanthropy needs to be more accountable, then start something to teach philanthropists who want to ensure their funding has impact. Don't give up on this sector without trying to strengthen it, for goodness' sake."

It was impossible to say no to Peter.

I spent weeks in the Rockefeller Foundation archives, seeking to understand what had been done in the past and what might be possible in the future. John D. Rockefeller had established the Rockefeller Foundation with hundreds of millions of dollars he earned after founding Standard Oil. A devout Baptist, Rockefeller tithed from a young age. Over time, his wealth, combined with his sense of duty, led him to make enormous philanthropic contributions. He helped establish the University of Chicago, provided funding for Spelman College (the first college for black women), and helped establish medical research centers across China.

Even before he had a foundation, Rockefeller's work helped eradicate hookworm infection in humans, which flourishes in unsanitary conditions. In the early 20th century, children across the South were infected regularly with this disease. Rather than think he had the answers himself, Rockefeller brought together the smartest people he could find in the field and learned that hookworm was an easily preventable disease: If people would stop going barefoot to their privies, they could dramatically reduce the risk of infection. Instead of limiting their efforts to ensuring the widespread availability of treatment, the Rockefeller team concluded that what was needed was massive public awareness that could be provided along with a boost to the country's public health services.

The team launched a media campaign through radio stations and town hall meetings. Rockefeller used his clout to convince southern governors to install a public health official in departments in 11 states. In less than 5 years, the disease had been eradicated in the South and a system to deliver public health had been established, one that provided a model not only for the United States, but also for the rest of the world.

Peter urged me to look at the proliferation of wealthy individuals—and this was prior to the dot-com boom. Already it was estimated that tens of trillions of dollars would be transferred from one generation to the next as the parents of the baby boomers died. Financiers were also beginning to earn sums that had been unheard of just a decade before.

"How can you help those who are interested in doing something important with their wealth?" he asked me. "What kind of program can you create that will help provide not only the skills, but also a spectrum of experiences that will enable individuals to understand issues and see themselves as part of the solution?"

After months of traveling around the country, discussing with philanthropists their own hopes and desires for learning, I started the Philanthropy Workshop at the Rockefeller Foundation. We would train a corps of philanthropists and provide them with the skills, knowledge, and networks needed to tackle tough problems. We knew our effort would be global; we would dive into many different issues and explore what had worked historically as well as what might be needed in the future.

Of course, I couldn't start anything until I spoke with John Gardner. I traveled back to Palo Alto to seek his advice. At a local coffee shop, I happily watched his deliberate movements, how much attention he paid even to making a sort of ritual out of a daily visit to a coffee shop. When John was with you, he was fully present. Though he didn't dress like a monk and could not have been more active in the world, he moved from a place of spiritual stillness that I craved in my own life. After listening to my dreams and plans for the workshop, he nodded with approval and said he thought it could make an important impact. Then he took a breath before imparting his thoughts.

"The one thing for you to teach," he said, "is that the most important skill needed is *listening*. If philanthropists don't first listen, they will never be able to address issues fully because they will not understand them. Second, philanthropists should focus on supporting others to do what they already do well rather than running programs themselves. There is such a disease among the newly wealthy especially, who think they are the only ones with good solutions. They should think about investing in great people in the social sector just like they invest in great people in the financial sector. That would help things a lot," he smiled, adding, "but the ego is a powerful burden."

I nodded in agreement, trying just to listen.

"Finally," he continued, "philanthropists should find innovations that release the energies of people. Individuals don't want to be taken care of—they need to be given a chance to fulfill their own potential. Too many projects create dependence that helps no one in the long run."

When I told him he was preaching to the choir, he laughed. "Then think *about* the choir. Think about community. People need to feel responsible to one another. Otherwise, we will breed successful individuals who don't feel connected enough to the greater society."

He paused and looked at me. "Think about how the middle and working classes fit into society. The intellectual elites who run society—the analysts and number crunchers and people who thrive on symbols and technologies—often have very little empathy for people with less. And when they *do* think empathically, they focus on the poorest of the poor and not the lower middle portion of society, though it is so critical to societal change."

In today's world, the elites are growing even more comfortable with one another across national lines, yet at the same time, less comfortable with low-income people who share their nationality. How we create those bonds of community that are truly global as well as national is one of this generation's great challenges.

I heeded John's advice and spoke to thinkers and doers across the country to put together a 4-week course given over a 10-month period. Each workshop would take 8 to 10 philanthropists who demonstrated a commitment to learning and to giving strategically. In the first year, they came from across the country, from Boston and Virginia, California and New York, ranging in age from 28 to 50, all with intrepid souls, to try a new course that included days spent in housing court in an effort to understand the perspectives of poor tenants and landlords alike, long discussions into the night, weeks away from home, and international trips. Today, more than 150 people from countries across the world have attended.

At the Philanthropy Workshop, we studied Rockefeller, of course, and Andrew Carnegie, another American industrialist who believed that men of great wealth had a duty to contribute to social, cultural, and economic life and improve the world. He wrote that "the man who dies, leaving behind him millions of available wealth, which was free for him to administer during life, will pass away 'unwept, unhonored, and unsung.'"

We read and discussed Aristotle and Socrates, Martin Luther King Jr., and Gandhi. We explored how best to make grants and investments, how to say no with grace, how to conduct a site visit, and how to understand nonprofit budgets. The idea was to ground individuals in substantive knowledge about issues and also to provide a framework for strategic thinking and moral understanding of how best to effect social change.

International trips were an essential part of the program. In India, we visited some of the most innovative programs in the country focused on education, on HIV infection prevention, on protecting the environment more effectively. The days were hot, long, and transformative. Two hours outside Calcutta on a 120°F day, our bus stopped in the middle of nowhere. We were on our way to visit an extraordinary community organizer to understand youth movements and the role of philanthropy in supporting them. The air was so hot you could see it. A few hundred meters in the distance, we saw a long ribbon of saffron along the pale horizon. Our guide pointed to the streak of color and started walking.

As we approached, we could hear ululating and singing. Gradually, we saw women dressed in oranges and reds and yellows standing in two lines, waiting to welcome us. As we walked through, the women danced and sang even louder, throwing marigolds over us. My white cotton blouse was streaked with the bright orange that seemed to melt into my skin and hair. The heat and passion and color and noise made me feel almost like I was hallucinating.

Inside the village, we sat together with the women and were handed cool coconut water—which had never tasted better. The women stood in the sun and made presentations about their work fighting for rights and for freedom. When they finished, they performed a beautiful Hindi song for us. The leader then turned to us and asked if we would do them the honor of singing something, too. All of the Americans looked at one another, none of us being used to spontaneously singing songs in front of strangers.

"Is there a song we all even know?" someone joked. Finally, we chose "We Shall Overcome." It felt appropriate, and at least we all knew the words.

We started singing, embarrassed and tentative at first, but gaining steam with each word. Suddenly, some of the village women stood to join us in their native language, clearly knowing the words. Midway through those determined lyrics, every person standing held hands and sang as loudly as he or she could in a mix of languages, yet with a singular spirit—50 Indian women smiling, and 8 Americans in tears.

In preparing for one of the first workshops, I visited Phnom Penh, Cambodia, in 1994, 20 years after Pol Pot had ripped the society apart, to meet an elderly Buddhist monk named Maha Ghosananda. As a symbol of peace and reconciliation, he was reviving the tradition of Dhammayietra, a nationwide pilgrimage across the country, including parts that were covered in land mines. He agreed to meet me at the temple where he lived, a simple place painted white on the outside, with neat wooden floors and open windows. Young monks shooed boys playing with guns around the temple, as the boys laughed and pretended to shoot at them.

On the second floor, Maha Ghosananda waited in his saffron robes, seated on a maroon cushion laid on a rice mat in a large, airy room. In front of him was another mat for me. Bowing hello, I sat on my shins, notebook open. Although I could feel his quiet strength, nervously I rushed through an introduction to what I was doing and told him how grateful I was to see him.

I felt like a young journalist, driven but totally out of my element.

He smiled and slowly bowed his head in acknowledgment.

"Would you tell me about the peace marches, how you have the courage to lead them, whether you have lost anyone along the way?" I asked almost breathlessly.

He looked at me, in no hurry to respond. With his hands clasped together, he said, "Each step is a prayer, each step is a meditation."

"You have made such a sacrifice with your life and are such an important spiritual leader," I continued, though I wasn't sure I even fully understood his first answer. "Those walks can take 45 days. Just the logistics must be an enormous burden for someone. Who helps you, and what can others do to support what you are doing? What is the right role for philanthropy? How many people know about the peace marches? I would think they are important not only for Cambodians, but also for the entire world to understand."

"We walk with compassion for the world," he answered.

My hyperenergetic style had never been so unsuccessful at connecting with another person before. Clearly, I needed a different approach.

"Maha Ghosananda," I said, "I am here out of deep respect for you and for what you are doing and want to consider how I might be able to introduce you and your work to others who might support it. Please forgive me for not even knowing how to ask the questions."

This time, he was quiet. He looked at me and I at him. Not knowing what else to do, I looked down and wondered if he wanted me to leave.

Minutes passed. Finally, Maha Ghosananda stood up slowly. I could see his advanced age then and was even more impressed that this man had withstood the evils of the Pol Pot regime.

"If you move through the world only with your intellect," he said in a direct and clear voice, "then you walk on only one leg." With his hands held in prayer, he lifted one leg and slowly and deliberately hopped three times. With the same deliberation and pace, he restored his foot to the floor. After a long breath, he started again.

"If you move through the world only with your compassion," he said, lifting his other leg, "then you walk on only one leg." Again, he hopped three times.

"But if you move through the world with both intellect and compassion, then you have wisdom." He walked slowly and gracefully, taking three long, slow strides. At the end he bowed his head again and then resumed his seat on the cushion in front of me.

"Thank you," I said to him, bowing again.

He smiled gently. There was nothing left to say.

Slowly, with each foot feeling the ground beneath it, I walked out of the temple and into the light.

CHAPTER 9

BLUE PAINT ON THE ROAD

*"There are only two mistakes one can make along the road to truth;
not going all the way, and not starting."*

—BUDDHA

In 1994, along with the rest of the world, I witnessed the horror of the
Rwandan genocide, as well as the brilliant inspiration of Nelson Mandela's forgiveness of his captors and historic inauguration in South Africa.
Coupled with an unfortunate encounter with personal violence on the
beach in Tanzania, these contradictory events solidified a worldview that
was growing more complex, grounded in the recognition of the potential
for both good and evil in each one of us.

On a bleak midwinter day in New York City, I received a call from
Dan Toole, my old friend from Rwanda days, who was then second in
command at UNICEF's Tanzania office: "I need you to come for a month
and review a microfinance program we've helped the government implement across the country. It's not clear it has been successful. Can you
come? And if so, sooner rather than later?"

I relished the idea of working with Dan again, contributing and learning. The chance to trade New York City gray for a patch of vibrant color
closed the deal.

From the window of the small plane that took me into Tanzania's
coastal capital, Dar es Salaam, I soaked in the turquoise waters and
watched the palm trees, their green heads flopping, skinny trunks bend-
ing in the wind. On the ground, the air was hot and humid. The buildings
reflected a history of colonialism and trading with Arab merchants who
came through magical Zanzibar, just off the coast.

At the UNICEF office, Dan and I sat in the little kitchen eating mangoes and discussing my "mission." The program was a cross between the microfinance work we'd done in Rwanda and the grants to women's groups I'd studied in Kenya. Dan explained that though loans were made to members of groups to help them pursue income, it was unclear who, if anyone, was repaying on time.

Tanzania had a history of efficiently distributing grants (but not loans) to its rural villages. Tanzania's first—and revered—president, Julius Nyerere, was a socialist who created a vast "villagization" scheme that aspired to bring good health care to every village in the country. His leadership did much to instill pride in Africans and respect among world leaders in the postindependence era. I remember the drivers in Rwanda often reading his texts and discussing his philosophies with great interest.

While socialism had failed, much of the Tanzanian government infrastructure at the village level was still in place. Unfortunately, I feared that structuring the lending program only as government grants might have hampered the possibility for its long-term sustainability. Dan counted on me to bring a critical but constructive eye to bear on the program and to present UNICEF with recommendations for moving forward.

Across Tanzania, I visited little villages in the lush mountains, where I was struck by the gorgeous scenery among which some of the poorest people on earth live. Tanzania, like Kenya, is a rich and varied country with a beautiful coastline, vast savannas, mountains, lakes, and thick, far-ranging forests. After weeks of traveling through the country, talking to rural women and government workers, I found myself not only awed by the beauty of the country, but also enamored of the kindness I found in the people.

At the same time, I was wholly dismayed by the lackluster performance of the government-administered program financed by UNICEF. Hardly anyone had repaid their loans, and I saw little evidence that any of the poor farmers or tailors were succeeding. There were no incentives for good management, and I met not a single government worker with real business or finance experience. Clearly this program was not moving anyone out of poverty, especially not in the rural areas, where poor women had such limited access to markets in the first place.

Back in Dar es Salaam, I met with Dan for hours to discuss all that I'd seen, as well as my thoughts on the future. He listened carefully and without defensiveness and ultimately felt that there were no surprises in what I was saying. He agreed with my key recommendation that the program be terminated. If UNICEF wanted to focus on microfinance, I said, it should invest in a microfinance organization and not rely on a government that had no systems in place for lending to the poor. I titled my report *The Cost of Good Intentions* and planned to write it over the course of a week while staying at Dan's large house on the beach.

Built "Swahili style," Dan's house had stark white walls, high-beamed ceilings, and tall, heavy wooden doors separating the rooms. A long wooden walkway of a light-colored wood extended to a pristine beach at the edge of the Indian Ocean's sparkling blue water. Pink sand shimmered beneath the hot sun. Outside my window I would watch fishermen drag their boats onto the shore as wooden dhows glided gracefully along the water. It was the season of Ramadan, when Muslims fast, and I thought of the discipline needed to work in brutal heat without food or water all day.

In reflecting on what I'd seen, I realized that I was beginning to recognize a pattern in the programs aimed at women's economic empowerment. Particularly in rural areas, women needed jobs and access to better, affordable services like health care and education for their children. Tanzania therefore required more investment in companies and factories to provide jobs; *and* the country needed to identify better ways of bringing critical services to the poor. Finance was one such service—there was no doubt about it. But the government should not have been a primary lender, not in Tanzania or anywhere. Instead, government should have provided the right incentives and infrastructure to enable self-sustaining initiatives to take root. Private enterprises, whether for-profit or nonprofit, could then deliver the credit and other services needed. By delegating everything to government, traditional aid efforts like this one missed the mark entirely.

After writing for a few hours, I decided to go running, though I'd promised Dan—and my friends at home—that I would avoid running by myself on empty beaches. My track record of running alone in faraway places included being attacked at gunpoint in Mexico, jumped in Brazil, badly mugged in Malaysia, and assaulted in Kenya. But the beach was peppered with people, and it was nearly 3:00 p.m. by the time I decided to take a break. I planned to run for only 15 minutes each way and would never be too great a distance from Dan's house.

I walked to the edge of the wooden walkway and looked to my left and right, taking in the quiet beauty of the afternoon. As I ran, I felt almost drunk from the feeling of sun on my skin, from breathing the salty air, from watching little kids splashing with their fully dressed mothers at the water's edge, and from listening to Bob Dylan's "Mozambique" on my Walkman. Life felt perfect.

Yet, it is so often in those moments of calm when the world feels right that suddenly it isn't.

I was just about to turn back home when, out of the corner of my eye, I saw three men walking down the beach toward the water, their deliberate steps a sure sign I was being targeted. After one man in a red knit cap called, "Mama, stop!" I took off like a lightning bolt. In the next instant, I was fighting all three men like a whirling dervish and screaming like a banshee, though this didn't stop them from grabbing my New York Yankees cap and Walkman. Somehow I kept hold of my silver bracelet, pulling it back from one of the thieves.

Nearly as quickly as it started, it was over. Suddenly I was free, running as fast as my legs have ever moved.

I didn't stop running until I was on the walkway to Dan's house. There I wrung out my sweat-drenched T-shirt and pushed the perspiration off my arms and chest in what felt like sheets of water that stung the deep scratches and gashes on my body. When I went inside, I saw my bruised face and swollen eyes in the bathroom mirror. I told myself to be calm, walked into the living room, sat down to write, and finally broke down sobbing an hour later. I wanted to talk to someone but didn't even have a phone.

Dan's gardener heard me weeping and approached me bearing cotton swabs and antibiotic ointment, mothering me in a way I craved but could not ask for. His attentions made my tears fall faster. He hugged me and told me he'd heard my screams as I fled from the attackers. I had no recollection that I'd made any noise after fleeing the men. Later I learned that the best response a woman who is being attacked can make is to scream and fight back, though my responses were simply gut reactions.

In recounting my tale later to Dan and others, I pushed away my most vulnerable feelings about the incident. I found it much easier to talk about the economic conditions that would prompt young men to attack women than to imagine what might have happened to me. Dan instinctively understood this reaction; he was a risk taker, too.

Though I realized there was a fine line between taking risks and being reckless, I craved being able to live life fully. Running on a beach with people on it in the middle of the afternoon seemed like a normal thing to do, and I ultimately didn't want to admit that something so simple could be off-limits. Even today, I struggle with the rules of the game for a woman traveling alone, though now I have a team of young people with me and I'm tougher on them than I was on myself.

I feared going to bed that night. After working until I could no longer keep my eyes open, I fell into a deep sleep. At about 3:00 a.m., the sound of a security alarm jolted me out of bed. I flew instinctively out of my room and banged loudly on Dan's door. Together we entered the living room to find that his stereo and CDs, his television, some furniture, and my computer had all been stolen. Most likely, the same men who'd attacked me on the beach had followed me and returned to rob us. Because they must have spent quite some time inside the house, it was likely that the guards had been paid off.

We spent the rest of the night in a sleepy police station recording everything that had been taken, though we knew we'd never see any of it again. Dan immediately fired the guards and later the same day hired armed guards from the country's best security firm—a good thing, because two nights later the robbers returned and cut a hole in the outside gate, though they never got close to the house.

In a week's time, I completed my report and got a ride into town to buy Fantas and cakes for the gardener and cleaner at Dan's house; they had both been so good to me. The driver from UNICEF dropped me back at the house with my goodies, and it was only after he'd left me there that I realized I'd forgotten my wallet and passport at one of the stores where I'd gone shopping. Not believing how careless I'd been, I fell into a frustrated, furious feeling of panic. I was ready to go home. Memories of the previous week's violence reemerged. With no phone at Dan's and no car of my own, I had few options but to wait for Dan to finish work, though I knew the longer I waited, the more I'd increase the chances of losing my things and, with them, my lifeline home.

The gardener and I started walking and knocking on the doors of houses in the area, one by one, asking each person if he or she had a phone we could borrow. Finally, we found a lovely couple who agreed to drive me to the stores. By now, several hours had passed. My heart was racing as I flew from store to store, stopping finally at the bakery, where a smiling woman handed me my wallet and passport, telling me she'd wondered what had taken me so long to retrieve it. I gave her a big hug and a tip and bought another cake, laughing that she'd reinforced my belief in human nature.

AFTER RETURNING TO NEW YORK the next day, I resumed my work at the Rockefeller Foundation, focusing on the Philanthropy Workshop, meeting incredible people who wanted to change the world, learning from the foundation's history. It was clear that the course needed to explore what didn't work with traditional aid and charity, as well as find successful examples, especially in Africa. Seeing the program's poor results in Tanzania had demonstrated how failure reinforces low expectations. Many of the women I met had shrugged sheepishly when I asked about their businesses, as if they themselves had never believed they would succeed in the first place.

Africa—like all communities large and small—needs success stories. Programs like the one I'd reviewed in Tanzania would do a greater service by focusing on a few things and doing them well. A pilot once told me that if you shoot for the moon, you'll have a better chance of clearing the trees. Programs serving the poor needed to do a better job of giving people the chance to aim high and believe in themselves—and of holding them accountable for reaching their goals.

One spring morning in April 1994, while riding the subway to work at the Rockefeller Foundation, I glanced at the front page of the *New York Times* and froze at the sight of the headlines about massacres in Rwanda. Among strangers on the train, I quietly shed tears of sadness, though I'd no notion of how bad things would become. I feared for the people I knew and for the country at large. For a tiny African country to make the front page of the US news, something terrible must be happening.

With each passing week, the news from Rwanda worsened: People were killing each other with machetes, studded clubs, with anything they could find. Longtime neighbors murdered one another; in some cases, fathers and mothers killed their own children. Though the stories seemed inhuman, impossible, we'd heard these tales before, in Germany and in Cambodia. On television I watched foreigners line up to board planes, leaving terrified Rwandans behind to face unknown fates. The memory of the Rwandan woman who'd told me that expatriates come and never stay haunted me—it still does. I wondered what I would have done if I had been there and felt ashamed that I wasn't sure of the answer.

My dreams filled with images of dead bodies, of being trapped beneath them, screaming to be heard. Inevitably, I would awake shaking like a leaf in a storm. As I struggled to comprehend these horrors, I realized that I didn't even know whether many of the women with whom I'd worked were Hutu or Tutsi.

I wrote the following on April 14, 1994, 8 days after the plane carrying the presidents of Rwanda and Burundi was shot down, unleashing the genocide:

Rwanda is exploding in an anarchical bloodbath of rampant, wanton killing. More than 20,000 lie dead, most of them murdered by machetes and spears. The killers see the eyes, hear the screams, feel the metal pushing through bone and marrow and sinew. In a town like Kigali, the killers know their victims. They have seen them in the street, said hello to them in the marketplace, exchanged pleasantries. Killers are related to their victims—husbands killing wives, brothers killing sisters. And the women are killing, too. I don't know how to think about the carnage in the city I knew so well—or at least I thought I did.

My friends ask my opinion, pushing me on why we should even be involved in countries "who refuse to move into the 20th century, let alone the 21st." All of your work, what has happened to it, they ask. I don't have a good answer for them, only that I know we could have avoided this if we'd paid more attention.

If only we had *listened*.

On the first day of the genocide, the army captured 10 "Blue Helmets," UN peacekeepers who were armed but not allowed to use their weapons. The Rwandan army castrated, mutilated, and killed the boy soldiers, showing the entire world their viciousness. The Hutu Power government of Rwanda understood that after the horrors of Somalia, the United States and Europe would be stopped dead in their tracks by images of 10 maimed blue-eyed blonds. As is so often the case, the supposedly insignificant understood the psychology of the strong, while the strong didn't have a clue about the other.

Had the West retaliated powerfully, immediately, and deliberately, even killing a few warriors early in the conflict, hundreds of thousands of lives might have been saved. Instead, bureaucrats argued endlessly until, in a country of 8 million, 800,000 were killed in 100 days. In some areas of Rwanda, 75 percent of Tutsis were massacred. Only near the end did the US government concede that this was not war, but genocide. By then, it was too late.

After the genocide ended in July, I wanted to work in the refugee camps, where I'd learned that Liliane and Prudence were living. Dan had been transferred from Tanzania to Rwanda to lead UNICEF's efforts at reconstruction, and I knew he would have hired me had I wanted to return. My mother and I argued fiercely about whether or not I should go. She felt strongly that I should focus on my best use, while I thought the notion of "best use" was arrogant in the face of an emergency. She said I'd made a commitment at the Rockefeller Foundation to run the Philanthropy Workshop and needed to honor it, emphasizing that what had happened in Rwanda should inspire me to be smarter in my thinking—and action—about solving problems of poverty. She argued that we all have different ways of using ourselves, and mine was needed for the longer-term view. I finally agreed not to go, though to this day I wonder if I made the right call.

It was against the backdrop of the horror of genocide that I now concentrated on understanding the potential of philanthropy to effect change in the world. Rwanda would always remind me of how serious the work of change is, how we have to build accountability into all aspects of development—and of philanthropy—and how the world really is interconnected. I would feel ashamed when I would hear people say "never again" in the media, feeling that these words were empty unless we helped build a stronger world economy in which all people could feel they had a vested interest in society.

Had the majority of Rwandans believed that they could change their lives through their own efforts and earn enough income to send their children to school, provide for their health, and plan for the future, it would have been much more difficult for morally corrupt politicians to instill a fear so deep it led to genocide. Private initiative and innovation driven by philanthropy were, I believed, our best hope for finding those ways to give the poor the opportunities they deserved.

In the years I oversaw the Philanthropy Workshop, I met wonderful people who would become colleagues and friends at a time when philanthropy was undergoing rapid change—moving from being dominated by a few older foundations to a flourishing sector driven by innovative individuals who had earned significant wealth and wanted both more involvement and more accountability in their charitable work. Ultimately, some of the workshop members would work with me in creating and building Acumen Fund, bringing their own creativity and networks to a shared endeavor to change the world.

While I was transitioning the Philanthropy Workshop to new leadership, the president of the Rockefeller Foundation, Peter Goldmark, and his able, elegant senior vice president, Angela Glover Blackwell, approached me to take on a new challenge. The Los Angeles riots had revealed America's fault lines of race, ideology, and class, which were growing in the 1990s. Angela and Peter worried that America needed to revitalize itself as an increasingly diverse democracy in a global society.

Angela spoke to me of "minoritarian leadership": "America needs leaders who are comfortable with diversity," she said. "The country itself is changing demographically, and we have a chance to play a different kind of leadership role in the world. I believe that women and people of color might have an advantage in leading diversity because they've been out-siders by definition."

I agreed with Angela, but wanted to learn more about the term "minor-ity leadership." She answered, "Individuals in the dominant group assume that the rules work because they've always seemed fair to them. On the other hand, people who view themselves as outsiders have had to learn to navigate the dominant culture in order to be successful. Becoming attuned to how others function and make decisions is a criti-cal skill set we need to inculcate in our next generation of leaders."

I thought of Rwanda again, of how the tiny country understood the psy-chology of the West and acted on it by castrating the Belgian UN soldiers. The leaders of Rwanda knew that the killing would unnerve the United States, especially given the public's response to US soldiers being dragged through the streets of Mogadishu, Somalia, months earlier. For its part, the West had paid no heed to Rwandan culture. Intuitively, I understood what Angela was talking about, but I wasn't sure how to implement it.

Peter and Angela asked me to create a program to identify, link, edu-cate, and inspire extraordinary young American leaders who represented diversity across boundaries of class, race, religion, and ideology. The program should be part-time, they said, and it should be transformative. Rockefeller would provide a budget, and I was to lead a team and make it happen. I felt flattered that they'd thought of me to do this, but also sure they'd found exactly the wrong person. What did I really know about leadership? I asked them.

Wearing a black turtleneck and skirt that made her appear even more regal than usual, Angela smiled and told me that of course I knew some-thing about leadership. "The issue is the new kind of leadership we need. You know how to listen. To do what you've done, you know what it means to collaborate across lines of difference and to be unafraid to take on big challenges. What you don't know intuitively, you will learn. The world needs this new program. We'll help you. Just say yes."

John Gardner told me that when you are young, sometimes the most important thing you can do is find the best leaders and follow them. Here were two individuals I admired deeply. Even though I couldn't see fully what I would be creating, I accepted on faith—and never looked back.

Angela helped me build a diverse team that included Jessie King, an Outward Bound instructor, and Rockefeller colleagues. I worked closely with Lisa Sullivan, a grassroots organizer who had worked with Marian Wright Edelman, founder of the Children's Defense Fund. An American original by all accounts, Lisa was brilliant and powerful, with a political science degree from Yale. She was also black, gay, and built like a truck driver. She always wore mascara and dainty earrings and could beat any kid in the hood in a game of pool while simultaneously winning him over to her side. I'd never met anyone like her.

At our first meeting, we eyed one another warily as we discussed our goals for the program and how to achieve them. We surprised ourselves by agreeing on the basics: The program would be action oriented; focus on solving problems, not just discussing them; and include reading and reflection. Two of my great privileges had been to serve as a teaching fellow at Harvard with the reknowned child psychologist Robert Coles, and to participate in an executive program at the Aspen Institute. Both experiences had taught me the power of using literature and great philosophical and political works as springboards into conversations about values and principles. I agreed with Plato that our world needs philosopher-kings and felt it was critical to combine action and reflection in building future leaders.

From hundreds of nominations, each year our team selected a group of 24 activist-leaders from all walks of life: community organizers, human rights activists, social entrepreneurs, even a fighter pilot with the US Marines. Each one was extraordinary in his or her own right. I loved knowing Rita Bright, a tall, thin, formidable African American community leader from Washington, DC. One of 10 children, Rita had lost a number of siblings to drugs and alcohol. She understood the low-income neighborhoods of Washington, earned the respect of the young men there, and made miracles happen on a regular basis. Once, she convinced the mothers in one of the most dangerous neighborhoods in DC to stand on the street corners where their sons dealt drugs in order to shame their boys into going home with them. She also started a community laundromat, believing fervently in the power of enterprise and the philosophy that God helps those who help themselves.

"Of course," she would add when describing the small business, "everyone needs a hand to get started. There is no embarrassment in using grants to train people and even to put the initial investment into these neighborhood businesses. Just give people a way to walk so that eventually they can run, and then you'll see them dance. Some of them will even fly."

When the group of 24 Next Generation Leadership (NGL) fellows visited South Africa, Rita met a group of very poor farmers who could barely afford the feed they needed for their pigs. Moved equally by their plight and their ambition, she pledged a sum of money to help, explaining in a matter-of-fact way that she would skip lunch twice a week and give the money slowly. "I've never felt as rich as I do right now after seeing what poverty really looks like," she continued, conveying with her eyes her deep and firsthand knowledge of how much crueler the poverty of a broken spirit can be than the poverty of income alone.

In spite of the privilege I found in knowing and working with the wise Rita Brights of the world, I still made every mistake in the book. In the first year I allowed NGL's group of 24 fellows to be held hostage in their discussions by a small group of activists who verbally attacked any thoughts with which they disagreed. Though extremely talented in their fields, those individuals rarely offered constructive solutions to problems and, ironically, represented exactly what we were trying to avoid in the program: leaders who were more comfortable flinging opinions than basing arguments on principles and facts.

My biggest flaw was that I was not being true to myself. In that first year, a young African American man intimidated me in front of the fellows by claiming I could never lead the group properly because I was white, privileged, and connected to the Rockefeller establishment, which he believed had done great damage to the world. Instead of confronting him directly, I stared like a deer caught in the headlights and tried defending myself as someone who had worked hard to cover university tuition and make my way in the world. I could almost feel the 24 fellows sink into themselves as I absorbed the young man's verbal blows without setting an example for both giving *and* insisting on respect.

It took months for me to understand that my biggest error had been trying to defend an implausible position. In a way, the young man was right—I *was* privileged. I'd been to some of the best schools on the planet and was raised by a loving family, and my white skin offered me significant access. The question wasn't whether I was privileged, but whether that privilege disqualified me from effectively running the program. I had responded to the wrong attack—and had done so lamely, at that.

Instead, I should have asked the young man why he chose to stay in a program when he disdained its host, the Rockefeller Foundation. He sounded like a trust-fund kid who spends the day badmouthing his parents while eagerly accepting their money. Indeed, the affiliation with Rockefeller provided him not only with instant credibility, but also gave him networks and contacts that afforded him significant access. In not confronting him, I let down the program and myself.

Though I was no longer the young woman staring at two champagne bottles and wondering what to do in the face of inequity, this question of navigating privilege in its many manifestations would continue to present increasingly nuanced questions. I'd learned that individuals gain privilege by their upbringing, beauty, athletic ability, or education, not simply from where they come or to whom they are born. My first-grade nun had instructed me that from those to whom much is given, much is expected. I was learning that this lesson had to be combined with Shakespeare's wisdom that one must "to thine own self be true." Add to this humility, empathy, a sense of curiosity, courage, and plain old hard work, and I was finally seeing the real path to leadership. Of course, humor is always a plus.

Among the Rockefeller program's fellows, I met several remarkable leaders, young and old, including a woman named Ingrid Washinawatok, a member of the Menominee Nation of Wisconsin, the wife of a Palestinian, and a voice for indigenous peoples across the world. Strong in body and spirit, Ingrid had a round, wide face, wore jeans most of the time, and loved sharing Native American legends and the philosophies of great Indian chiefs. We started a yearlong conversation about the role of the marketplace for tribal peoples who feel so far behind the economic mainstream.

I could listen to Ingrid tell stories for hours, but we never got to finish our conversation. While our second group was preparing to go to South Africa, Ingrid was working with the U'wa community in Colombia along with two colleagues—Lahe'ena'e Gay of Hawaii and environmentalist Terence Freitas. The three were helping an indigenous community threatened by US oil companies start a school system. On their way to the airport to leave, their car was stopped by rebels, and all three were tortured and murdered.

I thought of being jumped in Tanzania, about how Ingrid also must have been thinking it was a perfect day the moment before it suddenly wasn't. I thought about the adolescent boys of the rebel group who had no idea who she was or what she represented. The Next Generation Leadership group was in South Africa when we heard the news. A few days later, we met with Archbishop Desmond Tutu to discuss the work of the Truth and Reconciliation Commission.

He told us, "We are all children of God. You must remember that people want to be good, even if sometimes they are not. Ingrid's spirit lives inside of you now, and you must carry on her work. That is life and that is love." From then on, we would leave an empty chair when we met as a group to honor the memory of our greatly admired friend.

Hearing Bishop Tutu's words and thinking about Ingrid and the work of other leaders I'd known reaffirmed my own commitment to finding that place of common humanity. But NGL had taught me that just bringing diverse people together is not enough to foster productive dialogue. More powerful is enabling groups of people to work on a common venture, a common problem. And increasingly, the problems in the world are shared. Here was a Native American woman killed by Colombian rebels for doing work with an indigenous group that had been marginalized by an international oil company. Her life and death gave me a legacy to uphold, one of recognizing that all people, rich and poor, from all nations, religions, and backgrounds, are our sisters and brothers. From this place, everything else must flow.

Of all the people I miss from that era, Lisa Sullivan stands out. During the early days of building the Next Generation Leadership program, Lisa and I decided to take a trip to the Mississippi Delta, for we would later be taking the fellows there. We hardly knew one another then, and Lisa had let me know she wasn't sure about having me as a traveling partner in the real American South, a place she considered to be the home of *her people,* but I promised to behave myself. I arrived at the Jackson Airport on a cool fall day in a pleated skirt and heels. She wore jeans, sneakers, and a baseball cap. Perfect.

For a week, Lisa and I visited educators and church leaders, policymakers, prisoners, and businessmen. I showed my surprise at finding that 95 percent of public schools were black, while 95 percent of private schools were white—and my lack of awareness angered Lisa. I found her ideas on business to be knee-jerk liberalism and told her so. It took the extraordinary Unita Blackwell, the first black woman mayor in Mississippi (but unrelated to Angela), to remind us of how much we needed one another. Lisa could organize people like no one I'd known, and I knew how to build organizations. We shared a worldview, one in which all people had a chance to fulfill their highest purpose.

"Leading," Mayor Blackwell told us, "is a lifelong proposition—and the people who seem least like you are usually the people you need most."

Lisa and I were most devastated by the gambling industry's impact on low-income people. In 1990, Mississippi was the first southern state to legalize gambling, justifying the casinos as sources of jobs and tax revenue for the state. But the wages paid were low, while the toll gambling took on local communities was immense. In the Tupelo casino, Lisa and I saw mostly low-income people sitting in front of machines literally throwing away their meager earnings. And we saw this again and again in every casino we visited across the state.

At the catfish factories, we saw firsthand what an unfettered private sector can do to poor people in the name of job creation: All but one of the 400 catfish processing factories in the Mississippi Delta were owned by white men, and 99 percent of the workers were black women. The women earned minimum wage and typically stood in ice-cold, bloody water for hours cutting fillets of catfish, with few breaks for lunch or the bathroom. Until the late 1980s, workers were commonly maimed or killed by slipping inside ice-chopping machines. Many had to leave the job because of severe carpal tunnel syndrome.

As we approached a giant factory, Lisa pushed me to register with the guard at the metal gate. "Tell him you're a student," she whispered. "Otherwise, he'll think you're a spy. Tell them you're a student working on a paper about catfish."

"You've got to be kidding me," I replied.

When the guard sternly asked what I was there for, I nonetheless responded obediently, "Student."

On a quiet late afternoon, we walked into the front offices, where a uniformed, overweight woman in a white cap approached. "We are studying the catfish industry," Lisa told her when she offered to help. "We want to know how conditions have changed in the past year or so and take a look at the factory itself." She never asked the woman's name, and it wasn't offered.

When the woman asked if we had permission to visit the line, Lisa shook her head. The woman silently motioned for us to follow. Inside the factory, where the workers on the line sliced fish at rapid-fire pace, the din was fearsome. Though we wore rubber boots, sloshing through the freezing red water made me want to vomit.

Back in the front offices, the woman invited us to sit down at a white Formica table. Still, she didn't give us her name. Her massive hands were folded in front of her, and her lips stayed pursed together. Lisa told her stories of organizing in the Delta with the Children's Defense Fund, talked about her favorite foods and why she loved Mississippi. Finally, the woman began to soften.

"Things are a lot better now," she told us after a minute or two of silence.

"Why?" Lisa asked.

"The line is safer now, we can take breaks, and our hours are not as bad as they used to be. People aren't getting hurt as much."

"What happened?" Lisa pushed.

Leaning over the table, she looked at us and with her index finger traced a big, invisible U for "union." In whispers, she talked about how young Easterners had come down to Mississippi to discuss the power of unions.

The workers had risked everything, she said. "Some of us were fired and, you know, we didn't have no cushion to keep us eating. But we helped each other, and we kept at it, and we made it."

Mississippi is one of the poorest states in the country. At least one in three black men in his twenties at that time was under some sort of criminal supervision. The graduation rate for black male high school students was abysmally low, and the public health system was in shambles. This was another side of America, one that took Hurricane Katrina for the rest of the country to begin to see.

The Delta also reminded me of how easily capitalism can be manipulated to oppress the most vulnerable. Good public policy must accompany market-oriented solutions that are undergirded with an imperative of moral leadership. We need to ask more questions about who is awarded public contracts, who gains, who loses, and whether or not our public funds are doing the most possible for the most people rather than benefiting just a few. The premise of the Next Generation Leadership program was one that made me proud, but how could we extend the principles to a much larger group of leaders?

After running NGL for 2 years, Lisa and I both went on to build new organizations, mine focused on global issues, hers, on young people in Washington, DC. During late-night calls from our offices, we would commiserate about the long hours and loneliness. When we talked about the personal price we sometimes pay for trying to change the world, Lisa would remind me of one of her favorite songs by Sweet Honey in the Rock: "We Are the Ones We've Been Waiting For."

"We can't wait around for someone else to change things," she would say. A week after I advised her to take it easy, to take time to relax and regenerate, she died of an asthma attack. Lisa was taken too early from a world in desperate need of individuals with such courage, heart, intellect, and stamina, the ones who carry wisdom the way Maha Ghosananda had taught.

Knowing Lisa and visiting South Africa and Mississippi with NGL made me think about Rwanda and inspired me to return. If leadership was about having vision and the moral imagination to put oneself in another's shoes, then I had to try and understand what had happened in a place where I'd lived and worked, but might never fully know. I had to return and see what had happened to the women I knew. In 1997, I returned to Kigali, where I had learned firsthand the difficulties of navigating across difference. When all was said and done, here was a country destroyed because people feared one another.

When I boarded the plane at JFK, I expected to see the trees in Kigali weeping and the flowers all dead. I had an image of postgenocide Rwanda as a place that would seem perennially gray and depressed. After all, 800,000 people had died on its rich soil in a 3-month period.

But I was mistaken. Mother Nature had left nary a dent: The physical world was unchanged. Though memories would linger in the very air the people breathed, earth itself forgot the mass destruction in an instant. Of course, man-made structures suffered—churches and houses across the country had been destroyed. Buildings were riddled with bullet holes, and uniformed boys with machine guns stood at every corner. Barbed wire was wound atop high brick walls where wooden fences used to suffice, sometimes wrapped almost metaphorically by pastel morning glories slinking around sharp metal. And the light-filled sky was as blue as it had ever been.

I drove straight to UNICEF to find my friend Boniface the driver, who seemed so much older and more tired. "I found God after the war," he said, "and stopped drinking altogether. I nearly killed myself with too much beer trying to forget how badly people treated one another." A tiny Bible sat on the seat beside him and a rosary hung from the rearview mirror.

When I asked him to take me to the bakery, he protested: "Everything has changed, you know."

As we drove to Nyamirambo in silence, I thought about how much I liked Boniface, as well as the other drivers, now all dead—either from the genocide or AIDS. We passed the candy-striped mosque, a beacon above the area's rambling streets. The Muslims were the only group who didn't fight during the genocide, and the number of Muslim converts had risen significantly since then. A few Islamic schools stood by familiar little shops. Religion had played such a tragic, disappointing role: When thousands of people fled to the churches for safety, they found not sanctuaries, but killing fields. Some priests and nuns became modern Judases, and the masses, previously so beholden to authority, ensured that neither house of God nor shrine was sacred.

In a world turned upside down, I had come to see what was left of the Rwanda I had known. Just the sight of the mosque comforted me. I knew that Duterimbere had survived, but where was the bakery? Boniface and I walked down familiar streets, past tailor shops and video stores, until he finally pointed to a patch of blue paint by the roadside.

I knocked on the door, tentatively at first, but no one answered. When I knocked again, louder this time, there was still no response.

I had nearly given up when the door opened a crack and a skinny hand appeared. A young, birdlike woman with a red scarf wrapped around her head emerged slowly from the shadows.

I introduced myself in French. She just stared at me.

I repeated myself—to silence once again.

"I speak only English," she finally stammered. A refugee from Uganda, she must have moved here after the genocide and taken over the empty house. Perhaps she feared I'd come to take it back.

She said she hadn't heard of a bakery being on this spot.

Somehow it perturbed me to speak in my native tongue: "How long have you lived here?" I asked.

"Two years," she responded. "I sell milk from my house."

My house? I was sure the woman was squatting, having found the bakery empty after the genocide. This was happening all across Kigali, though I knew President Kagame was trying to address the problem. But this time it all felt so personal. I didn't like her possessive tone, though I also knew that she could have lost everything herself and was just trying to survive.

"Do you know your neighbors? Did any of them live here before?" I persisted.

She shook her head and closed the door before I could thank her.

I stood there in silence.

Blue paint on the road was all that remained of the bakery—blue paint that should have been green. For one brief moment, there had been a pocket of joy here in a place where women dared to have aspirations, to make their own decisions on their own terms. With the bakery gone, so were most of the women who worked there, I assumed. I thought of the Jewish concept of memory: Who will tell the stories so that people don't forget?

Though the bakery was destroyed, its lessons would go on and infuse other work—certainly my work. In an instant, a patch of blue paint made me want to do more. My prayer in response to what I saw after the genocide would manifest itself in a new organization yet to be invented.

As I stared at the blue paint on the road, what made my head spin was the fact that the women I'd known and worked with for years—Honorata, Prudence, Agnes, and Liliane—had played such dramatically different roles in the genocide as victim, bystander, and even perpetrator. I wanted to understand their stories, and from 1997 to 2000, I visited those women four times. What they shared with me changed how I think about any human crisis, be it genocide, the spread of HIV/AIDS, or the ravages of chronic poverty. To this day, they live inside me.

CHAPTER 10

RETRIBUTION AND RESURRECTION

"When I despair, I remember that all through history, the ways of truth and love have always won. There have been tyrants and murderers, and for a long time they can seem invincible, but in the end they always fall. Think of it—always."

—GANDHI

After learning that the bakery had been decimated, I feared discovering the fates of the women who had helped found Duterimbere: Honorata, Liliane, Prudence, Agnes, and Annie. I gave myself only a week on my first trip back, for I wanted simply to discover what had happened to the people I knew.

Once I learned that they'd played every conceivable role in the genocide, I decided to come back year after year just to try and understand, though I doubt I ever will.

On my second visit back, the first person I went to see was Honorata, Veronique's old sidekick who had helped guide me on visits with so many women's groups and had first introduced me to the blue bakery.

"God sent you back to me!" Honorata squealed almost exuberantly in her white cotton blouse and navy skirt, a tropical-patterned lemon yellow scarf wrapped around her head. This was not the Honorata I'd visited 2 years after the genocide had ended, when we'd both stood and wept, holding on to one another for dear life. Then she'd seemed a worn, weary, wilted stem and had uttered not a word of hope, nothing but despair. I remember seeing her walk toward me out of the shadows of her darkened office, seeming ghostlike, barely there.

This time, she was a magnificent blast of energy and light. Her eyes shone like the sun, and I couldn't help but smile just at the sight of how beautiful she looked.

Honorata's little pink house stood across the street from a giant, shimmering eucalyptus tree in her neighborhood of Nyamirambo, not far from where the bakery once stood. We sat in her small, clean, simple living room with walls painted robin's-egg blue and furnished with a plastic couch positioned in front of a small wooden table as well as a single bed covered by sheets printed with cartoon Smurfs. A large bowl of mangoes, bananas, and passion fruit and a vase of flowers adorned the main table—signs of life and renewal. On another table stood a large picture of a white, blue-eyed, thorn-crowned Jesus Christ, a plastic Virgin Mary, and a framed prayer about the need to trust God in all things.

God was everywhere in Honorata's life. She thanked the Lord in nearly every sentence she uttered, attributing everything good to Him. I respected her faith yet also wondered whether any unspoken doubt lingered alongside her deep conviction. Many Rwandans had concluded after the genocide that no benevolent God could have allowed such an atrocity, but if any uncertainty resided in Honorata, she didn't show it. And regardless of whether or not I shared her religious faith, it was undeniable that her strong belief imbued her with remarkable courage.

"Most of the women from the bakery were killed," she told me. "Now I spend a lot of time helping a women's group. I'm a widow now, like many of them. We accompany each other. It gives me great strength to work with those poor women—so many returned with nothing in their lives."

I thanked her for all she'd taught me when we worked together. Honorata's eyes welled up: "That was the *belle époque,* when we believed anything was possible. It was a time when women began to open their eyes to the external world, to see their lives in the context of something bigger. From 1986, we learned about other realities and other people. We shared the little we had for the common good, not caring whether a woman was from one ethnicity or another.

"The problems started around the time you were leaving the country," she told me.

In October 1990, the Rwandan Patriotic Front (RPF), a small but effective rebel army led by Paul Kagame, entered Rwanda from Uganda. The RPF's stated mission was to remove Rwanda's president and make it possible for exiled Tutsis to reclaim their citizenship. At the same time, the international community was pushing Rwanda for democratic reform.

This marked the beginning of fear. And with fear began the disinformation campaigns, the lying, and the manipulation by Rwanda's leaders to instill even more defensiveness—and paranoia—in an already insecure citizenry.

For the next 5 years, the question would be asked over and over: "Are you a Hutu or a Tutsi?" As tensions between the two groups increased, a growing hatred began to permeate everyday life.

I had never known Honorata's ethnicity, but if I'd been pushed, I would have guessed she was Hutu, just because she fit the stereotype of being a short woman with a broad nose. In truth, physical characteristics revealed little about ethnicity. I did know her mother was Tutsi—but ethnicity is handed down patrilineally in Rwanda. I'd also known that the genocide had taken scores of members of Honorata's extended family—nearly everyone on her mother's side—as well as her beloved husband and her identical twin sister.

Though she and her family were clearly targeted, Honorata and I never discussed her specific ethnicity, nor did we talk about our *multiple* identities: Honorata was also Rwandan, female, a social worker, and a mother. That's a conversation I would like to have had with her.

Instead I asked her to tell me her story. Holding my hand and taking a deep breath, for 3 hours she spoke, often in the third person. Maybe this was the only way she could bear to say the words aloud.

In childhood, there were three important women in her life. Her identical twin, Anunziata, was like "another branch on the same tree," her soul mate, her rock: "The most time we were separated was in the 15 minutes between our births," she told me.

The two spent much of their childhood searching fruitlessly for their mother, Collette, a woman known for her classic beauty, who had abandoned her family when the girls were young, possibly during the pogroms of the early 1960s. Or perhaps she fled to escape the girls' stepmother, who treated her with constant disrespect. After Collette left, the twins' stepmother abused them, forcing them to work like servants, showing them no affection.

"We used to pray to God," Honorata told me, "'Please show us where our mother is, even if she can be found only in the traces of a tree or a rock.'"

Loss and redemption were lifelong themes for both Honorata and her twin sister.

Ultimately, when the girls were adults, they discovered their mother in

Zaire, living quietly in a village, having had no further children of her own. Around the same time, Honorata also found the love of her life in a young engineer named Theodore. The young couple found a way to bring her mother, Collette, to Rwanda, married, and had four children, three girls and a boy. Anunziata married one of Theodore's close friends and moved to Butare, 2 hours away from Kigali. Still, the twins saw one another almost weekly. Eventually, Theodore was issued a house in accordance with his midlevel government position and Honorata's mother was able to move into the couple's old house in Nyamirambo, which she turned into a boardinghouse for young women. Finally, Honorata's yearning for family and closeness was fulfilled.

"Theodore promised he would love me forever," she remembered tearfully, "and in this he never failed me for a moment throughout his short life."

In 1994, as tensions rose in Rwanda, Honorata and Theodore discussed leaving the country, but were prevented from doing so by the impossibility of securing visas for everyone in their family. On April 16, 10 days after the genocide began, the Interahamwe marched into Honorata's neighborhood violently and unannounced. She and Theodore gathered their children and neighbors and immediately headed south to Butare, the only place in Rwanda not yet ripped apart. It was also the most educated part of the country, with a Tutsi majority—and Anunziata was there. The roads were too dangerous to drive to her mother's house in Nyamirambo, and Honorata's heart broke at the thought of leaving her, but she could see no other choice.

All across the country, government officials were whipping up the populace with a paranoid torrent of words and sermons played constantly on the radio. The genocidal government's message was consistent: The Tutsis had invaded Rwanda to regain power and subjugate the Hutus. Thus, the Hutus were in a "kill or be killed" situation. The citizens were restless, frightened, but they listened to their leaders. When the radio announced it was time to "clear the bushes," ordinary Rwandan citizens resorted to murdering their neighbors, cheered on by local authorities.

Despite these orders to rally the population to kill the Tutsis, Butare's prefect, Jean-Baptiste Habyarimana, refused to open the floodgates to violence. He maintained government services, ordered large stocks of food and fuel from wherever he could find them, and tirelessly held local meetings across the area, assuring people that they would be protected by law and should remain in their homes. He urged the citizens of Butare to exercise extreme caution when listening to the radio and reminded people repeatedly that there had been no "ancient tribal hatreds" in Rwanda.

With Habyarimana as a beacon of hope, thousands of Tutsis made their way to his city. Honorata and her family were among the throngs who miraculously survived the nighttime drive through the forests, arriving in Butare on the morning of April 17. On the same day, the president of Rwanda arrived with an official delegation that included our old colleague Agnes, one of the three parliamentarians who had helped start Duterimbere. Agnes's actions and Honorata's fate would be forever linked. The president summarily dismissed the prefect and commanded that he leave office immediately. I would learn only later that Habyarimana was the godson of Agnes's husband.

The exhausted ex-official walked out of the auditorium alone, speaking later to a crowd in the streets: Habyarimana never ceased pleading to stop the violence until he was drowned in a sea of rage and blood.

The government's grand plan was to ensure the collective guilt of every Rwandan, while exterminating every single Tutsi and moderate Hutu. Like a dark cloud inching across the sky, the government co-opted the weaker officials and murdered the ones who resisted. Habyarimana's replacement, Sylvain Nsabimana, an agronomist by training with a reputation as a lightweight and a dandy, claimed not to have wanted the position of prefect. Nevertheless, he managed to buy himself a new suit for his installation ceremony.

Habyarimana's dismissal unleashed the killing machine. On April 18, more than 10,000 people who had been hiding in the convent of the Bernadine Sisters were murdered. Honorata, her sister, and their families remained huddled in Anunziata's home for another 4 days, trapped, knowing that terror lurked everywhere.

The orange sun was descending in a foreboding sky on the evening of April 22 as Honorata's and Anunziata's families sat down to a meal of rice and beans. The scene was tense, filled with an unbearable masquerade of normalcy. Suddenly, a shot—then shouting and more gunshots.

Soldiers barged through the door. Young boys with banana leaves around their necks dragged adults and children alike outside until they counted nearly 40 people. Men were instructed to stand on one side of the street, and women and children on the other.

"I knew the time had come," Honorata whispered. "We recited the Act of Contrition right in front of the soldiers, and I said a prayer to the Virgin Mary, begging her to help us. Then I said the Act of Contrition again, with the children joining me."

I thought of the first words of this prayer that is part of the Last Rites, "Oh my God, I am heartily sorry for having offended Thee," and imagined her reciting it in the face of killers.

One of the soldiers snarled, "Your good Lord, where is he now?"

"Hail Mary, full of grace, the Lord is with thee."

A boy commander ordered the others to kill, and they shot each man once in the middle of his head, 6 feet in front of their wives and children. Theodore slumped to the ground, his slender frame folding into the muddy road. No one tried to run. Not a single man screamed. Not a single man survived.

The women and children cried and begged, pleading not to be massacred.

The head soldier turned and ordered the rest of his makeshift squad to kill the women and children.

"I felt the presence of the Holy Spirit then," Honorata said, her eyes turned downward. "I yelled to everyone to drop to the ground. The soldiers kept shooting, shooting, until they thought we were dead. Then they left, not checking to see who was alive. They didn't take our possessions. Maybe they knew we had nothing to take."

The rain pounded, drenching bodies and bloodying the street. Lying under a pile of corpses, Honorata thought she was dead. For what seemed like hours, no one moved.

Out of nowhere she heard a young, high-pitched voice asking if anyone was still alive. Honorata laid in shock, unable to utter a word in response. Another child shrieked, "Those who are still alive, try to save us."

Her daughter shook her and pulled her hair, crying, "Mother, Mother!"

She could do nothing but stare at her sister, Anunziata, lying next to her, hit by two bullets and barely alive.

Every other adult was dead.

Seventeen children were still breathing. Two were critically wounded: Honorata's 13-year-old daughter had been shot in the breast, another son of a close friend, in the thigh. But before she could think of helping the children, she had to somehow accompany her sister in her final moments. That was all that mattered.

Together the sisters prayed: "Forgive them, Father, for they know not what they do." Honorata asked the children to join them. Together, they recited the prayer three times.

Honorata told me, "Of all the adults, I was the least maternal and the least courageous—I was the wrong person for God to have left alive. But there I was with 17 children in my care. So I told God that our fates were entirely in His hands."

As she turned her focus to the children, the prayer of forgiveness and surrender gave Honorata a strength she had never known before.

Where to run? The churches were no longer secure. Thousands had sought refuge at chapels and cathedrals previously considered safe havens. Priests and nuns had turned over their congregations to die. With the children in tow, Honorata stumbled back to Anunziata's house, now littered with papers, food, chairs, and mattresses. By the time she returned to her sister, Anunziata was dead.

At dawn, workers from Doctors without Borders found Honorata holding her twin, keening and sobbing at the site of the massacre. She accompanied the two wounded children to Butare's hospital, where a MASH unit had been set up. Throughout the day, terrified, Honorata shuttled between the hospital and Anunziata's home, where the children were still hiding.

By the end of the first day, after community members learned what had happened, an old acquaintance found Honorata at the hospital and gave her $20, now all the money she had in the world. Other friends offered to take her children into hiding with them. Even strangers shared whatever they could to help her buy food for her children. When I think of how aid agencies characterize Africans as desperate for handouts, I think of Honorata and her support system, still functioning and generous in a brutish world gone mad.

For the better part of 6 weeks, Honorata remained at the hospital, comforted that the other children were safer outside town. "The soldiers would come into the hospital, see my children, and say, 'These children are offspring of *Inyenzi* [cockroaches].'" Other Rwandans came to the hospital to give her and other survivors whatever they could spare for medicines and food. In turn, Honorata did what she could for other patients, comforting them and praying with them.

By June, Honorata felt safe enough to brave another journey, this time to the refugee camps in the French-controlled Turquoise Zone near Cyangugu. My own memory of Cyangugu was one of beauty and magic: It is near a lush forest, one of the most extraordinary on earth due to its astonishing biodiversity. Home to 14 species of Africa's primates, 280 avian species alone, and thick with vegetation, the Nyungwe Forest is another world in peacetime. When camping there with a friend, I fell asleep looking at the stars from beneath the canopies of the high trees and awakened at dawn to loud chattering, surrounded by scores of colobus monkeys, their masked faces staring at us inquisitively. Now, that seemed like ancient history.

FIRST IN ONE CAMP and then another, Honorata began descending toward a nervous breakdown—and the state of her children wasn't helping matters. Her teenage children were suffering the trauma of loss, of war, and of the disappearance of normal boundaries. They had nothing to believe in and no sense of order or safety. The girls rebelled by donning miniskirts and blasting their radios, and they didn't want to talk to her—typical adolescent behavior that felt more confusing to Honorata, given her own state of mind.

"Why do we have to be wise and thoughtful?" her children would shoot back at her when she reached out to calm them. "Weren't you wise? Weren't you kind to everyone? And still they treated you like a dog. Still they killed our father."

The only people who listened to her were a small group of Canadian nuns who taught Honorata yoga and other exercises recommended to heal body and soul. They kept her close to them. For the first time in her life, Honorata allowed herself to be "accompanied."

"I always accompanied poor women and widows; suddenly, I needed others to accompany me," she recounted.

Love lies at the base of our common humanity. In parts of Africa, people say "I *am* because you *are*." Hindus in India greet one another with "*Namaste*," or "I bow to you," though spiritual leaders also interpret this as a way of saying that the God in me recognizes the God in you. War brings out the best and the worst in humanity, and genocide is no different. People killed one other by turning neighbors into "cockroaches" and nonhumans. But ordinary Rwandans also risked death to help one another. Sometimes—often—the same person did both.

Friends assisted Honorata financially. A Belgian priest offered to support her family, saying he wanted to be a "papa" of sorts. He recognized that her children refused to set foot in Rwanda again. He understood that she needed to go back to see if her mother was alive. And he helped raise the money to send her children to boarding schools overseas.

Honorata could barely discuss the day she said good-bye to her children. She'd been caught between knowing they would be safer and healthier in boarding schools outside the country and feeling that she herself had no choice but to return home to see if her mother was alive and to help the ones left behind.

She paused and took a deep breath. I looked at her, feeling exhausted and sad, yet seeing peace and calm in her eyes. If she could endure such suffering and still sit there with a beatific smile, what could I do from my own position of privilege? If I asked her where she got her strength, I knew she would attribute it only to God. But I also knew that much was due to the extraordinary woman sitting next to her—Collette.

WHEN THE GENOCIDE BEGAN, Collette was alone with 10 Tutsi girls in the boardinghouse for young women she'd set up in Honorata and Theodore's little pink house in Nyamirambo. Isolated, the girls and the older woman were easy prey. As angry young men with machetes encircled the house, Collette would lead the girls in long recitations of passages from the Bible, urging them not to look through the windows at the horror outside. Most upsetting to Collette was seeing the dogs that roamed the streets and ate the corpses of neighbors.

I remembered driving home one night when I was working with Duterimbere in 1988 and being attacked by a pack of wild dogs. It was around midnight when the pack began jumping on all sides of the car, trying to get in. One lunged onto the hood and I stared into his hideous face. I sped off and got away, but the viciousness of the animals still haunts me. Collette was driven almost entirely by her refusal to allow herself or the girls to face the indignity of being devoured.

"All people deserve a proper burial," she later told Honorata. "Death was a given. But I would not give up my dignity."

A blade of grass, in time, can push its way through stone: Collette and the girls remained in the house for 3 months. They grew food in the tiny garden, barely ate, and used parts of the wooden fence that circled the house as firewood. Daily, marauders came to the gate to taunt the young women with promises of salvation. The next day, the same boys would threaten to kill the girls, cut off their "fine" noses, or chop off their "long legs." Every day Collette sat in her chair and read the Bible, refusing to move. The soldiers began to believe that God was protecting Collette— and somehow, she and all 10 girls survived.

Like mother, like daughter. Immediately following the genocide,

Collette began working with widows. When Honorata returned, she joined her mother in accompanying those who had lost what she had.

Now Collette, Honorata, and the orphaned children had been joined in the pink house by Honorata's stepmother, whom she'd once considered evil. Honorata confessed to making a deal with God during the genocide: She would care for this woman if God let her survive.

"Time heals," Honorata told me. "I've heard my stepmother tell people how well I look after her. She once confided to a friend that she would have been much kinder to Anunziata and me during our youth if she'd known that I would end up taking care of her. But we never know, do we?"

Fire strengthens iron. "Before the war," Honorata told me, "I was comfortable. I worked without really knowing why. Living in the service of other people, I finally felt fully alive. I found the true force of God in being available to others and in accepting one's fate without complaining. I began to understand that God was sending me a message: You must radiate and shine despite the difficulties you have on earth. In spite of your own problems, comfort those women who have lost their husbands.

"In the end, goodness triumphs over the bad. It is our challenge to do good and to serve others without waiting for the good to be returned. I'm convinced that those people who cultivate universal love will have good fortune on earth. In serving others, I found light in a place of utmost darkness."

Through Honorata, I understood that resurrection happens right here on earth. I see her spirit and her resilience in women across the globe who have nothing, yet suffer great loss with almost unimaginable grace and dignity. Honorata will forever be one of my greatest teachers. Her story reminds me of the extraordinary power of the human spirit to withstand almost anything. Her story also speaks to the power of service, to living a life of purpose, and to keeping the flame of hope alive.

Honorata asked me to accompany her to visit the group of widows she supported. "They need to give you their stories for their own healing," she said. This notion of "giving" stories was new, but I would soon learn the power of bearing witness and of transferring pain through storytelling. By listening and acknowledging the truths of those women, I had the honor of playing a miniscule part in their healing.

Together, we met four women in a small room. They were Hutu and Tutsi, their husbands dead or imprisoned. All were living alone. Like Honorata, each woman took nearly 3 hours to tell her story. Like Honorata, each woman was full of grace.

For nearly 12 hours, we sat together, with nothing to sustain us but stories and tea. Each woman recounted experiences filled with horror and tragedy and the deepest grief imaginable. My head pounded, and I didn't know what to do with the feelings inside me. Finally, I asked how they could sit together and listen to one another's stories across ethnic lines. Didn't it generate rage? One's husband may have murdered another's—or another's son, for all they knew. Where did they find room for forgiveness?

One woman responded quietly, "We listen to one another and look into one another's eyes and we see suffering. It is that suffering that binds us. It is that suffering that reminds us that we are all human."

Her words resonated. In recognizing their humanity, I felt strengthened in my own.

NO ONE ESCAPED SUFFERING. Every Rwandan not only saw— or committed—horrendous acts, but everyone lost someone and, with that, part of their hearts. Hutus like Liliane, who were never targeted and never participated in the violence, still live with the shadows of shame and guilt. But so many ordinary Rwandans demonstrated the extraordinary courage and spirit that bode well for the country's future.

The first time I saw Liliane after the genocide, she seemed burdened with an almost unbearable depression. Honorata had suffered unimaginably, but she was already finding an inner peace that grew through the years, living in her former home and taking part in a survivors' group.

Liliane had been renting a small house in a slum ever since she and her family returned from the refugee camp to discover a Rwandan Patriotic Front (RPF) soldier occupying her house. Whereas Honorata's home was filled with light, the darkness of Liliane's rented place, by contrast, was appalling. Its center consisted of a meager living room, not bigger than 8 feet by 10, furnished with a small wooden table surrounded by a bench and three chairs. The concrete walls were riddled with cracks like river lines on a map and painted an ugly industrial green. The plain cement floor was so damaged in places that dirt pushed through the gray. A picture of a white Jesus Christ with a crown of thorns hung on the wall, and a plastic rosary was taped to another. A single naked bulb hung overhead, and the lack of air was suffocating.

Liliane's husband, Julien, was a doctor who continued working in the city's hospital through most of the genocide. Liliane remained at home, afraid to walk the streets, pregnant with twins and caring for their 5-year-old son, Augustin. She hid a close friend along with her friend's husband and young child in their house for weeks until it became too dangerous and the young family fled (the husband was killed, but the wife and child survived).

Toward the end of June 1994, the RPF took over the capital, and like most Hutus, Liliane and her family drove toward Goma, where a million refugees would quickly gather. On the first night, they reached Gisenyi, where Julien had worked for years in the hospital; Liliane went into labor 8 weeks early.

She gave birth in the middle of the night. By morning, one of the twins had died. The other, weighing less than 2 pounds, was so fragile that her skin could not be washed with water. In the midst of all the killings, the couple buried the dead child, mourning her short life in a way that countless children thrown into rivers or bashed with machetes and clubs would never be acknowledged.

They stayed at the hospital for nearly 3 weeks until the RPF took over Gisenyi, and then they fled to Goma. Privilege allowed them to find a hotel outside the massive refugee camps, at least for a few weeks until they'd spent the last of their money. With cholera killing thousands every day, Liliane was terrified to bring her baby to the camp, but she ultimately had no choice. She and Julien waited nearly 10 months before naming her Valerie and also giving her a Kinyarwanda name meaning Pearl, because there was nothing more valuable to them.

For 2 years, they remained in the refugee camps. It was bearable for Liliane because a village system emerged nearly overnight, with schools and clinics and even makeshift streets to give a sense of order and community. Family was close by, and she had managed to bring her photographs when she and Julien rushed from Kigali. "I looked at them over and over, remembering that life could be different."

Still, the Interahamwe ruled the camps with terror and brutality. "Right behind us were four small houses where a group of young men lived. They were maybe 16 to 25 years old. All had been in the army and none were married. It kept us living constantly in fear that something terrible could happen again."

In November 1996 Liliane's family joined more than a million people returning to Rwanda in a quiet, orderly procession. Most were terrified about what might happen to them next—what awaited them in a place they no longer knew. The refugees carried everything they owned in suitcases and baskets. They were a million ordinary people caught up in a genocide, penniless, walking for weeks, sometimes months, to return to a country where they were not wanted. Tens of thousands never made it back, including Liliane's mother.

On the first day, Liliane walked nearly 20 hours, with just water and sugar to sustain her, her 7-year-old son, and her 2-year-old daughter. She persisted by focusing obsessively on their house in Kigali, praying that it would still be there when they returned. She and Julien had bought it 6 months before the genocide and had already repaid a third of their debt. The house represented home and stability—everything.

Once in Kigali, she headed directly to her house, not knowing what she would find. Before reaching it, she encountered a friend who told her to turn back: "There's a soldier from Uganda living there. They are killing people who try to get their houses back. Just wait."

She could think of nowhere else to go. Without food or drink or stopping for the night, she turned with her children and retraced her steps all the way back to Gisenyi, about a 4-hour drive away. Though it wasn't home, Julien could find a job there in the hospital where he'd worked before—and there they had a better chance of finding another house.

Obsessed with getting her house back, Liliane stayed only a few months in Gisenyi before deciding to return to her home in Kigali, despite the grave risk she believed she was taking. But Liliane had title— proof of ownership—and President Kagame had promised that titled housing would be returned. She would bet her life on this.

RETURNING TO KIGALI CAME with a big price tag in the beginning: Liliane and the children had no choice but to move into a slum. Julien would remain in Gisenyi for the time being. The poor condition of Liliane's temporary quarters finally pushed her to find the courage to approach the soldier living in her old house. She walked slowly to the familiar house, knocked on the gate, and found herself standing in front of an imposing soldier dressed in fatigues. She took a deep breath, tried not to think about the women who'd been hacked to death, and told him her story.

He listened.

He refused to leave but agreed to pay her rent—not enough to cover their mortgage payments, but it was a start. She thanked him and then went home to thank God.

Nothing happened: The soldier never paid a franc, nor did he leave.

More visits, more negotiations; nothing changed. Liliane and Julien reached a point where they could no longer afford the mortgage on their home while also renting one in the slum. She began visiting the soldier weekly, each time asking him to leave.

One morning, she arrived to an empty house. The soldier had disappeared, taking everything that wasn't nailed down—every piece of furniture, every curtain, every picture on the wall. The stench in the empty, filthy house was nearly unbearable, but 5 years after leaving it, it was hers again.

A year after I first saw Liliane in the slum, I returned to visit her in the house she and Julien had so cherished. The house was by now light and airy and had three bedrooms—one for her and Julien, another for the children, and a third for her sister and her sister's child. Liliane had turned a fourth bedroom into a chapel to honor the deal made with God. The room contained an altar, a Bible, and several cushions to protect the family's knees while they performed their nightly prayers of thanks.

As it turned out, the soldier who had squatted in her house moved nearby, and Liliane's children would sometimes play with his. "There is no reason to hold anger against another person," she told me. "Too many of us have died over small conflicts. It is time to heal. I have my home now and I am grateful. Why should I bear a grudge?"

As she told me her story, she emphasized that refugee camps equalized everyone because of the terrible conditions in which they all lived. "There is so much to do in this country," she said. "So much healing, so much rebuilding."

In their own ways, women like Honorata and Liliane demonstrate daily an endurance and a capacity to dream that could change the shape of the world if only the world would open its arms to them.

CHAPTER 11

THE COST OF SILENCE

"In the end, we will remember not the words of our enemies,
but the silence of our friends."

—MARTIN LUTHER KING, JR.

If Honorata's story is one of rebirth, then Agnes's is one of a soul's weakening, a dive into darkness. Agnes was groomed to be a leader from the time she was a young university student studying law. For most of her life, she worked on issues of social justice, first as a judge and then as one of the first women on the African continent to serve in her country's parliament. Just months prior to the genocide, she was working to form a political party with moderate views, one that would have been inclusive of all ethnic groups. But somehow, she ended her career as a high-profile prisoner charged with crimes of genocide.

I wanted to understand her story. I had known her and worked with her on issues of social justice. She had been a woman of enormous potential, a pioneer in the women's movement, a role model for African women. Though I'd questioned her integrity while she was at Duterimbere, it was inexplicable to me that Agnes could end up a *leader* of such a cruel and murderous regime. If she could become part of a killing machine, then the capacity for evil was more common than uncommon. I'd read Hannah Arendt's *Eichmann in Jerusalem: A Report on the Banality of Evil*, but I'd never imagined I might actually know someone who could help lead a systematic effort to destroy an entire ethnic group.

I visited Agnes twice after the genocide, both times in Kigali's massive Central Prison. Built in 1930 by Belgian colonialists, the prison is a red brick fortress with a green metal door located at the edge of the city, about 100 yards away from the main road, at the top of a hillside.

With its red, red brick, it resembles an old factory from the Industrial Revolution.

If you walk far enough down the road in front of the prison, you can see green fields sloping downward to a verdant valley, rolling gently, then soaring upward into soft hills and a glorious sweep of sky, suggesting a sense of freedom and possibility. Originally built for 2,000 inmates, the Central Prison held more than four times its capacity 5 years after the genocide: 7,800 men and 600 women. There were few toilets, and the prisoners were fed only one soupy meal a day. I was told the men took turns sleeping, as there was insufficient room for everyone to lie down at once. Both men and women had been sleeping this way for up to 5 years at that time.

I arrived at the prison on a Friday—visiting day. Thousands of people, mostly women and children, had come from throughout the city and neighboring areas, some walking 5 or 6 hours, carrying baskets of food for their loved ones in the prison. The visitors were required to wait in the yard outside until they were permitted to see the prisoners, who depended on this food for their survival. The enormous toll all the preparation and travel took on the visitors was evident in their tired, weathered faces. The women wore colorful dresses and often carried babies on their backs, but waited motionlessly, staring with vacant eyes. Some sat quietly on the cracked dirt and nursed their children. Others murmured quietly among themselves.

This mass of women separated from the men inside represented one of the most severe social dislocations in the country. Every Friday more than 150,000 women and children brought food to approximately 120,000 prisoners in various Rwandan prisons. The women whose husbands served years in those prisons were like widows themselves in many ways, struggling to raise a family with no one to help them generate income or cultivate the fields. This loss of productivity in a country already devastated by war was staggering.

On the day of my visit, all of us waiting were kept at a distance of about 100 feet from the empty prison yard by a makeshift barrier, a thick rope tied to two poles. Three guards dressed in blue escorted two pink-clad male prisoners, one wearing green high-top sneakers and a red beret; the other, in yellow flip-flops, carrying three shiny new machetes wrapped in plastic. The five men laughed like old friends.

One of the guards approached me and took me to the director's office, then led me farther, to a small room with a single window covered by a pink curtain. I stood there alone, waiting and looking across the yard at a huge green door, wondering what lay on the other side.

Ten minutes later, Agnes emerged.

Though her head was shaved, she looked like a young girl, not the powerful former minister of justice of the genocide regime. She'd been an inmate for 3 years, 2 of them in confinement, and was wearing the standard prison uniform—a clean pink cotton short-sleeved dress with buttons down the front. I watched her walk toward me, swinging her arms and moving her head from side to side, seeming more little girl than woman. Freckled cheeks and soft brown eyes made her appear even more childlike, less capable of cruelty.

Of all the women at Duterimbere, I had known Agnes least of all and never fully trusted her. This day was no different.

"Jacqueline!" she exclaimed when she saw me, "I was just thinking of you!"

She held my shoulders and planted an exaggerated kiss on each cheek. "I didn't know you were coming," she said as if we were longtime neighbors reunited by a chance meeting. "Thank you for visiting me. You've been on my mind!"

I couldn't imagine how it would be me she was thinking about, and my own discomfort made my stomach turn. Though she still had not been tried by a jury of her peers, she'd been sworn in as minister of justice at the beginning of the genocide when the Hutu Power government had just begun forming. It was said by many that Agnes had made vitriolic and incendiary speeches, urging men to kill Tutsis and inciting women to encourage their husbands to work harder in their murderous and barbaric acts.

I feared her. I feared even coming too close to her essence. I worried that some of it might rub off on me. I had read that she had shouted out to a mob at one rally, urging, "When you begin extermination, no one, nothing, must be forgiven. But here, you have merely contented yourselves with killing a few old women." Was this the same person who just 5 years earlier had urged women to go forward with enthusiasm and build a better Rwanda together?

Many individuals believe that if women ruled the world, we'd finally have a chance at peace. While that may be true, Agnes stood as a reminder that power corrupts on an equal-opportunity basis. Agnes loved the trappings of power, and when all was said and done, she'd traded integrity and whatever good she'd built for glitter and gold.

Despite all I'd read about her involvement, I also knew that together we had worked to create an institution. My motives for visiting Agnes were mixed. I wanted, at least, to offer her kindness, though I was unsure what that really meant. I wanted to understand her, even if I had no desire to befriend her.

While I was still running the Next Generation Leadership program at the Rockefeller Foundation, I once convinced a South African freedom fighter that we should visit one of the generals who had overseen the country's security forces. The general was promoting the concept of a separate state for Afrikaners in South Africa. Though initially unwilling, the freedom fighter finally agreed to meet the general, but with the caveat that we could cut the meeting short if he became too uncomfortable. The meeting ultimately lasted nearly 2 hours, during which the two men found they shared a love of poetry. Afterward, the freedom fighter and I discussed the general's warmth and lack of self-doubt.

"He was only himself and didn't pretend to be anyone else," my friend mused. "Not like some of the white liberals I know who always say what they believe to be politically correct. At least I know who I'm dealing with here."

Though I no longer knew who I was dealing with when it came to Agnes, perhaps I could learn something from her.

We filled the first awkward minutes of the visit with small talk. How is your family? Did you ever marry? Always the first questions I was asked.

After much reflection, I had brought her a small box of chocolates. She tasted a morsel and beamed, looking like a blissful little girl again. I wondered what hell lived inside her head, what tortures she had created for herself. Externally, I saw nothing.

As she spoke, Agnes fingered the beads of a wooden rosary. I shared with her how much I'd loved the rosary when I was a little girl, though I hadn't held one for many, many years. Agnes had been trained by nuns whose belief in her had played a great role in her academic and career success. She had been one of the first girls in her school to attend university and had been one of Rwanda's first female judges and parliamentarians.

"Having someone believe in you makes all the difference," she told me.

I turned the conversation to Agnes's life in prison and to the general situation in Rwanda, and she plunged into a 20-minute rant. Her youthful face disappeared, transforming itself into a twisted mask of anger. She spoke through lips pressed tightly together, showing neat rows of perfect teeth, with eyes opened so wide you could see the whites surrounding her irises. I said little as she seethed about false accusations and the tragedy of the war, all the while rubbing the beads of her rosary.

According to Agnes, the RPF, the Tutsi-led army that had defeated the *genocidaires,* were to blame for having assassinated the president. On April 6, 1994, someone had shot down a plane carrying both the president of Rwanda and the president of Burundi, killing them instantly and igniting the genocide. No one discovered who actually did it.

"The RPF did atrocious things," she told me, "but the world sees this as only one-sided." She sucked in her breath. "Jacqueline, you will never understand what really happened because you are from the West. In Rwanda, we know each other. We know how things work. Both sides were killing. If you counted, you would find many more Hutus dead than Tutsis. I know people who were killed by the RPF all over the country in the first few weeks of April. Now it is convenient that the world has vilified the Hutus, so the Tutsis take no blame."

She likened the Tutsis to Jews—hungry for power. "The Jews lost millions and hold out those losses to the world, so they always have power. It will be the same with the other side here. The Tutsis have so much power now, and the world will be behind them for a long time. It could have been in their interest to see so many killed. That is why we need to discover who assassinated the president to determine on whom to lay the blame for this terrible war. You know, those who thirst for power will do incredible things."

I asked her what she remembered most about the work we'd done together.

"Personally, the thing that impressed me the most was the women, who learned they could do something more than they were used to doing. Before, the women would go to the fields, then wait all day to see what their husbands would bring home. When they learned that they, too, could work to bring home even more income than their husbands, they were eager to try. That interested me.

"They came to Duterimbere in big numbers," she recalled.

She reminded me of how hard we'd worked together. "Personally," she began again, "I had to combine the work with political responsibilities. We went to meetings that ended at 10:00 p.m. But we didn't complain. We didn't expect a salary from anyone or even reimbursements for expenses."

It was true that Agnes had worked as hard as any of the women toward building Duterimbere, though I didn't remind her that we essentially had asked her to leave because of her petty corruption.

She continued: "Duterimbere was founded by women who had been lucky to attend school, who had degrees, who had jobs, who wanted to do something for their sisters who hadn't been as lucky. We wanted to help women who weren't able to go to school. The country was getting poorer and poorer. There were more and more female heads of household who had to care for their families. Something had to be done to help them help themselves. In the beginning, that was our strength."

Without warning, a deafening cacophony interrupted her words. The women waiting outside to see their family members were finally allowed into the prison. First, at least 300 prisoners, all clad in pink, emerged in the yard, seating themselves on bright green benches, squeezed tightly one next to another, each holding a dark green plastic bag. A shrill whistle from the guard catalyzed the still-life market outside into wild action: 300 women and scores of children galumphed across the yard, their bags and buckets causing them to sway to and fro until they plunked down on the benches in front of the men. For 3 minutes, maybe 4, they threw fragments of information back and forth as loudly as possible. They were not allowed to touch each other. The din was unbelievable.

"Hello. . . . Are you well? . . . Is there news? . . . This child is sick. . . . That daughter just married. . . . Our mother died. . . . "

Almost as soon as all of the women had taken their seats, the guard rapped his baton on a bench and blew his whistle again. As quickly as they had appeared, the women moved away again swiftly and surely, as if these meetings had become as routine as brushing their teeth.

The prisoners shuffled back through the big metal door, each carrying a green plastic bag filled with the week's provisions. Minutes later, the whole process repeated itself. Three hundred men and 300 women poured a week's provisions from baskets into green plastic bags. Three hundred stories were shouted helplessly over a desperate babble. And at the bang of a wooden stick, both women and men retreated like a regiment of ragtag soldiers. By the end of the day, about 4,000 people would have been in that yard, leaving the confetti of incomplete stories in the air.

Agnes and I resorted to talking in the spaces between the mad shuffles.

As I listened to her speak, it occurred to me that Agnes might have taken a completely different road in the genocide, one that might have left her a hero instead of a perpetrator. For years, she worked closely with Annie Mugwaneza, the Belgian member of our group. Agnes and Annie were part of the founding group that created the Liberal Party in the early 1990s, a broad-based, moderate organization focused on a united Rwanda.

At the time, the West was pushing Rwanda toward multiparty elections. But you can't impose democracy without first establishing some foundation of civic education and understanding of what it means to be an active *citizen*—a lesson the world is still learning. Most leaders took the opportunity to form parties based not on democratic principles, but on an agenda of gaining power. In Rwanda, an enforced and empty democracy was another lit match in the powder keg.

In the beginning, Agnes and Annie tried to form a party based on principles of diversity and moderation. At one point the party apparently considered allying itself with the Tutsi-led RPF. But when a far-right wing eventually split off, Agnes left with it to join the extremist Hutu Power party. I'll never understand fully how or exactly when she made that decision and can only believe she followed power itself instead of risking her life for principles.

Annie Mugwaneza was one of the most vocal of the individuals calling for a diverse but united Rwanda and had to be silenced if the extremists were to be victorious. On April 6, the first evening of the genocide, the Interahamwe murdered Annie, her husband, and four of their five children. Hundreds of Hutu moderates and Tutsi intellectuals also died that night. There are none more dangerous to extremists than moderates.

Agnes ignored my question when I asked about her friend's death. She seemed to have lost herself in a swirl of words that had little connection to my questions.

"Let's take the United States, for example," she said. "Neither blacks nor Hispanics are the majority. If one day they seized power, if they started oppressing the rest of the population, you understand, that would be a problem. I don't know if you can imagine the blacks one day fighting and seizing the power. I don't think you could accept that."

"You're assuming those in power necessarily oppress the rest," I said.

She just looked at me blankly. Her fear and paranoia summed up the insecurity of a small elite trying fanatically to hold on to power in a society based on a strictly Hobbesian worldview. Power ruled in a zero-sum game.

In one sentence, Agnes laid out her view of Rwanda: "Those who had the power, who didn't want to let it go, had to use any means necessary not to lose it; and those who wanted it also had to use any means to get it."

As I listened, I realized there was only so much I could learn from her. She seemed to have paid the greatest price for her choices, sacrificing her very principles to become a force for evil. I'd been running a leadership program in the United States that focused on strengthening one's moral compass and building those things inside you that no one could ever take away. While I was visiting in Rwanda, nearly all the many women with whom I spoke who'd worked with Agnes remembered her as kind, intelligent, and warm. They were devastated that so much had gone wrong, that she had lost her way.

"She was among the strong women who energized the others to work and make better lives for themselves," one of her former friends told me. "She never should have entered into politics, for it is there that you become prey to power."

"I cannot think that she even knew what was being planned," said another. "When you are in politics, you become part of a machine."

I would listen to the women with a sense of wonder that they could believe Agnes hadn't known what was being planned despite the fact that she held one of the government's highest positions. At the time, if the minister of justice hadn't known what was happening, I would ask, who would have? Usually, they would just shake their heads.

When the guard returned to lead Agnes away, she gave me another hug. I thought of how she had traveled with the president to Butare to unleash the killings that would take Honorata's family from her. I thought of the good we all did together for a brief moment, fighting for women's economic justice. I played the same words over and over in my head: How had she gone so far astray?

I watched her walk away in her pink dress and shaved head, looking so vulnerable, still rubbing her beads, turning every so often to wave to me. I stood there, choked by suffocating sadness. A part of me wanted to push away what I'd just heard, to flee entirely from a situation that would forever seem incomprehensible. But Agnes had helped me internalize what I hadn't wanted to see before—monsters do exist, but not in the way I'd imagined them. I grew up believing in Frank Capra's world, where everyone was good except the bad guys who wore black hats and either died or found redemption by the end of the movie.

I *hadn't* imagined a bald woman with long eyelashes and soft eyes in a pink uniform, with whom I had built an institution of social justice.

Agnes is currently being tried in Rwanda, though she has been in prison for more than a dozen years. Such a slow road to justice must distort even further the woman Agnes was, while such a delay of justice for some of the genocide's top officials must chip away at and ultimately gash the souls of ordinary Rwandans.

The West wants easy answers for modern atrocities that revolve around ancient tribal hatreds, international aid gone astray, or political corruption. The real world does not oblige. Clearly, perpetrators must be held accountable for their actions, and justice must be done for victims—for everyone in the country—to heal. At the same time, our world's challenge is not simply in determining how we punish, but instead in how we prevent the kinds of atrocities that can come only from a deep-seated fear of the Other in our midst. Such fear is fueled in a world where the rich feel above the system and the poor feel entirely left out.

I determined to work on gaining more courage to put myself in others' shoes and more vision to enable me to create ways for them to help themselves. I wanted to become part of a movement to extend to *all* of humanity the notion that all human beings are created equal—for our world was shrinking even then. Somewhere along the way, Agnes must have put aside that notion of our shared humanity, possibly from a combination of real fear and the equally real desire for power. We'll never fully know.

IF RECONCILING WHAT HAD become of Agnes was impossible for me, I found myself confused and humbled by Prudence's story.

She had been imprisoned near her hometown of Byumba in the northern part of the country. Like Agnes, she'd been accused of category 1 crimes, meaning that she was allegedly a major perpetrator of the genocide. But the most complex aspect of her story was that Prudence was potentially neither victim nor perpetrator. Catholics speak of sins of *commission* and sins of *omission*. I assumed Prudence must have known what was happening, though many with much greater power to do something about it had also known, including UN officials.

My hired driver, Leonard, and I departed early one morning for the 2-hour drive from Kigali to Byumba. Jeeps filled with soldiers and trucks overflowing with Ugandan bananas drove straight toward us, swerving at the last possible moment to spare our lives. Boys on bicycles carrying enormous bundles of tall grasses extending 3 feet on either side of their skinny bodies careened down both sides of the narrow road. Goats chased by barefoot boys with sticks trotted past regal women draped in bright colors who were holding massive loads of firewood on their heads. A gray mist mixed with the yellow sunshine, lending brilliance to a teeming, beautiful morning in this land of a thousand hills.

Leonard drove his battered Nissan with a dour, depressed, and unchanging mien. He, too, had lost his family. Suddenly, just outside Byumba, our old Nissan broke down, and for all his efforts, Leonard couldn't restart the car.

He stepped out, walked to the front, and, like a surgeon, plunged his aging hands into the car's belly. Out of nowhere—always the case in Rwanda, where you can be in an entirely empty place and a minute later, surrounded by a crowd—two children approached the car and pressed their faces against my window. Both had closely shaved heads. The girl's round, black eyes were framed by thick lashes. The boy wore an old T-shirt with the neck stretched out of shape. I opened the car door and took in the length of their thin bodies. Her dress hung beneath her knees, and his shorts were rolled at the waist in an effort to keep them up. Both were barefoot.

They didn't say a word. As they stared, I held their gazes.

"Hello," I said.

Shyly, the little girl repeated my greeting. I wondered whether they were among the 400,000 orphans in the country.

"My name is Jacqueline," I said.

Their silence was more heartbreaking than any begging would have been.

I gave them each 300 francs—just a dollar. They took the money and ran, disappearing into the trees on the hillside. I remembered how the boy in my blue sweater had fled so many years ago.

We are connected, but the weave is sometimes fragile.

There wasn't a gas station until Byumba, another 10 miles away. As Leonard worked silently on the car, I moved to stand in the middle of the empty road, confused and a bit frightened by the sudden lack of traffic. Marauding gangs still had too much control in the north and west especially. With relief, I remembered the walkie-talkie UNICEF had issued me in case of an emergency, but the battery was dead.

Looking at the long road ribboning its way through the hills, suddenly I felt very small. As I stood with the defunct walkie-talkie in my hand, I said a prayer and waited.

Twenty, maybe 30 minutes later, a white jeep joggled by. I ran after the vehicle, waving my arms wildly. The passengers—both aid workers—agreed to drive me to Byumba and offered to help me get to the prison. From the jeep, I noticed a massive hill to my right that was covered with thousands of tents made of the ubiquitous UN blue plastic, lined up row after row. It looked like a canvas pasted with blue postage stamps from top to bottom. Twenty thousand Hutus were living there, still too frightened to go home. They suffered from insufficient water, disastrous levels of disease, inadequate food, a lack of latrines, and the stench of death. The RPF had killed thousands in this area, war crimes still a part of the country's wounds; you could feel the weariness in the air.

It was past noon when I reached Byumba's central prison, an old edifice with a capacity of 100 people now holding more than 1,000. We drove through the gate into a sweaty swarm of men. The compound, enclosed by a high fence, was wide open, with several brick buildings in the middle. All around me, men dressed in pink Bermuda shorts were fixing engines, shaping metal into useful objects, talking among themselves. One group was engaged in a boisterous competition to see who could do the most push-ups. In the bright sun under a cobalt sky, these boys swinging on bars and showing off to one another looked more postcard than prisoner.

For a split second I forgot where I was—until two men walked past me and stared with searing intensity, sending a chill down my spine. Alone, unguarded, and unarmed inside a prison overflowing with men accused of mass murder, I wanted to flee.

I moved quickly to the director's office. Alongside a wall, a row of barefoot women dressed in skirts the color of cotton candy sat doing needlework. They reminded me of cutout dolls all made of a single sheet of paper. They had the faces of grandmothers and next-door neighbors, of nurses and sisters.

It had been a decade since I'd seen Prudence, who, along with Agnes, had been one of Rwanda's first woman parliamentarians, but more important, had been a mentor to me. On my last day in Rwanda, we'd hugged so fiercely that it hurt. She had written my recommendation for business school; I hadn't yet found out if I'd been accepted, but she sent me off with all great wishes and confidence that I would make the cut. When I did let her know of my acceptance, she wrote me a wonderful congratulatory note that arrived on featherweight pale blue airmail paper and was filled with praise and caring.

Would she remember me, I wondered as I stood in my white T-shirt and khakis, looking like a Gap ad, waiting among hundreds of men for an old friend now on death row for crimes I could not imagine. She'd been accused of being a planner, just as Agnes had been, though many believed she hadn't played an active role. In an upside-down world, it was hard to ever know.

Prudence walked across the compound with a bright silk scarf of scarlet, lime, and turquoise draped over her shaved head. She seemed more petite than I remembered and yet oddly attractive. Even in prison garb, she stood apart.

With her head cocked to the side and her hand held to shade her eyes, she squinted in my direction as she walked. Recognition: She ran to embrace me, and I held her tightly, trying to conceal my nervousness.

"I can't believe you came all the way to see me," she said. "And here I am in prison. It has been so long, and I've thought of you so often and yet barely recognized you."

Sitting in the director's bare, dark office on two wooden chairs with our knees touching, I was again torn between my desire to know what had happened to Prudence and an impulse to disassociate myself—a mix of shame and revulsion. I held Prudence's hands, and she started weeping. We looked at each other, partly to assess, partly to remember.

She'd been in prison for nearly 2 years—arrested without charges. She described the conditions of the environment, explaining how the women slept on the concrete floor one after another, like cards. There were only two toilets for 80 or 90 women.

"You really must have a supernatural energy to survive here," she said. "We're all in such close contact with each other, touching even as we sleep. Right now, for example, everyone has the flu. I've not gotten it, I think because I won't allow myself to get sick. One survives thanks to one's own energy and thanks to God."

Prudence had held a high-ranking position in government before the genocide as head of the General Assembly—the equivalent of Speaker of the House in the United States. She explained to me that, unlike Agnes, her power was nonetheless limited after the Arusha Accord in August 1993. The Arusha Accord was a peace agreement built on a power-sharing negotiation between the Rwandan government and the RPF. A transitional government was put in place until general elections could be held, though, of course, they never were.

While I imagined that Prudence must have known something, my understanding was paltry at best. I wondered why she hadn't blown whistles, but could barely conceive of the stakes for anyone close to power. If she *had* known, she must have understood she would be among the first killed if she protested the policies.

Where is the line between knowing and participating? Prudence didn't believe she was guilty. Indeed, she told me she had returned from living for 2 years in the refugee camps along with everyone else to make her way home, assuming that everyone understood her innocence. Agnes, on the other hand, had fled along with other government officials to Zambia, where she'd been abducted by the Rwandan government. Prudence had just made it home to Byumba in November 1996 when she was arrested on the street and imprisoned. She was put in solitary confinement, though not charged. Soon after, she was transferred to this local prison.

I remembered her as kind. She was kind. She told me about the Tutsi housegirl she had hidden during the chaos. Yet here she was, accused— if not charged—with crimes of genocide.

The ambiguity felt toxic, infecting me with a sense of vertigo. "How did you get here?" I asked, barely audibly.

She shook her head, telling me she didn't know. "I walked back with the rest of the refugees because I was innocent and returning to my home. I never thought they would arrest me," she repeated for the second time.

"Rwanda was caught up in a great wind," Prudence said. "And now the country itself is the biggest loser." She went on to talk about the humiliation experienced by women like her who were innocent, but were now spending their lives in prison. I just listened. Even if she were only partly right, the humiliation of people accused of false crimes and sent to horrific prisons for years would deepen fissures of mistrust.

Later, a friend told me haltingly through tears about how she'd felt upon seeing Prudence return from the refugee camps, where my friend had also spent 2 years. "I couldn't look at her. Her hair was loose, and she carried everything on her head, like we all did. Prudence was never common—she was always extraordinary. It broke my heart in two to see her looking like a beggar woman. I suppose we all did, but it seemed so much worse to see it in someone who had commanded so much respect."

At the time of my visit, women already were beginning to play major roles in the reconstruction of Rwanda. They were starting businesses and building homes and representing as members of parliament in numbers that had never been seen before—in Rwanda or anywhere else on the continent. The sad truth is that the first three woman parliamentarians in the country, who had made such extraordinary strides for women, ended up with tragic histories.

Between 1991 and 1994, RPF soldiers reportedly killed two of Prudence's brothers in the north. We discussed the history of the unstable northern region of this tiny country. Many Tutsis had lived in exile for a generation and wanted to return. The RPF's movements and stories of war crimes generated deep-seated fears among Hutus in Rwanda. Politicians preyed upon this, turning fear into hatred, and ordinary people into killers. "It was a terrible time," she said.

When I pressed her on her involvement, she pushed back, restating that she was innocent. Prudence accused me of interrogating her along military lines, and she was right. I wanted to understand, and I *was* being aggressive. I felt trapped in a story of fear, identity, politics, and self-preservation and could see why what must never happen again so easily could unless we recognized our shared humanity and conquered fear itself.

Now there was distance between us. Who was I to step into her life after a decade-long absence, to show up at the prison and begin firing off questions? I understood why she didn't trust me. But what I sought in talking with Agnes and Prudence had little to do with trust; rather, in truth, I think I was searching for clarity from them to keep my own worldview in some sort of order.

As I said good-bye to Prudence, she thanked me for visiting her, saying that none of her friends had come.

"They're probably afraid," I said, and she gave me a wan smile.

On the drive back to Kigali, I felt so nauseated I had to ask the driver to pull over so I could be sick. Why had I thought I might find any clear answers in these prison cells? Maybe the gift those women had given me had more to do with accepting the *disorder* at the crucible of human existence.

A YEAR LATER, PRUDENCE was freed, declared innocent, though she never made an appearance in court. This time, I visited her at home, where she welcomed me with grand salutations and a long, warm embrace before walking me from her blue metal gate past the manicured garden filled with fruit trees and flowering bushes. On that day, this former high-ranking government official looked like a woman you might bump into at the supermarket, in black pants and a loose-fitting striped top. Her hair was styled with hundreds of tiny extension braids that nearly reached her shoulders.

We drank tea, exchanged pleasantries. When I asked her how she'd ended up being released, she responded softly, "There were never any charges against me."

She told me that after 2 years in prison, reclaiming a life was harder than she'd expected. She had grown accustomed to the coarse prison food and had problems sleeping in a bed after so many nights spent lying on the floor, pressed against women on either side.

"I had become nearly paralyzed from sitting all day and night in prison without moving much. I had terrible swelling in both legs. All night long I woke up, wondering where I was, forgetting that I was not on the ground."

But now she was a free woman—at least legally so, released without charges. Her eyes still had that familiar twinkle.

"And you know," she said, "if you pray hard enough and believe with your entire heart, miracles do happen."

THE NEXT YEARS WOULD not be easy for Prudence, but in time she would again become a contributor, due to her own resilience and the acceptance of a country still undergoing a remarkable healing process.

If Prudence had been just a bystander and that was her crime, then what about the rest of us who just stood by? The international community could have stopped the genocide if it had intervened. As our world becomes increasingly interconnected, we need to find better solutions that will include everyone in today's opportunities. Monsters will always exist. There's one inside each of us. But an angel lives there, too. There is no more important agenda than figuring out how to slay one and nurture the other.

CHAPTER 12

INSTITUTIONS MATTER

"God helps those who persevere."

—THE KORAN

When looking at what happened in the Rwandan genocide, we can conclude despairingly that the nature of humanity is evil—or we can focus on the things that endured: the extraordinary power of the human spirit, the exquisite dignity of some individuals on even the darkest days, and the number of people who helped one another during and after the tragedies in Rwanda simply because it was the right thing to do. It is from a place of hope, of the possibility of rebirth, of retribution, and even of optimism that Rwanda now has a real chance to become one of the developing world's success stories.

I have been touched deeply by what happened in Rwanda not only because it revealed our potential for untold cruelty, but also because it will forever remind me that in any good society, nothing justifies the powerful excluding the powerless from basic opportunities. And if the genocide reminded me of our fragility as human beings, it also reinvigorated my belief that providing incentives for people to do the right thing matters a great deal. Institutions are key in reminding us who we are meant to be and how we are expected to behave as community members and citizens.

We founded the microfinance bank Duterimbere on the assumption that women could not be excluded from the economy if Rwanda were to develop. The Rwandan founders dreamed that women could improve their conditions themselves if only they were given access to loans, markets, and some degree of business training. Though we made a lot of mistakes in the beginning, we created an institution that, for all its flaws, outlasted its founding group and has a life of its own, being run by and for Rwandan women and taking risks traditional enterprises would not consider. In retrospect, there is much I would have done differently, but seeing the Bank making an impact in so many lives 20 years later remains a deeply fulfilling experience.

Imagine Kigali in 1994, a few months after the genocide: Houses everywhere had been looted and many were burned to the ground. Computers and phone lines had been ripped out of nearly every school and building, and the public infrastructure had been entirely destroyed. Stunned survivors walked through streets in a state of collective shock and inconsolable grief while more than a million of their countrymen, nearly all Hutus, lived along with Liliane and her family in the refugee camps in Zaire.

To add to the overwhelming confusion, Tutsis who had lived in exile, some for more than 30 years as a result of earlier pogroms, returned to Rwanda. Those who had lived most of their lives in Uganda, including the new President Kagame and most of the soldiers of the Rwandan Patriotic Front, spoke English in addition to Kinyarwanda, not French, Rwanda's national language since colonial days. An entire nation needed to reinvent, rebuild, and reclaim itself.

A group of determined members of Duterimbere came together to be part of the country's rebirth, though the building housing its offices had been ransacked and the furniture and equipment had been destroyed. Most account records had disappeared, and loan documents were scattered in the streets and in nearby houses. Step-by-step, women borrowers began retrieving far-flung documents and slowly rebuilding the institution.

By 2007, I had a chance to see for myself what had become of their efforts. By then, Rwanda had again become a favorite cause of philanthropists and international aid specialists. I found myself in awkward conversations with wealthy individuals who spoke enthusiastically about the country: "An economic miracle," they called it, citing its 6 percent rate of economic growth, arguably a near-impossibility for a country still in a postconflict situation. They said it was "the perfect investment opportunity," a "democratic" nation with a population that "had moved on from the genocide."

Indeed, the country had seen extraordinary growth while maintaining peace, and has also demonstrated a commitment to women that stands as a model for the world. Rwanda proportionally has more women in parliament today than any other nation—something we only dreamed would happen when Prudence, Constance, and Agnes were the first. Moreover, women represent more than 40 percent of the country's entrepreneurs. President Kagame has also done a remarkable job of communicating that all of his country's citizens are Rwandans and should not define themselves by their ethnic identity. There is so much to be hopeful about—and proud.

At the same time, I bristled whenever I heard talk of Rwandans being "over the pain of genocide." I wanted to ask these philanthropists—and sometimes did—if they would be able to "move on" within a decade if they had to live next door to someone who had murdered their children in cold blood. I also wished for more humility and more answers about whether there was real equity in who was benefitting from growth.

Over 20 years, I'd changed. At one time I sounded just like those wealthy philanthropists, looking for ways to make a difference with an uncritical eye, certain of my ideas, not questioning whether there were countervailing forces that had to be reckoned with in order to achieve long-term success. The genocide had exposed the dangers of a country overly reliant on aid, illuminated the perils of government power concentrated in too few hands and dependent on systems lacking accountability, and shown the fault lines of idealism without tough pragmatism. I was returning more humble and ready to listen at a deeper level.

After arriving on an evening flight, I was instantly confronted by Kigali's distinctive scent, the sweet, burnt smell of roasted cassava, which made me both apprehensive and somewhat rueful, calling up in one aroma complex emotions about being back in a country so riven with contradictions.

Outside customs, my old friend Liliane stood waiting in the crowd, looking very formal in a cream-colored suit and matching pumps, her hair coiffed in elaborate plaits, her smile clear and brilliant. She enveloped me in a powerful hug, showing real emotion without a trace of restraint. Standing beside her was her husband, Julien; their 18-year-old son, Augustin; and Valerie, the surviving twin, now an awkward, beautiful teenage girl. Suddenly, I was back, feeling fully alive, ready to see and absorb whatever I could, happier just being in the presence of Liliane's unbridled spirit than I'd imagined I could be.

"We are your welcoming committee," she laughed.

That night we dined on shish kebabs and grilled plantains with chili sauce, like the old days. Liliane described with great animation the changes I would see the next day: high-rise buildings, upscale restaurants, even a posh cappuccino shop. I laughed, remembering my reliance on instant coffee and fat-fortified powdered milk 20 years earlier. At the next table, a group of men were involved in a heated discussion. I was intrigued by the way their voices would rise and then suddenly go quiet, a reminder that people still did not feel it was safe to talk politics in a public place. Later, I fell asleep feeling tenderness for the people and city of Kigali and also a sense that fear and mistrust were understandably embedded in the nation's fabric.

The next morning's light illuminated a frenzy of construction, not only in Kigali's business district but also in new suburbs, where giant houses were springing up for government ministers and a few highly successful entrepreneurs. Hundreds of boys wearing lime green jackets and helmets drove motorbikes that served as taxis, shuttling people back and forth across town for 50¢ a ride. Another league of young men in yellow shirts was selling cell phone cards, connecting people in this once faraway place to the rest of the world. Kigali was on the move, making strides well ahead of other countries in the region in spite of, or maybe partially as a result of, its national crisis. The change was exhilarating.

Still, I was struck by a startling feeling of sameness in the physical aspects of Kigali and found comfort in knowing most of the buildings, stores, banks, and roundabouts along the roads. The hilly streets were still graced with eucalyptus and bougainvillea and walls enclosing neat brick houses. Soldiers on some street corners and a barricade blocking the road housing the president's compound were further reminders that not everything had changed.

At a café where I sat for lunch, I met a Westerner who'd been in the country for decades. I asked him why he'd stayed so long and then remarked on the incredible progress I'd been witnessing. "Sure, things are getting done," the man with weary eyes and salt-and-pepper hair responded. "Rwandans are among the best at that. But there is a growing sense here that only one side is getting most of the benefits of development. The others resent that they've been left out of the system. It looks worse to them because some people here are getting very, very rich. Have you seen the houses being constructed? Mansions, some of them, almost all owned by government officials."

I reminded him that he hadn't answered my question about why he stayed.

"After all this time," he sighed, "this is my home, and I will never leave it.

"Why did you come back?" he asked me.

"Visiting friends" was all I said and then excused myself. I wanted to see what had happened to the women of Duterimbere 13 years after the genocide, 20 years after the institution was first created. I'd been in touch only sporadically since my last visit, 6 years prior. During that time my attention had been focused on building Acumen Fund, a new organization formed partially because of those early experiences with Duterimbere. But I also didn't have strong connections to the institution; it had seen several executive directors since my previous visit.

As the car moved toward the bank, I wondered how I would be received after so much time and so little contact. Would I be remembered at all? I told myself it didn't matter, though I hoped not to have been entirely forgotten.

It was thrilling to see a long line of people waiting outside the bank. The building looked clean and white, and I smiled at Duterimbere's familiar logo on the sign above the door. The people waiting were obviously poor, and there was a solid mix of women and men, something I hadn't seen in my day. I guessed the men were there for the for-profit credit union that Duterimbere had started, and smiled to myself at thinking about how organizations change and flourish, influenced by many hands and forces. Before entering to talk to the new executive director, I approached an older woman waiting in line, a red and yellow wrap around her waist.

"What brings you here?" I asked.

"I'm waiting to deposit my pay," she said, and her neighbors nodded. The woman next to her, holding 2,000 francs—about $4—was depositing her savings. More people sat patiently inside as three bank tellers tried to keep up with demand.

The bank's new executive director, Dativa, a tall woman with poker-straight shoulder-length hair in a smart pantsuit, welcomed me with a big hello and proceeded to introduce me to everyone in the office, pointing to the separate sections housing the for-profit credit union and the nonprofit, separate microfinance organization, which, together, served 50,000 clients. She then proudly showed me pictures of Duterimbere's 20th anniversary celebration, which had been attended by the first lady of the country and other dignitaries, including several woman parliamentarians and founding members of the organization.

Grateful for Dativa's generous reception, I congratulated her on how far Duterimbere had come, though I knew it hadn't been a smooth journey. Over the years, there'd been a number of severe financial stresses and staffing challenges.

"Yes," she affirmed, "but we're through that and are looking forward to more successful times."

In the third-floor library, a simple room with wooden, glass-fronted bookcases on the perimeter and chairs for meetings in the middle, Dativa found the training manual I'd written. She explained that recently Duterimbere had updated it to reflect the country's current realities. Eagerly I turned the pages of the earlier version, seeing my younger self in handwritten phrases and overly earnest explanations of business finance, such as the difference between *current liabilities,* debts the women could pay off quickly, and *long-term liabilities.* Unable to imagine that I actually went into this level of detail with our mostly illiterate clients who typically sold vegetables in the marketplace, I apologized to Dativa for all the poor women I'd tortured with my Wall Street credit training. We both laughed as she gave me a high five.

As we giggled at my expense, an affable-looking 50-year-old with straight black hair flecked with gray, wearing a long, traditional cotton dress in black and yellow and green, entered the library. Anne Marie, one of the earliest managers at Duterimbere after the genocide, was in charge of all training and program activities and would be my guide for the day. I liked her energetic style and smile.

I asked Anne Marie if she had grown up in Rwanda. She raised an eyebrow and smiled: "Already, you are placing people. Now I know you know Rwanda," she said, as if I had broken a code.

Sheepishly, I responded that the country still seemed very complicated; I was just trying to make some sense of things.

"Complicated, yes," she said. "No doubt. And it is good you understand it instead of ignoring the cultural context and realities of Rwanda. But there is more hope now, more of a sense that we can do something important. This is our chance. But we have to help one another live together as one people. We are trying."

Born and raised in the Republic of the Congo by Rwandan parents, Anne Marie had been living in Rwanda since a month after the genocide ended. She described coming to the country in 1994: "Kigali was in chaos then, and I was looking for an organization where I would feel proud to work," she told me. "I had experience with cooperatives and believed in women working together. My mother always said 'In union we are strong,' and I thought of her when I first saw Duterimbere's logo with the women marching together toward the bank."

I recalled the days when Dieu Donne had created that logo, working with Ginette and me, how he had laughed and said he agreed with Prudence that the women walked more like me than Rwandan women. I thought of so many struggles to conquer oppression or just survive. In union we are strong—all of us.

Anne Marie continued: "At the end of 1994 when I joined, everything was daunting, overwhelming really, but we pulled together. No one was without great suffering, but there was also no crime, nor were there voices raised in anger, even. We all helped one another. Sadly, since then life has changed."

The group of women members and borrowers who rebuilt Duterimbere went first to UNICEF for support and received a small fund to provide rehabilitation loans to solidarity groups, each formed by four or five women survivors. The group could borrow up to $50 for each woman on a no-interest basis. When all of the women repaid, they could borrow more. Duterimbere's team would "accompany" women borrowers trying to re-create their lives, giving them ideas for businesses, at times holding their hands to help them get through the really bad days.

One of those early borrowers was Charlotte, now the proprietor of an established restaurant in Kigali. Tall and fit with high cheekbones and black hair neatly pulled into a long braid down her back, she carried herself with no-nonsense professionalism in her matching black-and-white top and skirt. Anne Marie introduced me as one of the founders of Duterimbere, and Charlotte greeted me with the characteristic warmth of Rwandans: three strong kisses on the cheeks, each time accompanied by a hug in the direction of the kiss, and then completed with a handshake in a gesture of solidarity. Though she must have been in and out of her restaurant's kitchen all day, I was surprised neither by her freshly scrubbed scent nor by her firm grip, for everything about her seemed well cared for in a no-fuss way. We sat down at one of the white plastic tables on the back terrace to talk over a cup of coffee.

Her story began with 4 liters of milk.

"I had absolutely nothing but the clothes on my back after the genocide," she told me. "I was starving to death, and my daughter and I were eating grass around the abandoned house where we had taken refuge. But a friend in Kigali had heard of my plight and came to me and gave me 4 liters of milk. I handed one glass to my daughter to drink and sold the rest to a nearby cabaret that had been set up in town. I began to see what I had to do."

A year before the genocide, Charlotte had discovered she'd contracted HIV from her husband, and that through pregnancy she'd transmitted the disease to at least three of her four children. They and her husband all died of AIDS in 1993. "I am a fearful woman, not a courageous one," she told me through bursts of tears, "and I could only imagine death for myself then."

She paused to catch her breath and then said, "I am Tutsi and there was so much hatred then. How could I want to live?"

I had no words.

"In fact, when the fighting started," she continued, "I thought it better to die from a bullet than AIDS. I would walk into the streets when I saw the men with guns coming and ask them to kill me. They said they didn't want to waste their bullets on me. They knew I was going to die anyway . . . they didn't want to waste their bullets. . . .

"My daughter was safer because she was Hutu, given my husband's ethnicity, and so she stayed with my in-laws. I should have been a victim. I hid when I saw machetes but not when I saw guns."

With the $3 she earned from those first 4 liters, Charlotte bought more milk, earning enough to buy stock for the next day and to keep herself and her daughter alive. While visiting a friend's husband in Kigali's Central Prison, she met a woman from Duterimbere who told her about the rehabilitation loans. The next day, she formed a solidarity group with four women and took a $50 loan to buy more milk, a few glasses, and a table. Finally she was in business.

She sold milk from a roadside stand. Over time, Charlotte repaid her loan and then borrowed again, repeating the cycle several times over until she found herself able to operate a small café. She graduated from Duterimbere to its for-profit credit union COOPEDU and then to the commercial bank in her effort to buy shares in the cooperatively owned building that housed the restaurant. Duterimbere helped her with business planning and encouragement. She did the rest.

In Charlotte's busy open-air restaurant on the second floor of a building overlooking one of the main industrial market areas at the edge of Kigali, men and women sat at white plastic tables with red umbrellas, talking and laughing, sipping Fantas, drinking beers, and eating samosas. We nodded to the customers, said hello to the young woman behind the cash register, and walked into the kitchen, where a dozen men wearing blue cotton jackets stirred steaming pots of meat and vegetables, fried potatoes, chopped vegetables, and washed dishes.

Charlotte showed us the kitchen with a flourish of her hand and a self-satisfied it's-been-a-long-time-coming expression. The main cook took orders from the waiters through a hatch in the wall, the kind you see in diners the world over. Serving 250 meals a day, Charlotte's restaurant attracted lines of customers that ran down the stairs and into the street. In addition to the successful restaurant, she was running a catering business on the side. A government ministry rented one of the rooms for daily breakfast for 40 of its workers. She rented out chairs for events and owned the majority of the multistoried building housing her restaurant. She keeps growing the place, she said, to give herself "a sense of security."

I pushed her on what security really meant, and she told me she was not a philosopher. "I must spend a lot of time focused on remaining healthy," she said. Though antiretrovirals were free in Rwanda, she said, only Indian generics were *available* under that program, and her body would not absorb them. Her income from the restaurant enabled her to pay for European generics—but doing that entailed keeping her income level fairly high.

To grow her business, she was always seeking loans, but the banks rarely lent to HIV-positive borrowers, according to Charlotte, and they demanded 150 percent collateral. "So I found the collateral, purchased life insurance, and got a letter from my doctor explaining that I had been healthy for a decade." Ultimately, she borrowed more than $30,000 to continue her expansion: Charlotte would not wait for handouts.

Awed by her discipline, ambition, and audaciousness, I teased her for describing herself as a fearful soul. Charlotte smiled a gap-toothed grin. "My friend, I *did* know fear and wanted to die, but I am strong now and have my own business and hope for the future. Still, I have known every kind of prejudice. I was hated because I was Tutsi, hated even more because I was married to a Hutu, hated because I was HIV positive, judged because I was a woman. What does it matter who accepts me? Most of all, I must accept myself.

"I am not a philosopher," she continued. "I have only a simple dream: to get old without ever having to beg and to live without having to see that terrible violence again."

As I sat across the table and peered into her eyes, so full of life, I thought about how my dignity rests on hers and hers on mine. Though I wanted to collapse into a puddle of tears, I was glad I'd come back to this complicated land that had witnessed some of humankind's cruelest acts, but also some of its most courageous, generous, and beautiful.

I was astonished by what she had overcome and wondered how many Charlottes there could be. I knew I would meet Duterimbere's success stories, but what about the bigger impact a single strategy to make small loans available to the very poorest people so they could improve their lives had had? Charlotte was a true entrepreneur made even stronger by the trauma of having survived genocide. But real entrepreneurs account for a small percentage of the population. Most people are uncomfortable taking continual risks and imagining a future others cannot see. Microfinance is one important part of the solution, but it is not the only one.

My questions would have to wait a few days until I'd met more borrowers—and most of these women were successful, too. Alphonsine, stocky in stature and huge in personality, lives outside Gitarama on a farm where she raises European cows, pigs, and chickens and grows sorghum, bananas, tomatoes, and eggplants. After losing her husband, she started raising ducks in 1996 with a small loan, but no one in the marketplace wanted to purchase them. Though she lost money, she repaid the loan anyway and started borrowing to produce other agricultural products. Today, Alphonsine is one of the wealthiest members of the community. She told me she feels so lucky that now she spends a large percentage of her time training and showing other women how to build their businesses.

Asumpta, strong and straightforward with a decidedly urban image, returned from the refugee camps with no home, no goods, and few skills, but with a caring, stable husband by her side. An uncle loaned her money to buy a few pieces of children's clothing, which she turned around and sold for a few francs' profit. Over time, she expanded her business, always with loans and management support from Duterimbere. Today she travels twice a month to Dubai to procure at least some of the products she sells.

Proudly, Asumpta showed me her recently purchased SUV outside her tiny shop. "None of this would have been possible without those loans," she stated.

"Things used to be easier," she told me, "but now people like me who are just making it to the middle class are feeling so many stresses, yet we are the lucky ones. The poor are suffering more than they used to, and they are feeling poorer all the time. My old customers can't afford to buy children's clothes anymore. I'm worried that more must be done to help the people."

I thought back to the day in Veronique's living room when we had shared so many big dreams. Now the women who had dared to open bank accounts without their husbands' signatures for the first time in their lives were *running* the banks and holding major positions in government and business. Women could inherit land from their fathers for the first time. At least part of the change we had only dreamed about had happened.

Still, how could we reach the very poor with greater opportunities? I visited a few borrowers who were still making baskets and selling them to charities at a profit level that would surely keep them living in poverty for the near future. I met with people who bragged about fair-trade coffee projects as if they were the only answer to poverty in Rwanda, and yet history has taught us that change is rarely so straightforward.

Recently I heard a fair-trade promoter say in a speech, "You can change the world by drinking a cup of coffee." Those simple slogans are great for marketing, but should alert people to something false in easy promises. Poverty is too complex to be answered with a one-size-fits-all approach, and if there is any place that illustrates this complexity, as well as a better way forward, it is Rwanda.

Technology is one of the greatest drivers of change. When I moved to Rwanda 20 years ago, the tiny landlocked country had one radio station, no television, and a single newspaper that was printed weekly. People were more provincial because the exchange of ideas had been paltry. Everywhere I went recently, I saw young people with computers and MP3 players talking about international politics and thinking about a different kind of future.

Before coming, I'd e-mailed Liliane to ask her what gift I could bring for her. She begged me not to give her anything, so I asked on behalf of her children. The next day I received an e-mail that "Augustin had inquired about a new musical instrument called an iPod."

Though it took 13 hours to download iTunes, Augustin could now listen to his favorite music, Snoop Dogg and Tupac, though he was just learning to speak English. On the walls of his room were small posters of Nelson Mandela and Gandhi and Martin Luther King Jr. This child who spent his fifth through seventh years in a refugee camp was growing up to be like kids on every continent in the world and to know and share many of their myths and music and ways of communicating.

Liliane and Julien moved to a new house. Julien loved his work with an international NGO as a doctor focused on AIDS. Liliane was about to take a break from her work to focus on family, though she said she would seek consultancies. Because she wasn't as occupied with the office, she had time to cook. She spoiled me with nine different courses of Rwandan food, including fried tilapia and green beans, plantains and rice, meat stew, fried potatoes, and salad.

Together, Liliane and I visited the Genocide Memorial Center in Kigali, along with our young Tutsi taxi driver whose uncle is buried there. We held one another's hands as we moved through the rooms recounting the country's history and displaying photographs of loved ones lost, as well as testimonials from survivors.

Afterward Liliane told me, "I think we will not see another genocide in this country. If we have learned anything, it is the horror that can happen when people don't think for themselves, but instead follow authority blindly. We have to teach our children judgment in our schools and our businesses if we are to thrive truly as a country."

As for Prudence, unable to find a job after the genocide, she had returned to school to earn a law degree. Now she oversees standards at a major coffee producer in Kigali. On my last night in the country, I met her and her husband, Ezekiel. After about 30 minutes of small talk and beers, I asked her what she had learned since I'd last seen her.

"Before everything happened," she said, "my family and I had everything: a big house, two cars, four beautiful children, wealth, status, and even the title of being a parliamentarian. And then we lost everything. I was imprisoned, our things were taken, but most important, two of our children disappeared in the march back from the refugee camps. We never saw them again."

She went on to say that her time in prison was terrible for her, but it also was a time that allowed her to reflect on what was important and to develop a deeper faith inside herself.

"When you have everything," she went on, "you start to think that material things are most important. When you lose them all, at first you think you have lost yourself, as well. But with faith, you begin to see that it is *only* those things that you build inside—those things that no one can take away from you—that matter. Now we try to live from a place of love. And we understand that you can only have great joy if you also know great pain."

Though their children are both studying abroad, Prudence and Ezekiel will stay in Rwanda. "We can't imagine ourselves as refugees in another country," Ezekiel explained. "This is our home and we will stay here and grow with it."

Duterimbere had invited Prudence, one of the organization's founders, to attend its 20th anniversary celebration.

"I couldn't make it," she said, "because I had to work. It was still early days, and I was proving myself at the coffee company. But I have the certificate proudly displayed in my living room. Those were the best days of my life."

A hopeful little organization built to support women's economic activities 20 years ago has made a difference. The founding members of Duterimbere also helped create PROFEMME and the Women's Network and other enterprises that together advanced the women's agenda in a society that had little official place for them for generations. Hundreds of thousands of people have been touched by the loans made by the women's bank, and some of them have gone on to create real businesses that provided income and a sense of greater purpose to the borrowers and their families.

When I first moved to Rwanda, I could barely find it on a map. Today, Africa is on the front page of newspapers and talked about at family dinner tables across the world. Celebrities travel there, and many want to help, as do young people focused on learning and service. We are connected in ways we could never have imagined.

I will forever be grateful to Duterimbere and to Rwanda for teaching me about possibility, about the power of markets, the need for smart and carefully invested financial assistance, and the constant hope for rebirth. I learned that microenterprise is an important part of the solution, but it is not the only part. I also learned that traditional charity alone can't solve the problems of poverty.

Before we made the blue bakery a business, the women were demoralized, dependent, and still desperately poor. Big flows of aid can create as many incentives for corruption and mismanagement as for change. Markets alone won't solve the problems of poverty. Low-income people are invisible to most entrepreneurs, who don't see them as paying customers. Poor distribution, lack of infrastructure, and corruption all add up to a failure of markets to deliver to the poor what they want and need at prices they can afford.

What is needed going forward is a philosophy based on human dignity, which all of us need and crave. We can end poverty if we start by looking at all human beings as part of a single global community that recognizes that everyone deserves a chance to build a life worth living.

CHAPTER 13

THE EDUCATION OF A PATIENT CAPITALIST

"In the course of history, there comes a time when humanity is called to shift to a new level of consciousness, to reach a higher moral ground. A time when we have to shed our fear and give hope to each other. That time is now."

—WANGARI MAATHAI

In the final years of the 20th century, the dot-com boom was in full swing, 20-something-year-old millionaires were being minted on a daily basis, and interest in philanthropy was on the rise. At the end of 1999, I was sitting with the new president of the Rockefeller Foundation, Sir Gordon Conway, in his 22nd-floor office overlooking Manhattan, sharing my frustrations about traditional philanthropy, remarking that it often lacked clear measures and accountability and seemed at times more focused on making donors feel good than on effecting change.

The world needed a new kind of institution, I said, one built on the best lessons and precepts of philanthropy but also utilizing business approaches and concepts. I'd seen the rise of socially oriented companies and felt that deep changes were under way in both business and philanthropy. Leaning back in his chair, he looked at me as I spoke, listening intently, one eyebrow raised in a way that communicated either interest or skepticism, or perhaps a little of each.

I was breathless with excitement, dreaming about a different kind of "fund," one that would amass philanthropic money, have the flexibility to make grants or investments in both nonprofit and for-profit organizations, take a few big bets on enterprises that delivered critical services to the poor, so to ensure low-income communities could actually be part of the solution. We would build more transparency and greater accountability into the work at all levels and treat the poor as customers with a real voice, not as passive recipients of charity.

"How different is it from the work of foundations today?" he asked.

"The biggest difference," I said, "is that we wouldn't simply make grants, but we would invest in entrepreneurs who have vision and the ability to solve local problems with market-driven ideas and approaches. We would hire creative people with the ability to read financial statements and balance sheets, not just budgets. We wouldn't focus on specific 'projects,' but instead direct our efforts toward building strong *organizations* that we would gradually help bring to financial sustainability."

The philanthropic sector was already changing—the very word "philanthropy" felt outdated. The lines between the private and philanthropic sectors were beginning to blur: As more companies integrated a charitable mission into the very way they did their work, more nonprofits would become more businesslike, and more individuals would pursue second careers in giving back. The Rockefeller Foundation had been at the forefront of inventing philanthropy in its early days, and now it had a chance to help *reinvent* it.

Gordon drew in his breath and thought for a minute, and when he suggested I take a few months to explore the possibility of creating such a venture and do it on the Rockefeller Foundation's dime, I nearly fell out of my chair. This was a gift I hadn't imagined. As in the days when UNICEF had housed me and enabled me to help start Duterimbere, so now would the Rockefeller Foundation give me a powerful running start on a new dream, one that I couldn't yet even fully articulate but believed was badly needed.

The solution lay between the market and the traditional philanthropic model. For 20 years, I had been apprenticing, gathering tools while watching extraordinary individuals like Muhammad Yunus of Grameen Bank, Mary Houghton and Ron Grzywinski of ShoreBank, and Bill Drayton of Ashoka, learning to recognize other entrepreneurs and build networks of people who were capable of bringing about change. Now was the moment to stand on their shoulders and move.

I had been working on several concepts with a small group of committed philanthropists, most of whom had been members of the Philanthropy Workshop, the organization I'd founded at the Rockefeller Foundation. Cate Muther, former vice president of marketing for Cisco Systems, had conceived a technology portal to help change and facilitate philanthropy. To pursue the idea, she held regular meetings with

Stuart Davidson, a venture capitalist interested in the role of business in social change; Roberta Katz, former general counsel for Netscape; Tom Reiss of the Kellogg Foundation; and Tae Yoo, who had recently been appointed to lead Cisco's philanthropic work. It was an honor to be a part of this group who gave so much of themselves and were never short of new ideas.

Then an appealing alternative arose. The chief operating officer of a major financial institution approached me about building a philanthropic program for their clients worth at least $100 million. In the era of the dot-com boom, the circle of extremely wealthy people was expanding, and many were looking to do something important with their philanthropy. Here was a chance to help them. Moreover, the salary on the table was seven times what I'd been earning at the Rockefeller Foundation.

I was torn between the freedom to build exactly what I wanted on the one hand and the certainty of access to power and a real level of financial resources on the other. I had no money, no organization, and was facing a world of risk in striking out on my own. Having the backing of a prestigious institution with all the trappings—salary, title, and access—was very appealing. Though I had never made a decision based on income or title before, this was a new level of each.

Though either choice was good, one was truer to myself. Recently, a 71-year-old entrepreneur defined his breed as "the most stubborn and persistent people in the world. Entrepreneurs see possibility, an *idea,* and won't stop, regardless of the obstacles, until they make it happen. They aren't necessarily the smartest people in the world, but they are the ones who have the guts and the heart to do whatever it takes to make dreams come real." Then he added with a knowing smile, "They aren't always the easiest people to work with, either."

Seeing many of these qualities in myself, I knew I was more suited to trying to build something from a place of freedom and innovation. I thought of Aristotle's reminder not to confuse means with ends: If title and money could be conferred on me, they could also be taken away. I also knew that building a program inside a financial institution would mean dealing with a different set of constraints and challenges, especially in bad times (as it turned out, not even a year later, the dot-com bubble burst and the $100 million circle shrank overnight). Ultimately, I reflected on Goethe's invocation to "make a commitment and the forces of the universe will conspire to make it happen" and chose the uncharted path.

I began to think of what we were launching as a venture capital fund for the poor. We would raise charitable funds, then invest equity, loans, and grants—whatever was needed—in organizations led by visionary entrepreneurs who were delivering to low-income communities services such as safe water, health care, housing, and alternative energy sources. In addition, we would provide them with wide-ranging support on everything from basic business planning, to hiring managers, to helping them connect to markets. We would measure the results of our investment not only in the capital flowing back to the fund, but also—and more importantly—in the investment's social impact. Any money returned would then be reinvested into other enterprises that served the poor.

In the beginning, many people thought we were talking about microfinance, but the organization would be very different. We would not make tiny loans to women, but would invest hundreds of thousands or even millions of dollars in enterprises that aspired to reach at least a million customers. My passion was using business models to create effective, sustainable systems where government or charity alone had failed poor people. By investing in private innovation, we hoped to understand how best to make essential services accessible to all and to help lead the way to better models for solving public problems.

Raising the money intimidated me at first. We believed we needed both individual and institutional money because it would signify what the future could look like. Stuart, Cate, and Tae each pledged $500,000 of their personal wealth—acts of enormous generosity and commitment to a totally unproven idea, one they helped build and support with additional financing and significant time over the years. Ultimately, the Rockefeller Foundation committed $5 million and the Cisco Foundation, $2 million. This initial funding put us on the map and provided an early stamp of legitimacy, giving us a running start few organizations have—a huge luxury.

By early 2001, we had a business plan in hand and had raised more than $8 million, but hadn't yet named the organization. One of my favorite lines in literature is from a work by Tillie Olsen: "Better immersion than to live untouched . . . Yet how will you sustain?" I'd considered naming the organization Immersion. After all, doing this kind of work would require using all parts of ourselves—our heads and our hearts. And we would need moral imagination to put ourselves in the shoes of other people. It would mean having the courage as well to fall down and get back up and try to make progress all over again.

Though most women were comfortable with the name *Immersion*, men's reactions were typically to reject it, thinking it sounded too soft and murky. So I invited a group of friends and colleagues to a "naming dinner" at the Rockefeller Foundation, where we generated a long list of names for this new entity that would bridge different worlds, all with a focus on smart, strategic, targeted philanthropy.

My brother Michael, with whom I'd been in conversation since childhood about how to change the world, worked on Wall Street. He matched my sincerity with an edgy humor, suggesting that the name should be something like "Ain't Your Grandma's Philanthropy." As the wine flowed, the names became sillier. By the end of the evening, our group had amassed more than 400 names, most implausible, all creative and full of life. Something in this new idea was capturing people's imagination. Finally, with the help of my friend Antonia, who worked with a fledgling Internet company, we decided on Acumen Fund, a label we hoped would signify thoughtful, insightful, smart, and focused change—precisely what we were after.

Next we had to obtain approval from the IRS as a nonprofit organization, no easy task in 2001 given that there was no exact precedent for what we wanted to do. We were completely agnostic as to whether change came through nonprofit or for-profit channels; in fact, we believed it would come through both and often in partnership. Thankfully, our lawyers were able to register Acumen Fund as a public charity on April 1, 2001.

Changing the lexicon was the next hurdle. Traditional charity speaks of donors and grantees, but this passive language creates a power dynamic that might as well call the two groups the givers and the takers. I had seen so many dysfunctional conversations where a grantee would give a would-be or existing donor misleading and evasive answers because they feared losing funding if they told the truth about the difficulties of their work. And I'd seen those same grantees agree to do things the donors thought they should, even if it made no sense for the mission of the organization. It is hard to say no to someone who has the power to finance your dreams—or more to the point, your payroll.

I also took issue with the practice of donors typically funding only programs instead of institutions. "I want to be certain that all of the money goes directly to the people who need it most," prospective donors would tell me. That is a fine strategy for providing alms or direct charity. At the same time, no one would invest in a company and not expect it to pay for hiring great people, paying the rent, and keeping the lights on. We needed philanthropists to build powerful institutions in the social sector, too.

We committed ourselves to changing the traditional donor-grantee relationship. Our donors would be called investors. They were still giving us charitable gifts, of course, but we wanted them to think of themselves as *investing* in change, of taking seriously how their money was spent. We wanted to build incentives for more honest conversations; in fact, we would ask for big gifts to help build a real organization and then promise to tell them about failures as well as successes. After all, as investors, they were betting on long-term results and should feel like owners who would go through the ups and downs with us, just as they would with a company. I would tell them, "You don't get any money back from your investment. You get change."

While we had the luxury of starting Acumen Fund with significant institutional funding, we felt it would also be critical to build a community of individual investors from the start, people who would commit not only money but also their time and connections to the work. We sought to enlist 20 "founding partners" who would establish the initial base of money, intellect, skills, and networks on which we would build our institution. I asked each person to contribute $100,000 despite the fact that we had no track record and a vision that many people didn't fully understand.

Finding the first 20 was, of course, much harder than we'd imagined. More than a few Wall Streeters explained that they kept a strict division between the way they made money and the way they gave it away.

"You are trying to do both at the same time, and it will never work. Businesses operate for profit alone, and that is how they make good decisions," an investment banker told me one summer afternoon. "Your idea of combining business and philanthropy not only won't work, it is misguided." Needless to say, he didn't contribute.

Others felt the whole idea of solving global problems made no sense given the challenges at home. One of a group of financial investors and scientific experts at a dinner asked me whether "AIDS might actually be a natural culling process.

"Maybe trying to stop it," the scientist remarked, "is ultimately detrimental to the long-term health of this planet that is already facing the negative consequences of high population growth." I spent an hour or so trying to convince the group not only of how immoral I found that idea, but also how self-defeating and counterproductive it was in a world where disease flows easily across national boundaries.

With practice, as the message became clearer, I could discern more quickly which individuals would help and which ones were more focused on finding excuses rather than working on solutions. I also relied on my good friends to make me laugh and keep the big picture in mind after too many days in a row of hearing nothing but "no, thanks, but good luck."

Ultimately, the money came, at least as much as we needed in the early years. It is only now that I realize the true debt of gratitude I owe to each of the early adopters of this innovation, those first 20 founding partners, along with the Rockefeller, Cisco, and W. K. Kellogg Foundations, for they took big bets on what may have seemed—at least to some—an unlikely dream, but one which, if brought to fruition, could actually contribute to changing the face of philanthropy.

With funding and legal status finally in place, we hired a team of three in April 2001, including Dan Toole, our first COO. I couldn't think of a person I trusted more to start this journey with me. He already had been a vital partner, helping me think through parts of the vision, and would be instrumental in our early stages of growth. I also hired David Buxbaum, a crusty investment banker, Rustom Masalawala from Silicon Valley's technology sector, and Nadege Joseph, who became my trusted assistant.

In one of our first team meetings, I asked how we would differentiate ourselves from other nonprofits in terms of the culture of Acumen Fund.

"This should be a place where nonperformers get fired," David offered, and everyone agreed. If we were to hire excellence, then people had to know we were serious, and that meant letting individuals go if they weren't up to our standards or, more often, if it turned out they weren't the right fit for the organization.

After her prestigious Wall Street career, Margo Alexander, the first woman to head a major trading floor, became our board chair. She fit our desired profile of being both tough and compassionate and always curious about the world. Along with the rest of the trustees, she would give more of herself to this start-up than she—and the others—had probably ever expected.

The biggest early challenge our new little team faced was finding the entrepreneurs and ideas in which to invest. We had decided to start in health technologies with a focus on India and East Africa. I assumed that with our connections to foundations and the United Nations we would have no problem identifying social entrepreneurs in whom we could invest. We were looking for ventures with visionary leaders who were using business approaches to solve big social problems. Their enterprises were to demonstrate the likelihood of financial sustainability and hold the promise of reaching a million customers over time. We figured that in an area like health care and a geography that encompassed more than a billion people, we'd have no problem identifying "pipeline opportunities."

We were wrong. We talked to countless people, asking for advice and connections. Many pointed to wonderful innovators who were working at the community level but didn't give us confidence their ideas would actually grow, or *scale* in our language of business. We hired two summer interns who spent long days surfing the Internet, trying to identify possible candidates. Ultimately, we reviewed more than 700 enterprises, and none fit our three criteria of leadership, sustainability, and scale in part because we limited ourselves to the nonprofit sector that first summer, where we had greater contacts.

By the end of the summer, we were in a bit of a panic, and a wise CEO of a health care company gave me advice I will never forget. "Just start," he said. "Don't wait for perfection. Just start and let the work teach you. No one expects you to get it right in the very beginning, and you'll learn more from your mistakes than you will from your early successes anyway. So stop worrying so much and just look at your best bets and go."

Still, I argued, our vision depended on finding the right social entrepreneurs.

"So find the best entrepreneur you know and start from there."

A leader who represented our ideal was Dr. Govindappa Venkataswamy, who founded the Aravind Eye Hospital in Madurai, India. When this extraordinary man retired in 1976 at age 58 from India's Civil Service as one of the country's most lauded eye surgeons, he decided to found an eye hospital to help rid the country and then the world of unnecessary blindness. Indians suffer blindness disproportionately because of the higher incidence of diabetes among both adults and children, a result most probably of genetics and diet. The fact that millions in India are blind did not intimidate Dr. V. from starting an 11-bed hospital in a simple house.

Today, Aravind Eye Care System examines more than 2.3 million patients a year, performing more than 280,000 cataract surgeries that restore sight to people regardless of their capacity to pay. Each doctor performs, on average, 80 surgeries a day. The US average, in comparison, is six. If ever there were a social entrepreneur who fused tough discipline with powerful compassion, it was Dr. Venkataswamy. We decided to meet with him and see what innovation he might be undertaking.

I met Dr. Venkataswamy on a hot afternoon in the tiny Madurai airport in the state of Tamil Nadu, in South India. He was about 80 then, and I'd heard he suffered from rheumatoid arthritis. What I hadn't expected was the spirited lightness of this fine-boned, white-haired man with leathered skin. As he stood, a baseball cap on his head, he clutched a wooden cane with his mangled hand and I saw that he'd adorned one finger with a gold ring above the knuckle. This detail, in combination with his broad smile, reminded me of John Gardner: Dr. Venkataswamy was also full of sparkle, a walking example of integrity, and he saw beauty everywhere.

"You didn't have to come and get me yourself," I laughed upon introducing myself.

"Why not?" he asked. "You are our guest and I am happy to know you."

Dr. V.—as he was usually called—surprised me again by getting behind the wheel to drive me to the guesthouse. He swerved in and out of the traffic like a teenager, beeping the horn at least 15 times per minute as he talked incessantly about his model for change. I listened with amazement, trying to soak in the scene, feeling a sense of openness just by being near him.

"We run Aravind like McDonald's," he explained, "clean and organized, with every process known and understood so that we get maximum efficiency. Two-thirds of the patients pay nothing or nearly nothing, and yet the hospital is consistently profitable—and growing."

"How do you do that?" I asked, focusing my eyes on him, trying not to be distracted by the animals and the trucks and the children running in the dusty streets.

"We have these systems that I was explaining to you," he said, "and we simply don't turn anyone away. You will see how it works."

First we drove to the organization's guesthouse on a quiet street a few blocks from the hospital. It was a pristine building with cool white marble floors, a small eating area, and individual rooms upstairs. Mine had a bed and a ceiling fan, a small closet, and its own tiny bathroom.

Pictures of Sri Aurobindo, the spiritual leader Dr. Venkataswamy followed, hung on the wall. Everywhere you could feel a sense of quiet, respect, discipline, and grace.

The hospital itself was a lot busier, though a sense of groundedness and calm was pervasive. The 1,700 young women workers all wore saris in different colors, depending on the function they performed. I saw one doctor gently help a disheveled woman settle her sari more modestly on her frail, thin body. The pure grace in the doctor's interaction with the woman made me want to cry—this was the kind of compassionate care that is too often missing in US hospitals. For Dr. Venkataswamy, how you did things was as important as what you did, and he believed that great strength and spiritual fulfillment can come from the divine nature of work done well.

During the first year of Acumen Fund's existence, we looked specifically for health care technologies, thinking technology was a key driver of innovation for issues of poverty, an approach Dr. V. understood. For the first 30 years of Aravind's existence, the surgeons would simply remove patients' cataracts and give them thick glasses to enable them to see again. When the intraocular lens, which is inserted right into the patient's eye, was invented, Dr. V. knew this could revolutionize eye care. But the price, at about $140 in 1990, was prohibitive—and he'd learned that systems requiring the poor to wait for charity or government services would leave most of them waiting for a very long time.

The question for Aravind, then, was how to manufacture an intraocular lens that was priced to make eye surgery affordable to the greatest number of people, and ultimately, the organization developed a lens as good as any on the market at a $10 price point. Though the very poor still would be unable to afford this, a business model could be developed to make intraocular lens transplants accessible to huge numbers of people without depending on great amounts of charity or government support.

Early in the development of Aravind's lens (through its for-profit technology company, Aurolab), Dr. V. was approached by a pharmaceutical company that offered to purchase it with the intent of selling the lenses for $60 each, which would cut the existing market price by more than half. Though the sale would have provided major revenues to Aravind, Dr. Venkataswamy refused the offer, for his goal was to ensure affordability not to the middle class, but to the very poor. He knew the poor would never be able to afford anything near $60 and wanted to find a way to manufacture the lens for less than $10. Today, Aurolab is one of the world's largest manufacturers of intraocular lenses, exporting to more than 120 countries and selling the lenses for less than $2 apiece.

Aravind's simple business model was based on a sliding-scale pricing system whereby wealthier people paid the full cost of an operation and the poor paid a token amount or nothing if they were truly destitute. No one was turned away. Aravind at that time had two hospitals in the same location, and it differentiated ability to pay by offering full-service, air-conditioned rooms at the newer hospital to the paying patients. The "free" or lesser-paying patients were treated at the older facility and slept on mats on the floor, but every surgeon rotated between the two hospitals, so the actual quality of care was the same.

When we asked how Acumen Fund and Aravind might work together, Dr. Venkataswamy's team (comprised mostly of his seven younger siblings and their spouses and children, 31 family members in all) suggested we provide a grant for an experiment in establishing a telemedicine unit so that farmers in the field could have their eyes examined without traveling hundreds of miles to the main hospital. Aravind also wanted to use telemedicine as a teaching tool because it worked through five hospitals and wanted all of its students to learn from the best doctors, wherever they resided.

Telemedicine was a fairly new innovation at the time, especially in low-income areas. Essentially, it was a means of connecting doctors at a distance to patients through a computer with video capability. Given how far most rural villages are from high-quality hospitals, we intuitively understood the power of providing low-income people with access to talented doctors; however, we were unsure of how to build a business model that would enable Aravind to cover its expenses.

"Let us try and that part will come," Dr. V. assured us.

We made the grant and a year or so later, I visited again to see what had happened. Dr. V. walked me into one of the teaching classrooms in the hospital. The brightly lit room with wooden floors was filled with eager young medical students who stood when their revered teacher walked in. On the wide screen at the front of the room were live video feeds of four other classrooms in different parts of India, and in each of those rooms, the students stood for Dr. Venkataswamy, as well. Another doctor then took the floor, showing how to operate on an eye. Students in all four cities could see exactly what he was doing as if they were all in the same room.

Later that afternoon, I watched the doctors at Aravind diagnose the damage a swipe from a stick of sugar cane had done to the eye of a farmer who was sitting 300 kilometers away. The weathered farmer was terrified that he had lost sight in both eyes, which was tantamount to a death sentence: Blindness meant loss of the ability to produce income. The good doctors at Aravind could see that his healthy eye was having a "sympathetic reaction" and would return to normal after the wounded one was properly treated.

The cost to the farmer for this consultancy with some of the country's best doctors was an affordable few rupees: This could indeed be revolutionary. By 2008, telemedicine would be part of Aravind's normal business. It had been integrated into 16 vision centers in rural villages, each providing about 50,000 people with access in places where individuals previously had no access to high-quality eye care—and Aravind was treating about 150,000 patients a year. But 7 years previously, it had been only an idea—with a powerful team of entrepreneurial, results-oriented people behind it.

By the fall of 2001, we had identified other social entrepreneurs and were feeling more confident that a pipeline of talent existed and that there was power in our model. We'd also found new offices across the street from Trinity Church at the end of Wall Street. I loved the symbolism of the new location, for Acumen Fund would be built with both a hard head and a soft heart. I loved that church bells rang every 15 minutes, which would remind me of time passing and call me to be more present with the work we did. I liked that we would be right next to the World Trade Center, for our dream would be about all of humanity and our collective future.

We were set to move in on September 11, 2001.

I REMEMBER THAT DAY as if it were yesterday. The dawn revealed a perfect world, a pink sky folding into china blue as I ran the length of Central Park, thinking nostalgically of schooldays and of how much I love the rhythms of the East Coast seasons. It was fall, and I was looking forward to the year ahead and how much there was to do.

An hour and a half later, I was standing in our offices on the 28th floor of the building housing the Rockefeller Foundation, at Thirty-Eighth Street and Fifth Avenue, talking to David, our chief financial officer, as we looked through the big plate-glass windows down Fifth toward the World Trade Center Towers, near where our computers and furniture were in the process of being moved. Suddenly, a huge jetliner roared down the avenue, and we swore it was flying below the top of the Empire State Building, just a few blocks south of us. The plane continued until it neared the World Trade Center, then banked and plunged into one of the skyscrapers.

Though both of us were in shock, I thought it must have been an accident, but David recognized that it had banked. "That was an act of terrorism," he said. "That was no accident." Rustom had just returned from India, and both he and Dan walked up as David was shouting and pointing at the burning hole when the second plane entered the building. It was immediately clear that David was right. As we later watched both towers collapse, we knew the world would never be the same.

The next morning, our tiny team of four gathered in our borrowed offices at the Rockefeller Foundation. Like all New Yorkers, we wanted to do something—anything—to help. But we couldn't join the workers at the site, and it was already clear there would be few, if any, victims found alive within the rubble. The world's attention was turned on New York, and I wondered whether Acumen's prospective contributors would pull back now and focus on the city's challenges rather than international ones. We also needed to think of a way we ourselves could contribute.

The team decided to reach out and convene a roundtable to try and make sense of what was happening. We gathered our community of partners, team members, and experts, including a White House advisor on terrorism and a former *Wall Street Journal* writer who had covered the Middle East for years and had interviewed every jihadist from Ayatollah Khomeini to Osama bin Laden himself. The experts told us that the White House was already linking Saddam Hussein to the tragedy and predicted we would be at war with Iraq the following year.

After hours of discussing fundamentalism, terrorism, poverty, and possible solutions that focused on "soft power" rather than on forceful retaliation, I asked what an organization like Acumen Fund might do to contribute. The group reached easy consensus: "Build civil society organizations. Go to the Muslim world and provide examples of how people are working to give themselves a bigger stake and better chances for the future."

In Acumen's first months, we had focused on health care technologies in India and East Africa. Our early team knew little about the larger "Muslim world" despite our work in India, but we knew we could bring in people who *did* know. I remembered the health care company CEO's wise words, "Let the work teach you."

Though we explored the possibilities of doing something very quietly, by year's end, that evening's consensus was solidified via a million dollars in donations to Acumen Fund. A few months after that, in early 2002, we'd gone to Pakistan, and by the next November, just a year after that first roundtable, we had made our first investments. Working in Pakistan turned out to be one of the best moves we made.

In that first year of operations, we also gave a social entrepreneur a grant for his work on developing a $40 hearing aid that would later be tested and shown to be as effective as a $3,000 model. Like the services provided by Aravind, the hearing aid would be priced on a sliding-scale basis to make it affordable to the poor and provide revenues to the enterprise. When the test results came back after the initial trials, our entire staff whooped and laughed and cheered in the halls, sure this low-cost technology would disrupt the market and change lives. We hadn't expected such an early technological victory for the poor.

But as it turned out, it wasn't so easy.

We hadn't counted on the fact that most individuals are interested not in technologies themselves but in the services they provide. With cataract surgery, people go from being nearly blind to having sight and being able to work again; that change can be the difference between life and death. Given that a tailor, for example, depends on his eyes for his very livelihood, an investment in sight is worth the price.

Most farmers, tailors, shoemakers, and laborers can continue to work, however, with a loss of hearing. This is complicated by our human tendency toward vanity: Many feel a sense of shame at wearing a hearing aid, whereas no such stigma is attached to glasses. Consequently, individual demand for the hearing aids was low. There was—and is—still a major market for the devices among hospitals and other institutions, but, at least when we were starting, the market among the poor themselves was limited. The enterprise distributed 10,000 hearing aids, but we decided not to make a second grant or investment until we better understood the issues of distribution and demand. Price was not the only factor in delivering services to the poor.

In addition to the hearing aid, we also supported the early development of an electromagnetic immunosensor, a low-cost technologically advanced method of diagnosing diseases. From that experience as well, we concluded that we wouldn't invest in start-up technologies, especially when our organization was not set up to help develop the technology. Technology itself wasn't the answer, we realized, and we would contribute more to the world by understanding the distribution, pricing, and marketing systems for health care rather than simply the technologies involved.

From this and other ventures, we determined that despite Aravind's success, grants typically weren't as effective as equity and loans, especially when trying to create markets for the poor. An equity investment would make us real owners with the ability to negotiate with greater clarity. Loans and equity also would impose a market discipline that could lead to raising more traditional forms of capital over time—and that, we knew, was key to growing the innovations we wanted to support.

We were learning. By the end of the first year, we had modified our approach. We determined that we would no longer make grants, but instead invest equity in or make loans to social enterprises. We would establish metrics for what the entrepreneur hoped to achieve from the beginning and hold him or her to it, as we would hold ourselves to our own set of expectations and goals. This was the opposite of old-fashioned charity.

Our new approach also differed from the type of investment that a venture capitalist or private equity investor might make. Traditional investors doubtless would never touch the deals we were willing to contemplate. They were seeking returns of 25 to 40 percent and had a fairly short time horizon, usually 5 to 7 years. We were interested in enterprises run by social entrepreneurs who were unafraid to work in markets where individuals had minimal income, where the roads were terrible and infrastructure was sometimes nonexistent. Low-income markets also tended to be where corrupt politicians played, making promises that were never kept, but often requiring bribes or "speed money" just for providing the license to start a business that served the community.

We knew that the pipeline—the number of deals we could support— would be a challenge for a number of years, yet we were convinced that the many problems of poverty could only be solved if entrepreneurs were encouraged to overcome these hurdles. This meant we couldn't simply invest and expect quick results. We planned to work alongside our entrepreneurs, offering management advice and technical help and connections to a wider network of talent. We were also willing to be realistic about how and when loans would be repaid, remembering these businesses at the bottom of the pyramid could take a long time to grow and that our primary goal was not to make money, but to effect long-lasting change.

Our investment style was focused on what we termed *patient capital*—not traditional charity, not traditional business investment, but something in-between. Patient capital is money invested over a longer period of time with the acknowledgment that returns might be below market, but with a wide range of management support services to nurture the company to liftoff and beyond.

If it were easy to start a business serving the poor, patient capital would not be necessary. It's not easy. Social entrepreneurs focused on serving low-income markets work against all odds of success, facing enormous individual and institutional challenges. The only chance to overcome these hurdles is to combine an extraordinary entrepreneur with the kind of support that neither traditional investors nor charities can provide.

We learned the power of having strong teams on the ground. Varun Sahni, our India country director, a brilliant young man in his thirties with a degree from Columbia who had spent his early career at Unilever, opened our office in Hyderabad, hired a team, and surrounded himself with some of the country's best minds in business—advisors who were also keenly focused on the work of serving the poor. Varun has the talent and skill to be successful in a traditional private equity firm, but his personal quest is to help create a new industry that promotes equitable development. Early on he identified Satyan Mishra, a visionary entrepreneur who was focused first and foremost on supporting the poor by building a large-scale information distribution system.

I remember meeting Satyan when we had coffee at a New Delhi hotel along with Tim Brown, the CEO of a major design company called IDEO. Tim, an understated Brit who was living in Palo Alto, California, and working with big consumer companies, saw in Satyan the same infectious combination of qualities that Varun and I did: passion, commitment, and big ideas. When Satyan left the table to take an urgent call, Tim whispered to me that we'd just met the real deal.

The 30-something, balding man with a black mustache and honest face who wore conservative glasses over his serious eyes and carried pens in his front pocket was not one to dream small. His vision was to establish a network of tele-kiosks, one in each of India's 650,000 villages. A tele-kiosk, he explained, was a small store where a local entrepreneur would set himself up with a computer, a phone, and a camera. He would sell a range of services, from computer training classes to international calls to taking family photographs and sending them to relatives over the Internet.

"Much of the rural areas are cut off from real information," he said, "but for India to prosper, we need to bring the 300 million poorest individuals into the global economy. Connecting them to information and skills is one way to do it."

At the time, his for-profit company, Drishtee, already had built 500 kiosks, and Satyan was looking for additional funding in a combination of equity and loans. Here was a man who understood not only the preferences of the poor, but also how to build distribution systems that would reach them in an affordable—and sustainable—way.

Satyan knew what he was talking about when he spoke of rural villages; he had grown up in one himself in Bihar, one of India's poorest states. His focus on understanding his customer base, moreover, was so fierce that he typically spent a month or so each year living in his home village so he could listen directly to the people to gain a better understanding of their needs. As a potential partner, he urged me to visit that village with him.

At that point, we'd invested $1 million in equity in the company and loaned it $600,000 to help it expand. About a year later, I visited with one of our founding board members, Cate Muther. By then, the number of kiosks had more than doubled, but we noticed that most of the local franchisees were men and wondered where the women were. Satyan explained that women were actually his most successful franchisees, but they had no access to financing because so many of them had never been registered for birth certificates when they were born (as opposed to their brothers, who were expected to get real jobs and places in society and therefore needed official documents).

We asked why women performed better than men.

"Women come to work early and they stay late," he said. "They are very serious about what they do and I think they work harder to succeed. Apart from that, most of a dollar earned by a woman goes right to the family. It's not the same for men. So everyone benefits when we support more women to do this work."

Cate and I brainstormed on how to raise the financing to extend to women. I called Maria Eitel, who ran the Nike Foundation, because that organization focuses specifically on women's economic situations, just as

Cate's own foundation, Three Guineas Fund, does. Nike Foundation approved a $250,000 grant and Cate began spending many hours with the Acumen team and Drishtee to establish a larger lending capability to women that she herself would help finance.

Drishtee began to grow exponentially. By 2007, the enterprise was established in nearly 2,000 villages. Satyan invited me to visit his home village in Bihar. After an all-night delayed flight from New York to London, hours spent in Heathrow waiting, and another all-night flight to Delhi, I met two Acumen Fund team members, Ann MacDougall, our new general counsel, and Biju Mohandas, a former military doctor who knew India's rural areas. From Delhi, we took the 2-hour plane ride to Patna, the state's capital, and then started driving, this time on dirt roads riddled with potholes and covered with belching trucks and oxen carts, rickshaws, bicycles, and skinny men carrying enormous sacks.

Just outside Patna, the stench of garbage piled along the streets carried for miles. The refuse of civilization—paper, rotten fruit and plastic bags and cans—became part of the landscape, turning green fields into abstract paintings of blues and whites and browns more like a dirty moonscape than pastoral earth. We drove for 5 or 6 long, hot, and bumpy hours, and finally arrived at our tiny hotel, where we fell into our beds and then woke at dawn to drive another 2 hours to reach Satyan's village near Madhubani.

India is a contradiction of extreme wealth and extreme poverty living side by side. In Bombay, one of India's biggest billionaires was constructing a 27-floor mansion with parking for 168 cars, three helipads on the roof, and a staff of 600—all at a cost of a billion dollars. At the same time, 300 million people lived on less than a dollar a day. Bridging that gap and giving to India's poor, who represent a third of the world's people living in poverty, must become a priority for the nation's future. For Acumen Fund, it meant working harder with social entrepreneurs like Satyan to create the models that could help pave the way.

We had entered another world. Oxcarts and rickshaws moved slowly cutting through endless dirt roads bordering emerald fields. Women walked to the wells and holy men sat in front of temples, preparing for a religious festival. Only the very rich had electric generators, and even those who went to school told us the teachers never showed up.

When Ann asked one of the village women if she could use the bathroom, the woman led her to her backyard. The woman was by no means destitute. She lived in a brick house with separate bedrooms and her own walled yard. Ann told me she looked around to see where the outhouse was and it took her a moment to realize that there wasn't one. She looked back at the woman, who was happily waving her arm in a sweeping gesture to let Ann know that the entire yard was hers as a revered guest. She could squat in whichever part best suited her.

If this is what the better-off villagers did, Ann asked, how do the poorest ones take care of their hygiene? A doctor friend of Satyan's replied that open defecation was one of the biggest public health issues the area faced, reminding us that some health investments are best undertaken through effective awareness campaigns, not through medicines or direct services.

Against this backdrop, we sat in a circle under tall green trees outside Satyan's childhood home, cows lolling in the distance. Satyan pulled out his computer to show us the work he was doing to establish a business processing outsourcing (BPO) unit here. Already, he'd secured wireless, and sure enough, in this tiny village so far away from everything, we were able to check my e-mail and read the *New York Times*. Inside a small house, six young men sat inputting data for a bank in Delhi, all earning more than they had ever dreamed they could. A 17-year-old, too young to work at the BPO, introduced himself and showed us the Web site he had built.

Satyan took us to meet one of the kiosk entrepreneurs, a young man with a small face and pointed chin who greeted us with great warmth despite our arriving an hour and a half later than expected. The roads had flooded, and most were impassable. This wasn't a hindrance to his business, he informed us, because most people walked to his kiosk, where he sold photographs and computer services. He was bringing in more computers due to the high demand and had a phone to enable people to call whomever they wanted to. He also wanted to take us to a nearby town to see some of the art he sold through Drishtee Haat, the company's online crafts store.

As the sun was setting, we drove to meet some of the artists. Soon it was pitch-dark and impossible to see houses, let alone paintings, but we managed to fumble our way to one of the artists' homes. She came out with a scroll of paintings and two candles. The darkness alone made doing business impossible, and I felt a surge of frustration that something as simple as a single lightbulb could make all the difference yet be so inaccessible.

All of us, Satyan included, had an urge to try to fix every problem in the community. The children needed schools, and their mothers needed even more general education about health, hygiene, and nutrition. The farmers needed some form of health insurance so they could weather the inevitable catastrophes that befall a poor family and keep them in poverty forever. Satyan and I both are big dreamers. We can't help ourselves. But the conversation eventually turned to remembering what he was trying to do and what it would take to do it.

If Satyan was to succeed in creating a network of connections by having the tele-kiosks in even 10,000 villages, let alone 30,000 or each of the 650,000 villages across India, then his enterprise had to remain focused on one thing and do it better than anyone else. It required discipline and the humility to recognize that no single person can do everything. But if he did it, he had a chance to reach millions of people and change their lives fundamentally by helping them to help themselves, a goal worth focusing on and fighting for.

In 2008, Drishtee began expanding more quickly than Starbucks did in its early years, opening about four kiosks a day. By fall, the company was operating in more than 4,000 villages, creating more than 5,300 jobs and serving 7.5 million. What thrills me just as much is that the company is building a powerful distribution system through which it ultimately will be able to sell a multitude of products that can improve a low-income person's ability to change his or her own life. Acumen Fund's patient capital enabled Satyan to take great risks, experiment, and innovate in the early years. And we know that despite his enterprise's rapid growth, he is just getting started.

And so are we.

CHAPTER 14

BUILDING BRICK BY BRICK

Go to the people:
live with them, learn from them
love them
start with what they know
build with what they have.

But of the best leaders,
when the job is done,
the task accomplished,
the people will say:
"We have done it ourselves."

—LAO TZU

In India it wasn't a surprise to find entrepreneurs with enormous talent and drive focused on bringing basic services like health care, housing, and water to the poor. With more than a billion people, some of the best universities in the world, a powerful diaspora community, and a highly innovative health care industry, India seems to breed social entrepreneurs. I was far less certain of what we would find in Pakistan, an Islamic country characterized by the media as chaotic and overrun by terrorists and fundamentalists. I didn't expect to fall in love with the country. But life has a funny way of surprising you.

After a long week spent working in India with Acumen Fund, I was on my way to Karachi, Pakistan. As I sat in the Bombay airport thinking, writing, and waiting for my delayed flight, a Bohri woman abruptly walked over and sat down beside me, so close that part of her big thigh was almost on top of mine. The Bohris are an entrepreneurial group within the Muslim community who do a lot of business in Pakistan and India as well as East Africa. The women wear large capes with veils covering their hair, reminding me of Catholic nuns, though the Bohris seem to favor pastels or bright designs, often with lace around the edges. Their skirts are gathered and full. The older Bohri women often wear black shoes, reminding me even more of the nuns I knew as a young girl.

Why was this woman sitting so close to me when the airport was virtually empty? All around me were seats just waiting to be filled. The Bohri woman's face was eager and broad, the kind that makes you smile. She wore wire-rimmed glasses that could not hide twinkling eyes the color of honey. She was completely toothless. Though I wished for solitude, I had a hard time ignoring that face.

She talked a blue streak, leaving no room for idle chitchat. Her first sentence made me nearly laugh aloud. With no introduction, she asked, "Tell me, what do you do? Are you married? Do you have children?"

Though I didn't even know her name, I answered, "No, never married. No children."

"Ah." She clapped her hands together and smiled even more broadly. "I never married, either. But I could see that you are deeply happy sitting there all alone, but not lonely. I could see that you are one of the happiest people, the ones who serve the world."

I looked at her and said thank you.

"I am so happy, too, though I never married. You know, there are so many paths in a life. But the best are the ones where you are living the truth and searching for good and giving to others. Maybe that is what you are finding."

I was stunned. Maybe that is what I *was* finding. Maybe I just needed someone to remind me.

When our flight was finally called, my new friend walked up to the security woman and lifted her arms to the skies, ready to be patted down in full sight. Her cape lifted to reveal a shirt of green and white gingham—like the uniform of the blue bakery I had started in Kigali so many years ago—tucked into a big green and white skirt gathered at the waist that hit the tops of clunky, black lace-up shoes. Now she really reminded me of a nun, and I found myself grinning a silly, Cheshire-cat smile not unlike hers. It felt as if someone from the heavens had come to me, even if this toothless Bohri woman wasn't exactly whom I'd pictured as my guardian angel.

We'd been working in Pakistan because we felt it was the most geopolitically important nation on earth and because of our assumption that building civil society institutions that enabled people to have greater freedom and choice was critical to the country's long-term success—to any country's success. In 2002, just around the time *Wall Street Journal* reporter Danny Pearl was kidnapped and beheaded, we went to Pakistan and determined that the most compelling opportunities were in two areas in which Acumen had not previously been involved: microfinance and housing.

Roshaneh Zafar, founder and CEO of Kashf, now one of Pakistan's largest microfinance institutions, became our partner in bringing financial services to Pakistan's poor. Roshaneh is an extraordinary, indomitable leader with long, black hair and penetrating eyes, a slender frame, and fingers adorned with oversize rings. She is elegance, beauty, and fierce intelligence personified.

Her father told the story of how Roshaneh had started Kashf despite the odds. With a degree from the University of Pennsylvania's Wharton business school in hand, she'd been working in Washington, DC, at the World Bank when she called to tell him about her idea to start a microfinance organization to lend to women in Pakistan.

"Is this a call for advice?" he asked his daughter, "or just for information?"

He knew the answer to his own question. He also knew there'd be no convincing her not to do it.

She started in 1996 and soon hired her partner, Sadaffe Abid. Over the course of a decade they built an institution serving more than 350,000 women, earning Roshaneh the highest civilian award for service in Pakistan. But the road wasn't without its bumps. In their first year, it cost Kashf $8 to loan $1. The organization needed time to learn, and the funders needed to trust the leadership and have the patience to learn with them. Today it costs the institution less than 8 cents to loan a dollar to the world's poorest.

By 2002, 6 years after its inception, Kashf was serving 12,000 women and moving toward operational self-sufficiency. Acumen Fund supported the organization's growth with a long-term loan priced below market—patient capital. Recently, Citibank led a $32 million round of financing for Kashf; and Acumen Fund invested $1.5 million in Kashf's holding company as it has now created a commercial bank for the poor. Kashf now lends to more than 320,000 clients, and Pakistan can boast of a model microfinance institution that is setting a standard for the world.

Microfinance's success rests on the ability of low-income women to borrow and pay back small amounts of money in a short period of time. Housing is a more challenging issue. Half the people in Karachi, a city of 15 million people, live as squatters, usually paying rent to slumlords. At the same time, due to the growth of the cities, land speculation is rampant, which leaves little that is affordable for low-income and even middle-class people. Even if a poor person has an opportunity to purchase a home, he or she has no access to a mortgage; in fact, many commercial banks view low-income areas as "no-go zones."

The question was whether you could structure housing finance and development to make it affordable and accessible to all people, not just the very rich. There was also the question of trust: Even when housing schemes were made available, developers too often failed to deliver on promises to bring real housing to low-income areas. And the poor were always hurt the most.

A few rare individuals, such as Tasneem Siddiqui, experimented with different approaches to low-cost housing.

During my first visit in 2002, he explained the philosophy of his organization, Saiban: "We go to the people and live with them, build on what they know, listen to them, and help them do things for themselves."

In his tiny office in his first development, Khuda-Ki-Busti, or City of God, about 18 kilometers outside Karachi, the air was sweltering, but Tasneem didn't seem to notice. Balding at the crown, with longish white hair, Tasneem, in his wrinkled pants with oversize glasses framing intelligent eyes, reminded me of an absent-minded professor.

But this man was a true activist: "I learned incremental housing through 30 years of trial and error," he said, "first in East Pakistan (now Bangladesh) until the war in 1971, and then back in Pakistan."

The concept of incremental housing was based on Tasneem's knowledge about the buying decisions of very low-income individuals. "People in the slums are market oriented, but they usually can't afford to construct the entire house at once. The people gain dignity by doing things for themselves, and our job is to make it possible."

Saiban encourages people to start small with what they can afford. Over time they can expand their houses.

"When we started, we knew the biggest challenge would be to confront people's fear that we might swindle them. All of the rules for Saiban are written on the exterior walls of our offices. Everything is transparent so that everyone, buyer or not, knows our rules. There are no surprises."

He walked me outside in the blazing heat and pointed to the blue writing on the wall of the office building. The Urdu script was large and beautiful, easy to read, and apparently easy to understand.

"But how does it all work?" I asked.

He chuckled and gently shook his head. "It wasn't easy in the beginning. We had to work hard to find our first buyers. We were asking people to live in a new place with no services, a fair distance from their jobs and communities. But there were brave souls willing to take a risk. They would pay $170 up front for the land, and then we required them to live in the courtyard for 10 days. Usually, they would come with some basic covering to protect themselves, but their willingness to sacrifice helped us differentiate the real prospective home owners from the speculators who wanted to buy and then flip the houses. You see, you can't just ask a person if they are poor enough to qualify for a house, but we could learn a lot about their commitment."

"And the hardest part?" I asked.

"Trust. In addition to being transparent with the rules, our manager has lived here among the people since the beginning. He helps resolve disputes 24 hours a day. We listen to the people and let them choose the kind of house they want to build. The poor want a roof over their head, a feeling of safety, services they can rely on. We didn't bring it overnight—it is why we call this incremental housing. In time, this has become a beautiful community."

Today, more than 20,000 live in Khuda-Ki-Busti, and dozens of viable businesses have sprung up to serve it. Churches coexist with mosques and a Hindu temple. A bus service runs into town regularly at an affordable price. Saiban is a model for change.

Tasneem next focused on experimenting with the model in a different place, this time using private land because free public land had become almost completely unavailable by 2003. His starting point: a large plot of land about a 40-minute drive outside Lahore, in the Punjab region of Pakistan. If Karachi is like New York City, Lahore is more like Boston, an intellectual center, just a bit slower, and lovely to behold, where community ties are stronger than in the more urban, individualistic city of Karachi.

Acumen Fund agreed to lend $300,000 to Saiban to purchase land and register it for development. Tasneem was lucky to find Jawad Aslam, a young 30-something Pakistani American businessman with an entrepreneurial streak who had grown up in Baltimore and worked in commercial real estate development until the events of 9/11 convinced him to move to Pakistan and contribute as best he could. Of medium build, Jawad typically dressed in traditional clothing, wore a neatly trimmed beard, comported himself with humility, and worked hard at making things happen for very little money. In his first year at Saiban, this successful US-born businessman earned about $450 a month.

"I want purpose in my work," he told me. "I wouldn't trade it despite the headaches and sacrifices."

Acumen Fund's country director, Aun Rahman, and I flew to Lahore to meet with Jawad about a year after he arrived. Aun was also in his early thirties, more than 6 feet 2 inches tall, with light eyes and a shock of black hair. He grew up in Karachi and attended private school there. After graduating from the University of Chicago, he worked for several years at a prestigious consulting firm. Still, he understood the challenges of low-income markets. He'd spent a year as our first Acumen fellow working with Saiban in the slums outside Karachi. The experience opened his eyes to the realities of the poor and reinforced his commitment to doing things differently, which made him the right person to lead our efforts in Pakistan.

We were eager to visit the site, though Jawad did his best to lower our expectations. "I know you won't believe that a year has passed and we're still not registered. Just please don't think I've not worked hard enough, for work is all I do. And since the land isn't yet registered since we refused to pay speed money, you realize we will be visiting an open field, yes?"

"What are the registrars like?" I asked, imagining brutes intimidating buyers to pay bribes for the right to own title on something for which they'd paid.

Jawad laughed out loud. "Think instead of a one-armed 31-year-old, as skinny as a broomstick, who used every excuse in the book to avoid me. I can't tell you how many times he canceled meetings because 'it was raining.' And there was nothing I could do about it if I were to play by the rules—which I was determined to do. For a year, despite all my running around and begging, I made little headway."

In most countries, there is big corruption at the highest levels, and then there is the often more destabilizing petty corruption that becomes so common that people experience it simply as the way things work. Petty corruption—paying someone to get your child into school or to avoid a speeding ticket—is ultimately deeply corrosive.

"I've learned that a lost year or two is sometimes inevitable with new initiatives, especially," I assured Jawad. "Sometimes the lost year is due to unanticipated bureaucracy and corruption; at other times, it comes from the need to convince people to try something new or from delays in getting materials or finding the right staff."

Jawad nodded gracefully, knowing that it is only when some people refuse to play that the game has any chance of changing.

Finally we arrived near the land for the new development. We parked the car, walked under an archway, climbed across railroad tracks, and found ourselves moving through the dusty, narrow alleyways of an enchanting village. Children carried soaps and other sundries on their heads. Women sat in doorways peering from beneath brightly colored shawls. Little girls held hands and swung their pleated skirts as they skipped along the brick road. As we neared the edge of the village, we could see emerald green fields of rice against a perfectly blue sky. Everything felt beautiful.

The taste in the air was fresh and healthy, something missing from Karachi. For as far as I could see were fields of rice, young boys driving donkey-drawn carts filled with grass to sell at the market, and, mostly, empty space. This was country living—and only a 40-minute drive from the slum. I imagined it would feel like heaven to move here from a low-income urban neighborhood.

About a quarter mile or so across the field stood another small village, though it wasn't clear how much interaction occurred between the two. Jawad pointed to a newly dug fishpond and to rice fields that would flourish in the wet season. Aun and I nearly danced around, just standing on the place where we could dream together of a community for low-income people.

"It won't be long now!" I said gleefully.

"Not now that there is a fishpond!" Aun added.

Jawad teased us for our optimism, but we wouldn't stop dreaming.

Another 6 or 7 months passed before Jawad's efforts were finally rewarded and the land was officially registered. His next challenges loomed larger: finding the right people and materials to construct houses and battling the monsoons. When I visited Lahore again, Jawad invited us to go out and see the development. This time Aun and I were accompanied by our colleague Misbah, who left a 10-year career at Citigroup Pakistan to work with Acumen Fund.

After meeting for a quick coffee in a hotel in downtown Lahore, the four of us piled into a hired car and headed outside the city. As I stared out the window, I was mesmerized by the soft hue the afternoon light was casting across the world, kissing the romantic silhouettes of minarets and the swollen rooftops of mosques. Before reaching the crowded part of the city, I soaked in the more pastoral parts of Lahore, the tree-lined roads along the wide river bend, the enchanting gardens outside private schools for boys complete with enormous green fields for cricket matches and polo games. Women walked hand in hand alongside the road, some in modern Pakistani dress, some completely covered in the traditional black hijab. Like Karachi, Lahore is a city of contrasts.

Our car moved to the city center and then slowed to a crawl through the crowded streets, accompanied by horse-drawn carts and donkeys, three-wheelers, vans and trucks, men carrying baskets on their backs and pedaling bicycles with huge boxes attached to the seats. Families atop the funny-looking humps of decorated camels trotted alongside our car. Big painted trucks, true artisanship in action, roared past, all overflowing with waving boys. Bearded men walked slowly in their white kurtas and businessmen rode in the backseats of shiny Mercedes-Benzes. Mangy dogs—part of the scenery in every developing country—rambled along the roads while random shopkeepers put out their wares.

We passed the Lahore Fort, an impressive citadel built in the 1500s, and the breathtaking Badshahi Mosque, whose towering walls and onion domes glow magnificently at night in a sea of lights. All of us remarked on the many beautiful minarets, the mix of modern and ancient, the beauty of Islamic architecture, and how we might one day integrate more of that beauty into the housing we were building.

As we had the first time, we turned off a dirt road at a blue sign for Saiban, passing fields of wheat, some of it harvested into neat bales. On this quiet afternoon, farmers walked alongside buffalo and sheep as old men cycled past. Again, we walked through the little village and came across the giant field where the housing development was scheduled to go. But this time, there was actually a single house, beautiful and glorious at least to our eyes.

"That's ours," Jawad said excitedly, "but you might not want to walk down the path to get there."

Normally dry, the dirt road slicing through the rice paddy was full of mud from recent flooding. "We can just look at it from here," he added.

But we'd been waiting a long time to see that first house, and we wanted a closer view. Jawad laughed as we gingerly followed him barefoot through the mud after taking off our shoes and rolling up our pants legs.

I loved the sensual feeling of soft earth squishing between my toes and the movement of water across my legs, though I imagined myself falling splat into the muck in the dress pants and pale blue silk jacket I'd worn to a morning meeting. A dark-skinned boy in a turban cut a dramatic figure in tangerine orange as he sat on his haunches at the edge of the rice paddy. Huge, horse-drawn carts of grass rolled along, slowing near the horizon as cormorants swooped back and forth across the bright green fields.

It took maybe 10 or 15 minutes to reach the house, and we couldn't have been prouder. At 500 square feet, it was large enough for a family, with two rooms, two bathrooms, a small kitchen, and a courtyard. We must have snapped a dozen pictures in front, which was already painted with the rules, like Saiban's main office outside Karachi.

When I put down my camera, I looked at Aun and Misbah and Jawad with their shoes in their hands and so much pride in their faces. I thought of what these children of Pakistan—so incredibly bright, competent, and committed—could have been doing with their lives instead of being here in a field, working to surmount enormous hurdles to build houses for the poor. I reflected for a moment on how lucky I was to be able to work with them and how much I wanted to support them as leaders. Their generation is the future of Pakistan.

We congratulated the men working at the demonstration house, but refused an offer of tea. The sun was setting, and I wanted the team to return before dark. As we walked across the field, we spoke about the importance of this first house—how crucial it was to come and celebrate because life is short, victories are hard-won, and hope comes not from playing it safe, but from working on good in the world, as my angel had reminded me at the airport.

Suddenly, *BOOM*. Gunshots rang out from behind and young men flew past us, obviously panicked. I grabbed Misbah's hand and we quickened our pace. With the bullets coming more rapidly, we moved as quickly as we could, planting one foot at a time in the mud, trying desperately not to slip.

In the village ahead, we could see a man in a pale blue shirt shooting high into the air, surrounded by young men. Our choices were limited: We were in the middle of a narrow, muddy road cutting through a field of rice paddies, caught in cross fire. There was no going back. Though it didn't seem that anyone was shooting directly at us, men with guns were running toward us from both directions, and the sounds of bullets flying seemed to be everywhere. We kept moving forward, running as fast as we could.

As we neared the village, we saw a group of men grab a young man in a black shirt with a red stripe down the front. Everyone was yelling, and the man looked terrified. I assumed he was somehow a culprit, but we didn't stop to find out. We raced through the narrow walkways in the village. Misbah, still holding my hand, suddenly told me to stop.

"What is it?" I asked her.

"Pull down the legs of your pants," she said. "You never know who or what is causing the trouble right now. If we look disrespectable, we'll stand out even more than we do now."

Meanwhile, Aun said he could hear people shouting that there were foreigners in the village. We walked rapidly while trying to hold ourselves with some semblance of calm, focusing on the path ahead, though my brain seemed to split apart as if I were watching what was happening to us from above—a coping mechanism.

I focused mostly on getting my young team out. As we moved, I felt a profound feeling of love for them. At the same time, I watched the little girls in dresses running behind the boys with guns rather than seeking cover. To them, these boys were not frightening. They were heroes and guardians of their security.

We escaped safely, and it was only later that we learned that a group of four or five robbers had driven in a small car to the far village, vandalized some of the houses, and then jumped back into the vehicle for their getaway. The car got stuck in the mud along the path, and the robbers jumped out and fled in every direction. The villagers chased after them, calling men from the distant village for help by shooting in the air—not unlike the whooping I remembered being used as a signal by the guards in Rwanda when trouble occurred.

No one in the village was hurt that night. With no police force on which they could count, the villagers took protection into their own hands. Most households seemed to have a gun. Poverty is about not only income levels, but also the lack of freedom that comes from physical insecurity.

After the incident, the villagers decided our group was no fly-by-night shop: We were committed. When Jawad came to work that next morning, he was greeted by many fewer skeptical eyes. Within days, the first person signed up to buy a house. Jawad and Saiban were on their way.

Sales were slow at first. Very-low-income people can't afford to think far into the future and rarely have the savings for a down payment. Because this project was built on private land, a down payment for each plot was three times what it had been in Karachi—nearly $600, a princely sum for most people in the target market. And Lahore's community orientation made it harder for people to leave their homes, however inadequate they were, to take an uncharted course alone.

Potential buyers also feared a 15-year mortgage. One severe sickness befalling the family breadwinner could put the entire family behind. Though the Saiban mortgage payments, about $30 to $35 a month, were less than what people paid to rent in the slums, the concept of a long-term loan was frightening.

But Jawad kept talking to people and, one by one, they began to come.

Fast-forward to late 2007. We drove from Lahore back to the village again, but this time we were able to drive along the dusty access road to see the first 50 dwellings on two blocks, housing nearly 300 pioneering residents. A park stood in the middle of the first block, a perfect square of well-kept grass ringed by pink and white flowers. Benches lined either side, and many of the home owners had planted flowers beneath their windows. I wondered aloud whether we would ever be able to measure the changes in how human beings see themselves in the world.

I met a man I guessed to be about 60 because of his pure white hair and weathered face, but he was closer to 40. He'd lived in the slums for most of his life and came to Saiban to start a new chapter with his family. He also laid claim to being the first person in the development to take a mortgage.

"The people here, they are very patient," he said. "At first, I asked them why would I take a loan for one amount and then have to pay you several times that amount back over the next years? They tried explaining this over and over but never made a good argument."

"And how did they convince you, finally?" I asked.

"I used to pay about $38 a month for my rent in Lahore. And I never owned any property. Now I pay $30, but this time it is helping me buy my own house for my wife and children. I am thinking about the future."

Fifty feet from the houses stood a one-room brick schoolhouse. Tiny shoes were piled outside the door as the schoolchildren sat on the floor with books in hand, reciting English words for their three young teachers. In the midst of turbulent times in Pakistan, a country in a race between extremists and leaders building the framework for a more civil society, the school was a profound symbol of progress and achievement. After 3 years, the project was assuming the shape of a real community.

DR. SONO KHANGHARANI UNDERSTANDS community. He was born one of Pakistan's roughly 2.5 million Hindus. Nearly 80 percent of the Hindus living there are from the Dalit caste, the lowest social group, historically consigned to serve as leatherworkers, carcass handlers, street cleaners, and landless laborers.

While the caste system is no longer as prevalent in Indian urban areas, even today in many rural areas Dalits are excluded from living in some places and attending certain schools. Some rural teahouses even keep special cups and utensils for them to use so that higher-caste people won't be sullied by touching the same items. It was this fear of touching that led to the common name for Dalits, Untouchables.

Dr. Sono's father was a cobbler, and by tradition, the son should have followed in those footsteps. But a twist of fate occurred during the partition of India and Pakistan in 1948. Thar, the vast desert region where Dr. Sono was born, is so remote that many Hindus remained in Muslim Pakistan. Dr. Sono completed university and, though faced with opportunities unimagined by his parents, nonetheless chose to return to his community, where too many people still work as bonded laborers toiling in brick-making and carpet-weaving factories or farming tiny plots on feudal lands.

What brought Acumen Fund to this desert place where the poor live in mud huts, own just a few pots and pans, and eke out hardscrabble lives on arid land? The story actually started in India with another social entrepreneur. My colleague Yasmina Zaidman and I met Amitabha Sadangi in 2004, when Acumen Fund was starting to build a portfolio focused on bringing water to the poor. Amitabha, in his forties, had been working for nearly 20 years with poor farmers in India, designing and distributing affordable implements to increase their productivity.

His organization, IDE India, had distributed hundreds of thousands of treadle pumps, rudimentary devices that farmers connect to water sources and activate by standing on them, pumping their legs as if they are on StairMasters. These simple technologies were helping farmers triple and quadruple their income levels, so Amitabha was encouraged to design something for farmers who had access to only minimal levels of water—the poorest of the poor.

Amitabha has one of the world's great smiles, at once conspiratorial and sparkling. He is a solid, sturdy man with a trimmed beard and flashing black eyes. Despite his diamond bracelet and gemstone rings, his laughter and easy way with farmers—and, most important, the way he listens—elicits trust in the most rural areas. Amitabha is always who he is, without ever trying to be someone else.

I was excited by his can-do attitude and pragmatic approach to farming. "Did you ever see drip irrigation in Israel?" he asked me. I had indeed. Drip irrigation was simply a matter of connecting long, skinny pipes to a water source and then extending them down the length of a field, each one along a row where seeds will be planted. Extending from the pipes are microtubes, tiny straws that drip water by the stalk of the plant. The concept was brilliant, but it was designed only for use by large-scale farms, where the systems could be most profitable.

Amitabha looked at the technology and determined that he needed to make it affordable for the poorest farmers. "We needed to follow three core principles," he told me. "The system would have to be so affordable that the farmers could cover the entire cost from the sales of their harvest in less than a year. Second, it had to be fairly easy to use. And third, it had to be infinitely expandable. If the poorest farmers had funds to irrigate only an eighth of an acre, that would be fine because once they earned income, they could buy a second system to double the amount of land irrigated and take themselves out of poverty."

He was frustrated that several of his donors loved what he was doing but hated that he was selling the systems to such poor farmers *and* that the manufacturers of the system, as well as the distributors, were making a profit.

"How can I explain to them that there are 260 million smallholder farmers in India? We have so many millions living on less than $1 a day—and to reach them, we must focus on providing financial incentives to ensure systems are well built. There is charity involved, no doubt, but we need to build systems that will last."

Yasmina and I agreed wholeheartedly and Acumen Fund supported Amitabha's work, eventually helping him to create a for-profit company. Over the next 4 years, Amitabha's organization would sell more than 275,000 systems and see nearly all of the farmers who used them double their yields and incomes, and some even more than that.

I shared Amitabha's story with Dr. Sono in Pakistan when I first met him in the Unilever offices in Karachi. I was struck by his amiable face, the way his eyes smiled, his salt and pepper hair parted on the side and his obvious delight in just about everything. Dr. Sono's eyes widened as we described what drip irrigation was doing to help Indian farmers change their lives. He could imagine a partnership with Unilever, as the company was committed to working in Thar, and with Acumen Fund because the farmers were so eager to change their own lives.

Immediately Dr. Sono decided he wanted to try introducing drip irrigation to the farmers in Thar. We agreed to try our first technology transfer from one investment to another, this time from India to Pakistan. It would be challenging, partially due to the political tensions between the two countries, but we also believed that fostering this kind of learning and trade was a powerful way to build relations. And Dr. Sono seemed to be a great bet. Like Amitabha, he loved working with poor farmers, had built a community of trust, and had committed his life to his work. And like Amitabha, his eyes sparkled when he spoke.

Dr. Sono's first step was to visit India and see for himself what IDE India was doing. It took months to obtain a visa to New Delhi, and only after he arrived did he learn his travel was restricted to certain cities that didn't include the farms where IDE India was working in Aurangabad. Importing the systems caused further difficulties, but these were two men for whom the word "impossible" had little meaning. While it meant another "lost year," Dr. Sono never lost enthusiasm and got to work establishing a demonstration plot so that local farmers could see the drip irrigation in action without taking the risk themselves.

Farmers in general are rational decision makers, but they are a risk-averse lot. Their entire livelihoods—and reputations—depend on successful crops season after season. Risking new technologies could mean losing an entire harvest—disaster from both a food and an income perspective. Dr. Sono understood this, as well as the need to build trust not by telling the farmers about the power of drip irrigation but by enabling them to see it with their own eyes. With Unilever's support, he created a demonstration plot and then, after one successful season, convinced 20 farmers to experiment with the systems on a portion of their land at his expense. Only when they saw increased productivity was he able to sell 100 systems to farmers in Nagar Parkar whose land, all told, accounted for about 1,000 acres, thus starting the first real experiment.

I drove to Thar with Aun to meet Dr. Sono in his office in Mithi, 5½ hours outside Karachi, a long, hot drive (the temperature hovered at about 115°F) through sparse and beautiful scenery—huge tracts of land punctuated by a sugarcane factory here or a brick factory there. Everywhere the land was cracked and seemingly empty of life.

Dr. Sono greeted me with a big hug. I couldn't help but feel happy around him. He hadn't been to see the farmers in Nagar Parkar for a month or so himself and urged us to eat quickly before we got back in the car and started driving the 2½ hours to our destination.

As we moved along the single road through a monochromatic, moonlike desert landscape, the heat intensified. Despite being in an air-conditioned vehicle, sweat poured down our faces. I kept cool by looking at the furry camels sitting below scraggly trees, knowing I had to feel better than they did. With a deep breath of satisfaction, Dr. Sono exclaimed, "Don't you just love the desert in springtime? The air is so fresh and there is so much color everywhere!"

"Please forgive me," I told him, "but I see a palette in shades of gray and tan, and to be honest, I'm not thinking the air is so fresh. It feels like we're caught in a cookstove."

"Then you aren't looking hard enough. See the little buds in all of the trees out there? Look at the pinks and oranges and purple flowers everywhere," he said as he pointed at the horizon. "It is the festivity of spring in those small, small colors. Ah, I love this place."

I asked the driver to stop for a moment and got out of the car to explore. Sure enough, if you looked closely enough, you could observe the beginnings of riotous color, all wanting to explode, held closely in the trees and bushes and flower stalks alongside the road. He was right. Color was everywhere if you didn't insist on the obvious, making it all the more powerful and compelling.

As we traveled in early 2008, the food crisis was just beginning. The farther we got toward what felt like the ends of the earth, the more I understood how the farmers here were facing a perfect storm. The only way they'd historically been able to access water was through wells, which wealthier farmers powered with diesel fuel. Now the cost of oil made operating the wells prohibitively expensive for even the better-off farmers. During the dry season, poor farmers would walk for days to labor on bigger farms for usually no more than 50¢ or a dollar a day. With this they were expected to buy food for their families. High prices now made that untenable.

Dr. Sono's experiment depended on providing the farmers with water. Solar power was beyond their capacity to purchase, so he negotiated with the government's Poverty Alleviation Program to provide 80 percent of the cost of a solar pump and his organization covered the rest. With infrastructure free for the farmers, those in the experiment had to risk only the cost of the drip system itself. Whether it would work, neither of us knew.

Two and a half hours into this second leg of the drive, we finally reached our destination. At the distant horizon, I saw a sliver of yellow expanding slowly until we could make out an enormous field of sunflowers, bright yellow and green against the blue sky. The vision made us giggle like little kids.

"This is the dry season in the desert, when it is so hard to grow things on small farms," Dr. Sono laughed. "Can you believe it?"

At the end of the field, we stopped to admire the sunflowers growing 7 feet tall. Breathless, I felt a deep emotion well up inside me, perhaps because of the presence of new life, of birth on fallow land, of hope in a place too easily forgotten and abandoned. The drama of nature was one of gentleness, of sustainability coming from little plastic pipes laid along the earth's surface, conserving every drop of water and giving life where nothing but starched hunger had stood before.

As Mary Koinange used to say in the Nairobi slums, "Water is life."

At once, nine tall men began walking toward us from different parts of the field—a father and his eight sons, all dressed in farmer whites, each one more handsome than the next, surrounded by 15 or 20 little boys. Together this family owned about 7 acres that served as their sole livelihood, though it was possible to cultivate during only 6 months of each year. Rajan, the father, was a tall man whose green plaid turban capped a wise, leathered, mustachioed face with kind hazel eyes that reminded me of my father's. He gazed proudly at the flowers that would be sold to the government at a guaranteed price.

Behind him, eight large blue solar panels angled toward the sun stood behind a well that pumped enough water for the drip irrigation. "How is it working?" we asked.

"Not a single problem," he smiled.

The tiny lines of IDE India's drip irrigation tubing lay in straight rows beside the healthy plant stalks. Sons and grandsons eagerly pointed to the workmanship required to properly lay out the field. "Our need for pesticide is greatly reduced," said one of the sons.

Rajan didn't know yet how much income the field would generate. "But," he added, "this is the best yield we've ever seen on this land, even in the good seasons."

I tried imagining a family of 50 people trekking across the desert in 110°F heat with only their livestock in tow to test their luck as day laborers.

"I am an old man now," Rajan told us, "and this is the first time in my life that I've remained on my land. Finally, we can plan for the future."

He pointed to a compound of little huts at the edge of one of the fields. "Come and see our home."

Built on slightly higher ground, the compound was a circle of sleeping huts, each constructed of mud and a thatched roof. The doorways were small and low, requiring visitors to duck upon entering. The main hut, where the grandmother and eldest wives slept, contained only a clay storage trunk and a small shelf built along the wall with circles of bright-colored paint above it. A few plates and utensils stood on the shelf, "out of children's reach," the grandmother told me.

In the middle of the compound, a depression in the ground, about 2 or 3 feet long and 1½ feet wide, served as the stove. The women wanted to find something safer because in the windy season sparks could too easily be blown to the roofs. A stone mortar and wooden pestle sat beside the cooking area, waiting for the women to grind grains and leaves into family meals.

Next to another hut alongside two clay vessels holding grains stood a large mill, a flat stone that turned with great effort to transform wheat into flour for the women to make chapatis. There were blankets on the floor of each hut, though I didn't imagine they would provide much warmth on cold desert nights.

The women, young and old, were captivating, dressed in gauzy skirts and sequined tops in brilliant colors that reminded me of peacocks and other exotic birds. The married women wore white plastic bracelets on their arms, sometimes 50 or more. Their lips were painted pink, and many wore dark kohl, making their eyes even more arresting. Most wore colorful veils over their dark hair.

The grandmother, slender and beautiful, wore a bright turquoise top and a fuchsia and blue veil. Though her dark skin was weathered by the sun and she had birthed a dozen children, she looked like a young woman.

"You must be happy not to have to leave your home this season," I said to her.

She smiled broadly and pressed her two hands together in a warm greeting.

"Did you used to fear leaving your things behind before?" I asked.

"What things?" she laughed. "We have only a few plates and cups for drinking and some urns for carrying water. The only ones who come here when we're gone are the termites, and they eat the straw from our roofs. There are no other guests."

"But the termites must appreciate you, at least."

"Oh, yes," she laughed, "very, very much."

We asked Rajan what he would do now that he had income.

"My children and their children have never attended school," he told us. "I would like to see my grandchildren educated."

Someone asked him if that included his daughters. "Yes," he answered.

"But they might stop veiling and become more progressive," the man challenged.

Rajan responded gently that it would be a good thing for the girls. "I want them to attend school so that they will not be so discriminated against and also so that they will not discriminate against others."

There is no more powerful reminder of the dignity to be found in making one's own choices than Rajan's endless sunflower fields shouting out "Life!" in the arid desert.

The market can serve as a listening device: Through our experience with drip irrigation, we began to see the power of providing smallholder farmers with different inputs along the supply chain so they could increase their productivity. Think of all the opportunities to improve a farmer's crop. In addition to drip irrigation, improved seeds and fertilizers that are priced affordably can improve yields by 30 percent. Farmers also lose 30 percent of their potential proceeds because there are no storage facilities. We're exploring a solar tunnel that can dry grains more quickly so a farmer will ultimately have more to sell. Transporting the produce is another issue. And so is finding markets that will provide adequate profit margins to the farmer. If we think about the 400 million smallholder farmers as producers upon whom all of us rely, then there are myriad ways to support their growth and income and feed the world.

Of course, the more we learn about how to sell productive inputs to farmers, the more we learn about the distortions the aid industry can foist upon those same farmers. When there *is* a crisis in a place like Kenya or southern Pakistan, the United States and Europe will send "free food" that is purchased at highly subsidized prices from their own farmers rather than sending the money to purchase the produce of local farmers. The world has a long way to go, but these relatively small experiments are teaching us how much is possible if we build trust, show the farmers what is possible, provide them with technical assistance, and connect them to markets.

William Gibson wrote, "The future is here; it is just not widely distributed yet." It shouldn't be all that difficult, but we have to increase our sense of urgency and allow farmers to change their lives and change the world in doing so.

CHAPTER 15

TAKING IT TO SCALE

"I would not give a fig for the simplicity this side of complexity, but I would give my life for the simplicity on the other side of complexity."

—OLIVER WENDELL HOLMES

It's hard to imagine a greater contrast to Pakistan's harsh desert clime than the lush green hills of Tanzania. There, in 2004, in a tiny village called Usa River, I met another unforgettable man for whom a simple technology was life changing. His name was Eliarehemu, and his hut was situated on a stamp-size patch of dirt that had a single stalk of maize growing outside his front door. He was wearing the only clothing he owned, an ancient, tattered, dirty hat and a ripped shirt he buttoned hurriedly as we approached. His pants, unworthy of even a scarecrow, were a patchwork of threads sewn over places where they had torn apart. His hands were battered, thick, and tough, like sandpaper to the touch, but his smile was likable and easy.

At that time, he'd estimated his earnings as a day laborer in nearby fields at about $6 a month, but he was quick to tell us that malaria often kept him from working. "Sometimes it is so hard to move when you have malaria. You just stay inside and shake and try to sleep off the terrible ache in your head."

Like many low-income Africans, Eliarehemu lived nearly full-time with the disease, scrounging together a few cents to buy chloroquine tablets when he felt sick but unable to take the entire treatment due to the cost. As soon as he felt better, he'd cease taking the medication, consigning himself to living in a weakened state. The presence of rice fields throughout Usa River meant there was a lot of standing water where mosquitoes bred, making malaria endemic. By failing to complete the required chloroquine regimen, Eliarehemu and hundreds of millions like him also contributed to making the disease more resistant to the drug, exacerbating the problem.

In that first year, Eliarehemu told me spiritedly that he was feeling healthier, though he looked old, worn down, and deeply impoverished. "I am just too happy now that I have this bed net," he said, never mentioning that he had no bed under which to tuck it. He simply connected the bed net to the rafters of his house and then let it drape to the mud floor on which he laid his body.

What struck me most, that first time meeting Eliarehemu, were his gratitude and joy despite how little he had in the world. A simple gift of a bed net, something to which everyone should have access, changed his life.

"You see, I sleep peacefully through the night now, without the noise of mosquitoes circling and biting," he told me while holding his hands to his face like a baby napping, smiling with contentment.

Each year I visited Eliarehemu, he appeared healthier, and with health came more work and income. He'd seeded a garden of corn, which had begun to flourish, and built a fence around his hut to keep the animals away from his crop. Two shirts hung on a simple line strung inside his modest home. All the while, we were developing a sweet acquaintance. I took photos of him at each visit and once brought him a bag of fine chocolates.

Three years after I met Eliarehemu, he remained free of malaria and stood proudly by the stalks of maize now literally towering over our heads.

"I have enough now," he said, "to feed myself through the year. And maybe next year, there will be some left to sell." He continued to work at nearby rice farms to earn cash and had begun studying at the local church in the evenings.

"Oh, yes!" he exclaimed in English, though I hadn't asked a question. "I am feeling strong now."

"Where did you learn English?" I asked, laughing.

"The pastor is teaching me," he said.

Then he switched back to Swahili and asked me to come into his hut. On the floor was a mattress with sheets, and for the first time, the bed net could be tucked underneath it.

When I asked his age, he said with a smile, "I am 66 years old."

Since he could now properly tuck in the bed net, he'd moved the bed net material that had covered his eaves to the latrine outdoors.

"I know that the mosquitoes can infect me if I leave in the night to go to the bathroom, so I need protection there, too," he said sagely.

I could only imagine what it must have felt like for Eliarehemu, at age 66, to have a soft place to lay his head for the first time in his life, to sleep on a cushion instead of the cold dirt floor. I also saw matches and soap and a couple of bowls, all new—purchased with the efforts of a man who finally knew what it felt like to be healthy.

Still in the hut, Eliarehemu leaned over and whispered, "Do you remember those chocolates you brought to me the last time?"

When I nodded, he grinned widely. "I ate one piece, just one, every night for nearly 3 months and, oh, the happy feeling it gave me."

I told him I'd try to find more, though I couldn't promise the same quality. He shrugged and said he'd be happy with anything, as long as it was chocolate.

It was the first time he'd even hinted that he wanted something from me. He was a poor man, but a proud one. I promised to bring chocolates next time and then shared some photos I'd taken of him over the past 3 years.

At the first one, he grimaced and whispered, "I am so old, so old."

"Oh no," I said, "you were sick then. Now you are healthy and beautiful. You've even become a bit fat."

He shook his head worriedly. "I am too old."

Quickly, I turned the pages and showed him a recent photo of himself standing in clean clothes, sporting a much fuller face and figure.

"Ah, I see! I see!" he exclaimed as a wide smile spread across his face. He then patted me on the back and pronounced each of his words slowly and carefully, his eyes dancing, as he happily exhaled. "We've done well."

He had done well indeed, and except for the gift of a simple tool—just one bed net, plus some belief from people around him—he had done it all himself.

ANECDOTES ARE POWERFUL IN that they show possibility. One bed net used regularly vastly improved a poor man's health, restoring his strength so that he could work, farm his own land, increase his income, and change his life. There is a strong correlation between investing in health care for people and enhancing their ability to earn income, and with higher incomes come increased investment in their children's educations and lower population rates.

The question then becomes how to ensure that hundreds of millions of nets are distributed effectively and used properly by the people who need them. But that cannot be the only question, for anecdotes can also be misleading. While bed nets are one answer, they are not the only answer. Continuing to look for entrepreneurial innovation enables us to find better and better solutions to extremely complex problems.

Malaria is one of the world's biggest killers, taking the lives of between 1 and 2 million people every year. About 90 percent of these cases are in Africa, and three-quarters of those who contract malaria are women and children. I will never forget my bout with malaria when I lived in Kigali, nor the people I knew who died from it. What it means for Africa is staggering losses of life and human productivity.

Imagine a million people—the entire population of a big city—dying every year. It's estimated that the continent loses about $13 billion yearly because each time someone gets the disease, she or he usually stops working for a week to 10 days. If you take the most conservative estimate of 300 million cases and reduce it by the 150 million cases in children, then you are still looking at a minimum of 150 million lost workweeks each year.

In 2002, we were approached by representatives of a collaboration of UNICEF, Sumitomo Chemical, and Exxon Mobil to see if we might participate in an effort to manufacture a long-lasting, insecticide-treated bed net in Africa for distribution there. Traditionally, people used simple polyester-based nets to cover their beds at night, but there were two big problems with them. First, they ripped easily, and once there was a hole in the net, mosquitoes could easily sneak through to find their victims. Second, continued efficacy required that a person dip the bed net in an insecticide every 3 to 6 months. Humans being humans, few users went to the trouble of dipping the nets. Most of the bed nets in people's homes became fairly worthless after just a few months of use.

Sumitomo Chemical Company of Japan had developed a method of impregnating a polyethylene-based netting material with organic insecticide and created a bed net that could last for 5 years without redipping. The technology itself could revolutionize malaria control. The challenges, however, were to produce enough bed nets to cover a majority of people, to distribute the nets so that people actually got them, and to ensure that once they had a bed net, they used it properly.

Critical to producing the bed nets was identifying an African entrepreneur capable of taking this new technology, transferring it effectively to Africa, and financing a new, unproven venture. This is where Acumen Fund came in.

After reviewing a number of different businesses, Anuj Shah of A to Z Textiles emerged as the best entrepreneur on whom to take a risk. Based in Arusha, Tanzania, the family-owned company had already operated successfully for a quarter century in a tough business environment. Employing 1,000 people, it produced both textiles and plastics. Anuj, the CEO, was smart, ambitious, driven, and hardworking, and had a reputation for follow-through. Acumen Fund provided a loan for the first bed net–weaving machines, and the company worked with Sumitomo to bring a new bed net–manufacturing process to Africa. I remember thinking that if the company produced 150,000 nets a year, we would have made a major contribution.

On my first visit to A to Z, I was reminded of factories in Bangladesh that were efficient, clean, bright, and busy, with women everywhere. Upstairs, Anuj pointed to rows and rows of women sitting behind their sewing machines, producing nets and then handing them over to quality control for testing and packaging. To check the quality of the nets, the women would hang them and stand inside, examining them for unintended holes and tears. They looked like Matisse dancers, fluid figures moving gracefully in a world of blue gauze. The feeling of productivity was everywhere. Anuj proudly told me that production rates were already comparable to those in China.

I sat next to a beautiful, round-faced young seamstress who had worked at the company for 8 months, sewed 160 nets a day, and earned enough at A to Z to move into town and pay for her father's cataract operation. She was in no hurry to marry. Before working there, she'd been selling vegetables on the street, but with a real job, her life was completely different. That was in early 2004.

By 2008, due to the relentless entrepreneurial spirit and determination of Anuj and his team, more than 7,000 women were working with A to Z. Assuming that each job helps support five people, that means more than 35,000 individuals are directly touched by production of a much-needed item for the health of the poor. In quantitative terms, it translates to more than $3 million in new wages to the local economy.

Anuj's third-generation company now supplies 16 million nets a year, more than 10 percent of all long-lasting insecticide-treated nets globally. A to Z is now providing enough bed nets to cover more than 20 million people a year, helping them retain their productivity while saving thousands of lives.

At more than 70,000 square feet, the company's new factory, a joint venture with Sumitomo, is enormous, well lit, and always humming. Women and men alike wear uniforms; there is an aura of professionalism throughout the facility. Though energy supply is still a major problem in Arusha, A to Z has a room full of generators that kick in during the daily brownouts so that work can continue uninterrupted.

The production of a lifesaving product is just the beginning. Identifying the right approaches to marketing and distributing it is where the challenge lies. While most long-lasting bed nets are given away free with support from the Global Fund and UNICEF, many players, including government and aid agencies, each with its own set of incentives, have to be figured into the equation. Moreover, the roads in many parts of Africa are difficult to travel and sometimes impassable. All these factors are challenging obstacles—and great opportunities.

While Acumen Fund believes in the goal of promoting universal access to life-saving bed nets, we are also committed to experimenting with various private sector approaches to distribution. We and A to Z agreed to try selling nets at different price points, not only to low-income consumers but to companies that had an economic incentive to protect their workers from the disease. Innovation requires experimentation; no one has the answers for solving poverty yet. The total price needed to make and then distribute a bed net to a poor woman in Africa is about $10. We knew that some level of subsidy was needed and wanted to determine how much in order to make the nets available to everyone.

One key assumption we made was that there might be room for a small private market, given that overall production of the long-lasting nets wasn't large enough to reach everyone. This was corroborated when my colleague Molly visited a village of about 4,000 in Zanzibar and saw that a free program had delivered 700 nets to pregnant women and children, the groups included in the United Nations' Millennium Development Goals. The village chief was tremendously grateful for the gift but frustrated that the other 3,000 villagers had no access. Because only giveaway programs were made available—and these were bound to serving only pregnant women and children under age 5—there were no bed nets in the local markets for other people to buy. Having seen the effectiveness of bed nets, many of those villagers were willing to pay as much as $4, but they couldn't find them at any price.

We experimented with selling bed nets at different prices and studied what people might be willing to pay for bed nets in various situations. While some villagers were indeed willing to pay $3 or $4, the majority of rural East Africans moved more quickly to buy them at a $1 price point, and still, a large group couldn't afford to pay anything. To complement this, A to Z agreed to experiment with building a small sales force of women to see what would happen if they tried selling bed nets door-to-door.

The first approach was to build a sort of Tupperware model whereby individual women would sell nets door-to-door and at small house parties. In the first month, three of the women absconded with 17 nets. Having anticipated some amount of stealing early on in the process, A to Z had required the women to leave behind a minimum of two guarantors at the factory, each of whom would be responsible to make full payment for any missing or stolen nets. They held to their policy and no nets were taken after that.

One of the most charismatic saleswomen demonstrated how she pitched the sale of nets to her neighbors at a trial house party. The typical public health language of "shoulds" and "musts" was nowhere in evidence.

"You put the bed net on your floor," the big woman with two long braids bellowed in her baritone voice, "and all the bugs go away, not just the mosquitoes. Can you imagine? You can sleep the whole night long because there is no buzzing in your ears—and your children will do better in school because they won't be so tired."

She continued, "The color is beautiful, and you can hang the nets in your windows so that your neighbors know how much you care about your family." Almost as an afterthought, she mentioned that the bed nets would protect the children from malaria.

Beauty, vanity, status, and comfort: These are the levers that are pulled the world over as we make our decisions. The rich hold no monopoly on any of it. But we're a long way from integrating the way people actually make decisions into public policy instead of how we think they should make them.

A to Z experimented with a number of distribution channels, and two proved promising. Tanzanian companies were willing to buy the nets at a price of $3 or $4 and sell them for the same price to their employees through a payroll-deduction program. A to Z also sold nets off its own trucks when distributing other products in rural areas. Boys with bicycles would buy the nets and then resell them in local markets.

Finding such modes of distribution reminded me of Haddy, the Gambian fertilizer seller I'd met years before. The solution focused on building on systems already in place, systems that worked for the poor and increased their overall levels of choice. I also thought of Charlotte, who wished she could accept the free antiretroviral drugs but appreciated that at least she could afford the European pills in the marketplace that suited her body's needs.

Indeed, when we talk to women in rural areas, they push us to think of more creative solutions altogether. It can be hot and sticky under the nets, and you are vulnerable to mosquitoes if you walk around inside the house or go to the bathroom at night. Consequently, we've been working with a brilliant scientist who has lived for more than two decades in Africa and has been developing a way to cover the walls of a rural home to protect the household not just from malaria, but from all sorts of insect-borne diseases.

We started with a single approach—financing a technology transfer by investing in an African entrepreneur to bring a critical good to Africans. Through the work, we learned a lot about how people make decisions and what it might take to build an alternative distribution system. We also learned that while free bed nets are key to reaching the masses, there is also a place for market mechanisms that put malaria bed nets in shops so anyone who needs them can get them without having to hope that a clinic will provide them, at least until public health policies are reliable enough to ensure truly universal access.

Public health is the thorniest area for change, but not an impossible one. So much can be learned by listening to the market: Indeed, this process may lead to insights about how to price insurance products for the very poor so we'll have a more rational system for bringing affordable, critical goods to them in a way that is reliable and accessible. Malaria bed nets might be one component of such a program, which would have to be built from the perspective of the people who actually use it.

What also makes the process of growing solutions to poverty complex is the noise we hear in the media and among thought leaders who believe their way is the only way. They suffer from a paucity of listening skills— just at the time when listening has never been more important. Today's media are highlighting a major debate between those who think that everyone in Africa should be given a free bed net to protect him or her from malaria and those who believe that the bed nets should be sold at an affordable price.

The free-nets side cites fast coverage ratios and immediate reductions in malaria. And it's true: Malaria rates fall dramatically when an entire village is given free nets. Social marketing advocates—those who believe that nets should be sold—argue that giveaway programs typically result in quick fixes that don't last and point to evidence in Ethiopia and other countries where, only a few years after net distribution, actual usage rates fell precipitously. This, too, is true.

So often we ask ourselves the *wrong question*. When it comes to a disease like malaria, the question should not be whether bed nets are sold or given away free. Both distribution methods have their place in a broader attack on the disease. The question instead is, What does it take to eradicate malaria? Without a reliable source of bed nets, people may find themselves abruptly cut off from a supply when they most need it. It's not "either-or," but rather "both-and."

We have to be careful, as well, that the world's focus on bed nets doesn't hold back other potential innovations. The Bill and Melinda Gates Foundation has put hundreds of millions of dollars into researching a malaria vaccine, and efforts are under way to create a line of house paints that kill mosquitoes but are safe for humans to touch. These are exciting possibilities that will work only if the world learns how to collaborate in a system-wide assault on the disease.

In the 21st century, private-sector approaches fueled in large part by creative philanthropy will be vital to solving public-sector problems. Almost nowhere is such innovation needed more than in supplying water. Poor farmers in arid regions can't find enough of it to irrigate their crops. People the world over contract diseases from dirty water; an enormous global burden of disease is due to unsafe water and poor sanitation. Increasingly, we're seeing skirmishes that may lead to big wars in this century over who has rights to water.

Meanwhile, the water table in India alone is declining by 6 meters (20 feet) a year. Solving water-related issues is key. Again, no one has all the answers. If they did, we wouldn't have a world where 1.2 billion—or one in five of us—have no access to a glass of clean water.

As with public health, our approach to water at Acumen Fund has been to experiment and innovate to find solutions that can inform the public debate and show the way to wide-scale change. In India, for example, the platforms of many state governments have held largely that water is a human right and should be given free to everyone. At the same time, more than 180 million Indians have no access to safe, affordable water.

Since Acumen Fund started working on water, I have been invited numerous times to sit on panels focused on determining whether water is a human right or its ownership should be privatized. Again, the question is wrong. People need water to live, and there is no better intervention to improve health on a global scale than bringing safe, affordable water to as many people as possible. But how do we make sure it can be distributed to the poor in a sustainable way? How do we ensure that all people have access at least to the minimum amount of water needed to live healthy lives? We're trying to find those brave entrepreneurs who are determined to discover the answers.

Tralance Addy is a Ghanaian entrepreneur who, after a long career at Johnson & Johnson, turned his energies toward creating a company that would deliver safe, affordable water to low-income rural communities. He identified an ultraviolet filtration technology developed by Ashok Gadgil at the University of California at Berkeley, and set off to introduce this new technology to the developing world. In the Philippines, Tralance learned that he was selling the wrong thing to poor villages: People didn't actually care about what kind of technology was cleaning their water. Instead, they wanted a service that was reliable, affordable, and safe. Tralance thus shifted his focus from the technology to building the right distribution system.

We met Tralance when, armed with these lessons, he decided to establish the business in India. Along with other early investors, Acumen Fund made an equity investment of $600,000 into the new company that now had a simple business model. WHI would sell a $50,000 filtration system to a local entrepreneur with the capability of running a small business serving around 5,000 people at village level. Individuals would buy the water at affordable prices, and the revenues would eventually cover the costs of running the company. Tralance had a vision of serving millions this way, and we bet that he could do it, though the odds were against him. Long distances, lack of bank credit, terrible roads, and a sense of fatalism among many villagers meant that only the most patient of investors would ultimately be rewarded.

I and several Acumen partners went to visit WHI's first facility in 2005, when the company was establishing new operations in India. Our first stop was Vijayawada, a small city by Indian standards with a population of about a million people. We'd taken a long, hot, overnight train ride from Hyderabad to arrive just before dawn so we could drive another 3 hours to visit the company's first village operation. We were all eager to get a better sense of what it took to bring safe water to people who'd not previously had access—to underserved markets that had been for too long invisible.

Despite the early hour, the city was teeming. Colorful trucks overflowing with baskets and fruits, furniture and people, rumbled along Vijayawada's crowded early morning streets. Women walked with pots of water tucked under arms covered with colorful bangles. Others carried metal containers on their heads. Morning is the time for fetching water. Three-wheelers and bicycles competed audaciously in a dangerous game of chicken with the big bully vans and trucks that often carried signs on the back saying, "Please sound horn, please."

As soon as the car reached the outskirts of Vijayawada, we found ourselves on a narrow road lined with palm trees and green fields as far as the eye could see. Thatched huts dotted the landscape, and every so often we would come across two women in saris of fuchsia or chartreuse fluttering against the blue sky. Potholes riddled the road, and we weaved carefully from side to side. Then the road was smooth again, though I doubt we ever exceeded 30 mph as we passed bicycles, people, and cows. Women laid just-washed brightly colored clothes on flat rocks to dry in the sun. A white Ambassador car whose hood was bedecked with yellow marigolds puttered along with its old men and women passengers nodding to the past.

Flowers for celebration, for mourning, for making life more beautiful: India is filled with flowers—jasmine and gardenia, marigold and bird-of-paradise. An ox stood alongside a cart painted with folkloric landscapes: Life was beautiful.

After a 2-hour drive, we entered a village area called a *panchayat* and moved along a single road toward clusters of houses. In the distance, we could see the WHI structure, an alien-looking, diamond-shaped dome colored electric blue. People had come to the site using all sorts of forms of transport. Boys walked forward with plastic containers and filled them from one of the three taps. Young men drove up on motorbikes and bicycles, rickshaws and three-wheelers. One man pushed a huge cart that carried 9 or 10 of the 15-liter containers. On average, the center was already selling 300 containers a day at their first facility—an early sign of success.

I was struck most of all by the fact that not a single woman approached the plant to buy water. I remember standing next to a man years ago as we watched a woman carrying not one but two pots on her head still walking gracefully. As I marveled at her expertise, the man had said, "Well, you know, women are built for that. They have stronger necks relative to men."

"I see," I had hummed, not wanting to get into this particular conversation with a stranger on the street. I remembered the same sentiment voiced so many years ago by Chowdury, the man who drove me through the desert on a motorcycle. For 20 years, I've seen attempts made to reduce women's labor based on the assumption that the more time women have free from daily chores, the more they can increase their income, care for their families, even have some leisure. But most attempts failed. Now, with no focus on gender, for some reason this new plant was enticing men to carry water. Of course, they weren't carrying the water themselves, but hiring boys with bikes, rickshaws, and taxis. But what mattered was the change itself.

A poultry farmer with a handlebar mustache and a big, intelligent smile explained that he purchased, on average, 10 containers a day. He fed the water to his chickens—about 7,000 of them, a big jump from the 5,000 he'd been raising before he had clean water, which, he said, made medicines unnecessary and enabled his chickens to grow about 20 percent more quickly.

He was there to ask WHI to allow him to pipe water to his farm, but they refused, explaining that it would be too easy for people to steal water by drilling into the pipes. The farmer wasn't convinced. He said he would pay for it, protect it, and take care of it. The group asked him to think about purchasing a water storage unit instead, at least as an intermediate step. This would allow him to control flow and reduce time spent carrying water. I was struck by his entrepreneurial spirit and sophistication. He knew he was the company's most important customer, and he was bent on changing his life.

We wondered aloud why not every villager was rushing to buy safe drinking water. After all, the farmers' chickens were visibly healthier, and families drinking safe water would likely see much lower health care bills. But technical changes are easier to effect than behavioral ones. To reach out to the rural villagers, WHI thus decided to partner with Naandi Foundation, a local NGO that understood the communities where the company hoped to work and had great experience in helping villages adapt new technologies, build distribution systems, and work effectively with local governments. This kind of partnership between for-profit companies having skill in delivering goods and services and nonprofits with an understanding of poor communities and a will to ensure they are protected is an important model for the future, one that depends on the blurring of lines dividing private and public sectors.

As one of the first investors in WHI, Acumen Fund has been working with the company for more than 4 years. In that period of time, we've collaborated on a number of projects, including redesigning the original plant structure so that the existing outlets are streamlined, simple to build, unobtrusive, and easy to maintain. WHI deserves credit for experimenting with its design, recognizing shortfalls, and changing quickly to a better model.

We also worked together to bring bank credit into rural areas so that villages could borrow the capital needed to install a plant in the first place. Acumen Fund used our *patient capital* to provide a 30 percent first-loss guarantee to ICICI, India's second largest commercial bank. We could have lent directly for village operations, but this approach would bring more money into underserved areas. Over time, we reasoned, if the business model worked, the banks would become more comfortable with lending and we could reduce our guarantee.

As it turned out, in less than a year, because of WHI's track record, Acumen was able to provide a second guarantee with a 15 percent loss coverage. In other words, this time, a $1 million guarantee from Acumen released $8 million in commercial loans to build rural water systems.

After spending a few hours at the water facility, we walked through the village. Most people lived in thatched huts or concrete houses, all of which were neat and clean. Women gathered at the wells, gossiping and laughing while they pulled the water from the ground. They still carried the well water to the river's edge for washing. All along the river, women were laundering their clothes: Water was at the center of life. Young schoolgirls in green skirts and white blouses carried their books, and white egrets sat atop haystacks and cattle. As both men and women worked in the surrounding fields, at least some of their children were being watched in a tiny day-care center next to one of several small temples: a clear source of community pride.

Since that visit in 2005, WHI has grown to serve more than 200 villages with more than 350,000 customers. And it has raised more than $12 million in additional capital. Now the goal is to issue a large bond in order to reach millions of people with safe water.

Recently, I visited another WHI plant, more urban but still seemingly in the middle of nowhere, at the edge of a beautiful lotus pond ringed by palm trees and little houses with thatched roofs. Like many of the WHI installations, the plant was situated close to the government water source that provided free but undrinkable water. This way, customers could pick up the free water for washing and then pay for what they needed for drinking and cooking.

Most of the people in the village worked as laborers in the nearby rice mills or as farmers, earning between $1 and $3 a day. In the case of this WHI site, the Lions Club had donated the initial plant, which the community was responsible for running as a viable business. A cheerful village resident managed the plant on a daily basis and oversaw several employees while also talking incessantly to a stream of customers waiting to purchase their families' water supply for the following few days.

A mustached customer wearing the uniform of an engineer, a checked shirt with a pair of reading glasses tucked in the pocket and a baseball cap, sauntered up to the plant. In fact, he turned out not to be an engineer, but a day laborer working on odd jobs. But you could sense his drive and ambition by the very way he walked and dressed. When I asked him when he had started buying water from WHI, he replied that he'd started on the first day of the plant's existence.

Previously, he'd had to walk a fair distance to pay a high price for safe water. He liked the WHI price of about a rupee per liter, enjoyed the taste of this water more, and appreciated the plant's proximity to his family's home. I asked whether his life had changed. He nodded, saying that the family experienced less diarrhea and other common diseases. He thought the price was right and the service, satisfactory. As I watched the man place his filled container on his bicycle and pedal away, I thought about how smart he was, how much he would do for his family if only he had the opportunities.

If Acumen Fund were a normal investment firm or even a socially responsible investment firm, we would be thrilled by the growing financial progress of WHI and leave it at that. But we started Acumen Fund because we believed the markets were the starting point and not the endgame for solving problems of poverty. Our team wants to understand what it takes to bring the greatest number of people safe water in a way that is affordable, reaches millions, and sustains itself over time.

It was important to track what people did with the water once it arrived at their homes. WHI sells the water in 15-liter sanitary plastic containers, which is a great start. However, a problem arises when some customers pour the water into contaminated clay pitchers. People in rural Andhra Pradesh—from the poorest Rajput woman to a maharaja—all seem to prefer clay to plastic or glass for their water because it has evaporative qualities that make it serve as a natural cooler. This we discovered while collaborating with the design firm IDEO, which shares Acumen Fund's belief in systems that build customer-focused solutions. Though IDEO works with some of the world's largest companies, the framework for listening to people of any economic stratum is the same. IDEO preferred not to try and convince low-income people that they should switch to plastic water containers, but rather to see whether it was possible to design clay containers that could be sanitized regularly.

We also have been working with the Gates Foundation and a global research organization to listen to the poor to try and understand what really happens when people start drinking safe water. We want to gain insights into how to get more people to do so. Changing any kind of behavior is not easy. And in places like rural India, most people think water comes from God, so there is a lot of pressure to accept whatever God decides to give you. Convincing people that they nonetheless have a choice about the kind of water they drink is neither easy nor free. It is why nonprofit groups like Naandi are so important to the larger solution.

In this case, Acumen Fund works with WHI, a for-profit company that partners with Naandi, a local NGO. We guarantee loans for and have a working relationship with a commercial bank, ICICI. We work closely with the Gates Foundation and with the nonprofit Research Triangle Institute and have embarked on a joint venture with a for-profit design firm. Most villages that want to install a plant are required to get the blessing of the local *panchayat,* or government official. And the communication and negotiation, the learning, failing, succeeding, and learning all over again require real and long-term commitments from the different players involved. It isn't a simple solution, but the problem isn't simple, either, though each part of the answer is pretty straightforward.

It is this commitment across sectors, disciplines, geography, and profit status, as well as a focus on a common goal that enables WHI to thrive and increasingly become a symbol of what is possible in using markets as part of a solution. WHI is bringing one of the most precious resources on earth to the world's very poor and doing so in a way that makes sense, creates jobs, and respects the integrity and needs of all people. Doing this well requires a certain kind of leadership, one that starts with listening, knows how to collaborate, is not satisfied with easy but incomplete answers, and is driven by finding solutions for those with the least in a single world community. What is exciting is that we're starting to find such leaders and can see many more coming along the long row we need to hoe together.

CHAPTER 16

THE WORLD WE DREAM, THE FUTURE WE CREATE TOGETHER

"Few will have the greatness to bend history itself;
but each of us can work to change a small portion of events, and in the total
of all those acts will be written the history of this generation."

—ROBERT F. KENNEDY

Thirty summers have passed since I gave away the blue sweater that ended up on a little Rwandan boy. Since then, the world has greatly changed. The boy I encountered had never seen a television show, made a telephone call, or taken a photograph, whereas his counterpart today, an urban youth wearing secondhand clothes in Kigali, is likely to have access to a cell phone and the Internet. As for my counterpart, today's 20-something professional working in Kigali won't feel the isolation I did; she is likely to e-mail and call her friends on Skype at least once a day and check her local newspaper on the Internet to learn about the goings-on at home. We have the tools to know one another and the resources to create a future in which every human being, rich or poor, has a real chance to pursue a life of greater purpose.

I have changed, too. After more than 20 years of working in Africa, India, and Pakistan, I've learned that solutions to poverty must be driven by discipline, accountability, and market strength, not easy sentimentality. I've learned that many of the answers to poverty lie in the space between the market and charity and that what is needed most of all is moral leadership willing to build solutions from the perspectives of poor people themselves rather than imposing grand theories and plans upon them.

I've learned that people usually tell you the truth if you listen hard enough. If you don't, you'll hear what they *think* you want to hear.

I've learned that there is no currency like trust and no catalyst like hope. There is nothing worse for building relationships than pandering, on one hand, or preaching, on the other. And the most important quality we must all strengthen in ourselves is that of deep human empathy, for that will provide the most hope of all—and the foundation for our collective survival.

I've learned that generosity is far easier than justice and that, in the highly distorted markets of the poor, it is all too easy to veer only toward the charitable, to have low—or no—expectations for low-income people. This does nothing but reaffirm prejudices on all sides.

I've learned how profoundly the world is interconnected in a single economy linking all parts of the globe. Extraordinary wealth has been generated by this global economy, and millions of people have been lifted out of poverty. Yet it brings as much danger as hope unless and until every single one of us gets a fair chance to participate.

I have learned all of this through the extraordinary people I have had the privilege to know, the colleagues with whom I have worked, my fellow travelers, and the family and friends I have loved. One of my favorite lines from Tennyson's "Ulysses" is "I am a part of all that I have met." And they—every one of them, good and bad—are a part of me.

A grandmother and a little girl, one from Kenya, the other, Pakistan, stand out as reminders of the extraordinary capacity of the human spirit. I met Beatrice, a member of Jamii Bora, a nonprofit organization started with the savings of 50 beggar families in Nairobi that has grown to more than 200,000 slum dwellers. Acumen Fund has been supporting the organization's efforts to build and sell 2,000 houses in a new, ecologically sound development.

A woman with a wide, square face, her hair pinned neatly in a bun, Beatrice had rodlike posture and looked at me directly when she spoke. She bore and raised eight children in Mathare Valley, one of Kenya's poorest and toughest slums, where I danced with the women on that rainy night so long ago. She worked constantly, never resting, earning little but still ensuring that all of her children were raised properly and given a good education; this was one of her proudest accomplishments.

No one could have prepared her for the shock of learning that her eldest son and his wife were dying of AIDS, leaving her to care for their four children. A year later, another child passed away, and then another.

By 2000, every single one of her children had died, leaving her with a dozen grandchildren to raise, though she had neither a husband nor a real source of income.

"I was so desperate," she said, her hands clasped gently in front of her, her round eyes shaded with sorrow. "I thought of making porridge and putting poison in it to end the lives of the children and myself. I could think of no way to take care of everyone."

A friend told her about Jamii Bora and helped her save so she could earn the right to take a loan from the organization. Beatrice borrowed enough to start selling french fries, and as she succeeded, she borrowed more and more, adding rooms to her house so she could rent them, and establishing a water kiosk as well as a butcher shop and a hair salon.

Today, Beatrice has five businesses, 11 employees, and 21 rooms for rent. Her eldest grandson is training to be a lawyer and three others are in high school. All of them work—at times, with her.

Or at least that was the situation a few months before I wrote this passage, just a week after Kenya's questionable December 2007 election results unleashed widespread violence and unrest, devastating the slums where Beatrice and most of the other members live. Jamii Bora's intrepid founder, Ingrid Monro, a Swedish woman in her sixties with pale blue eyes and blonde hair tied loosely in a ponytail, told us that nearly half the members of the organization, who have worked so hard to lift themselves out of poverty, had been affected, but were still working to recoup their losses and to help those who lost even more. What happened in Kenya is a reminder to all of us of the dangers inherent in a world with a rising gap between rich and poor, especially in the developing world, where more than half of the population is under 25 years of age.

The psychology of poverty is so complex. It is so often the people who know the greatest suffering—the poor and most vulnerable—who are the most resilient, the ones able to derive happiness and shared joy from the simplest pleasures. Think of the women dancing in the slums, the fortitude of Charlotte after the genocide, the goodness of Honorata.

That same resilience, however, can manifest itself in passivity, fatalism, a resignation to the difficulties of life that allows injustice and inequity to strengthen and grow, to solidify into a system where people forget to question until an event or series of events wakes up the next generation. For adolescent boys especially, the excitement and camaraderie of doing battle can outweigh the dreary prospects of a future driven by low expectations and even fewer hopes.

It is not just Pakistan and Kenya that are feeling the strains. Bihar, India, where Drishtee operates, has seen the rise of a Naxalite movement, an offshoot of Nepalese Maoism, whose adherents reject modernity through their armed militia groups.

People need to believe that they can participate fully in the decisions that affect their lives and have a stake in the societies in which they live. This is why it is so critical to identify and invest in those rare entrepreneurs who see true human capacity in all people and are working on ways to unleash it. Ingrid Monro told me that Jamii Bora belongs to the whole world.

"After all," she said, "all of us came from people who were this poor at some point. Why do we continue to separate ourselves?"

I felt Ingrid's sense of hope, global citizenship, and human connection when I met Maryam, a little girl in northern Kashmir who lived with her father, trying to survive in a makeshift house after the devastating earthquake in northern Pakistan. I noticed that beside the temporary shelter for her family was a miniature one, like a little dollhouse.

When I asked who would live there, Maryam, who was standing with her little sister, responded, "Our dolls."

She pointed to a group of cloth dolls she had created. For each one, she wrapped fabric around a small stick, creating a tiny head, and then dressed the body with colorful fabric so that each doll had a dress and a veil for propriety. She had cut out faces from magazines and pasted them on the little heads. There was a glamorous blonde in a veil who reminded me of the heroine of *Bewitched*, a brunette, and even a handsome man. The levels of creativity and humor were thrilling.

Nine-year-old Maryam was wearing a white headband and a pale green gossamer veil that hung loosely over her dark brown, shoulder-length hair. Her clothes were pretty and clean, and I noticed that her hands were hennaed with daisylike flowers.

I asked who did her henna.

"Myself," she said shyly. "I like beauty."

Her 6-year-old sister Mona hung on our every word.

I told her I liked beauty, too, and that she was an artist and an architect. Blushing, she pointed to the temporary shelter she had built next to the permanent dollhouse, which had a corrugated tin roof and plastic sheeting on the walls and held a small wooden bed and a water jug just like her family's own shelter. Despite living in a conservative area where women were rarely given the same chances as men, Maryam could dream aloud because her father was different. You could see it in the way he spoke of his future, in his actions, and in his insistence on educating his daughters. Maryam also had a spark inside that made her stand out.

I asked if she wanted to become a businesswoman and if she would consider selling me one of her dolls—and, if so, for how much. She replied that she would gladly give me the dolls as a gift.

"Oh, no," I said, and tried to explain the value of a small business transaction, of selling just one or two dolls that she could remake and maybe sell again. She shyly nodded her agreement, and I gave her and her sister each a 100-rupee note and a pen.

The girls looked at the crisp notes in their hands and ran into the temporary house, returning with a bag to make this a truly professional transaction. She would have let me choose whichever dolls I wanted. I didn't want to take her favorites, so I asked her to choose those she didn't like as well. I received the gorgeous blonde and the brunette, leaving her 15 or 20 family members.

Despite the geography, cultures, years, and religions that divide them, Maryam and Beatrice have a common spirit. Neither is looking for a handout, yet both are constrained by societies that see them as "others," as poor females with little to offer. As I worked with Acumen, I met more and more individuals like Maryam and Beatrice. Each time I did, it strengthened my resolve to find more solutions that started with the poor as *customers*. At the end of the day, finding the answers to a fractured world must begin with encouraging and honoring the discipline and ambition, hard work and generosity of so many billions who want the same things we all do.

There is a powerful role both for the market and for philanthropy to play in creating this future. Philanthropy alone lacks the feedback mechanisms of markets, which are the best listening devices we have; and yet markets alone too easily leave the most vulnerable behind. By thinking about the Beatrices and Maryams of the world as our ultimate customers, Acumen can support entrepreneurs who have the same values in creating solutions that will enable the poor to help themselves.

The entrepreneurs who will help us create a future for all people are individuals who exist in every country on earth. They are the Roshaneh Zafars and the Dr. Venkataswamys, the Amitabha Sadangis and Dr. Sonos. They are the ones who see a problem and don't stop working on it until it is solved. They refuse petty ideologies and reject trite assumptions. They balance their passion for change with an ability to get things done. Mostly, they believe fundamentally in the inherent capacity of every human being to contribute.

At the same time, today's most effective leaders have a pragmatic bottom-line orientation that results in focusing on measuring what they accomplish, building institutions that can sustain themselves long after their founders have gone. The world will not change with inspiration alone; rather, it requires systems, accountability, and clear measures of what works and what doesn't. Our most effective leaders, therefore, will strengthen their knowledge of how to build organizations while also having the vision and heart to help people imagine that change is possible in their lives.

A potential donor asked me if I really believe we can teach leadership. "Leaders are born, not made," he said decidedly.

I not only disagree with that but also believe that we can—and must—infuse our young people with the qualities of leadership. More than any academic subject, judgment, empathy, focus, patience, and courage should be studied and cultivated. As our world gets more complex, smart and skilled generalists who know how to listen to many perspectives across multiple disciplines will become more critical than ever.

In 2006, we started the Acumen Fund fellows program to build a corps of leaders with the skills, networks, and moral imagination to help solve the tough problems of our time by using their understanding of how to build sustainable businesses that are appropriate for local contexts. The program is a mix of action and reflection, for it is much easier to teach a young person how to create a spreadsheet and do financial analysis than it is to navigate the emotional and political labyrinths that so often dominate developing economies.

Each year, we select approximately 10 extraordinary young people between the ages of 25 and 45. They apply from all over the world, bringing with them experiences ranging from working in investment banks, to serving as doctors in rural villages, to starting their own organizations. After spending 2 months in New York learning about the work we do and meeting dozens of leaders, they spend days reading and discussing literature and poetry—Aristotle and Martin Luther King Jr., Gandhi, Aung San Suu Kyi, and Nelson Mandela, among others—to help them begin to hone and then ground their own philosophies for change in the pragmatic realities of the work we do.

On the third day of the fellowship in New York, we take away their cell phones and wallets, give them only $5 and a New York City transit pass with two rides on it, and ask them to come back at the end of the day ready to share their perspectives and insights on how New York City's services for the poor might be better designed if low-income people were considered customers, not just charitable recipients. There is always nervousness in the morning as the fellows leave the building for parts unknown.

They return in the evening with wide eyes and thoughtful gazes, often carrying piles of documents that low-income people are required to fill out for each service they need.

"I worked as a management consultant at McKinsey and went to Harvard," said Adrien, a fellow from France, "and I found the reams of paper you need to navigate confusing. Imagine how you would feel if you were homeless and uneducated."

Catherine, an American, spent 7 hours sitting in a hospital emergency room in Harlem, listening to the stories of a man who waited patiently alongside her.

"By the end of the day, I was so frustrated, wondering what would have happened if I were really sick. But more tragic was the acceptance by so many people, as if their energy for change had been sapped from them."

Wangari from Kenya sat for hours in a soup kitchen with a group of women, listening to them tell her how this was the only place they felt they belonged. She puzzled over the difference between Kenyan notions of community and those in the United States. "Maybe there is room for more emphasis on community here and not just on the individual," she mused.

I loved listening to them, for they were learning in my own country what I had seen in poor communities the world over.

Beyond young people, there is a groundswell of successful individuals who want something more than the financial rewards of professional success. Neurological and psychological studies on human happiness bear out the fact that after reaching a certain financial level, an individual's receiving an incremental dollar does not correlate with the same increase in happiness. Moreover, scientists are finding, not surprisingly, that the one factor that does bring greater happiness is serving others. Of course, these scientists define happiness, much as Aristotle did, not as an episodic moment of bubbly lightness, but as a deep sense of meaning, purpose, and, ultimately, abiding joy.

Seth Godin is not someone who immediately jumps to mind when thinking about developing rural economies. He is a New Yorker, a hero of Silicon Valley, a marketing guru and author of the book *Purple Cow* who also pens a highly popular blog. He has a capacious brain and a heart of gold to match. After working on global issues for Acumen Fund, he traveled to India for the first time in his life to spend a week with some of our entrepreneurs on his own time, at his own expense, offering his consulting services for free.

Satyan Mishra, the entrepreneur who founded Drishtee, was open to Seth's key insight from the visit: that most of the "kiosk entrepreneurs" are, in fact, much like McDonald's franchisees, seeing the opportunity for business and income. Consequently, Satyan agreed, each franchisee should be given a precise blueprint for operations that details everything from services offered to marketing strategies. A fraction of franchisees will indeed be more entrepreneurial: I met one who sent fliers to schools so students would bring them home to their parents. This technique worked well for the kiosk owner and would be shared across the network: systems matter.

Satyan and Seth now talk regularly. Both are richer for it. So are the more than 7,500,000 people in some of India's poorest villages who benefit from their collaboration.

Making the collaboration work means building a relationship based on trust and respect. Seth thinks Satyan is one of India's great entrepreneurs, one made more amazing by his focus on helping people get out of poverty. Satyan gains immensely from hearing business success stories and insights from Seth's experiences with global corporations. Neither is always right, nor does either have all the answers. But together, they are a lot smarter for knowing one another.

What is important is that individuals bring what they do best to the world. After the Pakistan earthquake, I met Adnan Asdar, a contracting genius with laughing eyes, an energetic spirit, and a quick and generous smile. He was standing in his makeshift office in Muzaffarabad wearing a red-checkered scarf around his neck, a sweatshirt, and jeans. While overseeing the building of a new hotel in town and still owning a number of companies that he founded, mostly in Karachi, he decided after hearing about the earthquake to give a year of his life to making a contribution.

He committed to the Citizens Foundation, an NGO in Pakistan, that he would oversee the building of 5,000 houses for people who had lost everything. To do this, he brought together a band of volunteers from Pakistan and the diaspora—as far away as New York—young people who wanted to do something positive for their country. I asked one of the young men why he was working 16 hours a day in the cold for no money and no social life. He told me he was a *burgher* in Karachi, meaning a "rich, spoiled kid." He had attended a boarding school in Kent, enjoyed the pleasures of life, and didn't do much of anything, by his own definition. I told him he must now feel like a rich man.

He looked at me and responded, "Actually, I feel like a *man* . . . finally."

By the time I'd met Adnan, he'd overseen the building of 1,000 temporary houses to get people through the winter. His success was due not only to his good heart, but also to his being one of the country's best project managers. The experiences of Seth and Adnan and others like them make me wonder if there isn't a place for a senior fellows program to attract the best and brightest midcareer and retired professionals who are seeking greater purpose in a world in need of their skills.

Every one of us on earth, rich or poor, has something important to give. Acumen Fund's chief administrative officer and general counsel Ann MacDougall joined after a 17-year career at PricewaterhouseCoopers, where she held a variety of important positions, including global deputy general counsel. Her 12-year-old daughter, Charlotte, an angel-faced beauty with bright green eyes, decided she wanted to contribute as well, so she held a bake sale at a New York craft fair, and invited local potters to give a percentage of their day's profits. With their help, Charlotte was able to raise more than $350 in a single day. She saw what she could accomplish, taught people in her own words about this work that serves the poor, and inspired a whole lot of adults.

I stood at the podium at Acumen Fund's Investor Gathering, thinking about the hundreds of people who have contributed to making a collective impact in the world. Because of efforts big and small, from multimillion-dollar contributions to one envelope we received stuffed with 20 $1 bills from a 7-year-old girl, by 2008 Acumen Fund had been able to approve more than $40 million in investments in 40 enterprises serving the poor. Through the entrepreneurs who run those companies, we were able to help create more than 23,000 jobs and bring basic services like water—and therefore health—to tens of millions of very-low-income people around the world. Today, more than 350,000 people in rural India are buying clean water for the first time in their lives. Thirty million people have access to lifesaving malaria bed nets each year. A hundred and fifty thousand farmers have doubled or tripled their family incomes because of drip irrigation. And this is just the start, the beginning of our own journey, in which entrepreneurial initiative is paving the way for significant social change.

As for Acumen Fund itself, we were in the midst of raising $100,000,000 to invest in such enterprises. We had teams of people in India and Pakistan, Kenya and New York City, young people from around the world who could be doing anything they wanted but have come to see this work as the most interesting, challenging, and meaningful on earth. I thought of Brian Trelstad, Acumen's chief investment officer, a modern Jimmy Stewart–like character, whose former boss at McKinsey told me he was one of the best hires he'd ever made. Brian actually contributed to the first business plan for Acumen when he was a summer intern, and he continues to be a leader of innovation, now as the architect of a major metrics platform called PULSE that Acumen hopes to see used to measure impact across the social sector. I also thought of Yasmina Zaidman, a young heroine to many business school students because of her example of how to live a life.

I believe this next generation will change the world. Everywhere I go, I meet young people who are hungry and ready to contribute. University students and freshly minted MBAs from across the globe ask me what skills they'll need for meaningful work in serving the world. They should gain skills in the functional areas of business—marketing, design, distribution, finance—as well as in medicine, law, education, and engineering, because we need more people with tangible skills to contribute to building solutions that work for the poor. And they can be of service in this area by working for NGOs, progressive corporations, or governments.

Our team has come to see the work not just as investing patient capital. Although this is at the center of our mission, we've learned repeatedly that money is not enough. These young people around the globe are focusing their lives on change because they believe in a world where every single one of us can have access to the services, tools, and skills that will enable all human beings to pursue lives of greater freedom, opportunity, and, ultimately, purpose.

In one of my last meetings with Dr. Venkataswamy before he died at age 87, as we walked together at 4:30 or 5:00 in the morning, I asked him what he thought about God. He was quiet for a moment and then answered, "For me, God exists in that place where all living things are interconnected—and we know it when we feel the divine. For the world to heal its suffering, we need to combine tough determination and bring solutions to poverty with this sense of ourselves not as isolated individuals, but as beings who need one another and depend on one another."

A mile or so from Aravind sits the Meenakshi Temple, built in the 15th century, the world's largest Hindu temple with a capacity of a million people. With its thousands of carved and painted gods, its rooms filled with statues, ancient pillars, giant Ganeshas and Shivas carved from granite and marble, the temple has an awesome presence. My favorite room is the hall of 985 pillars: It was explained that 1,000 pillars would be too perfect. Humans must live with their own imperfection.

Dr. Venkataswamy's beautiful niece Pavi took me to the temple early one morning. As we walked through the massive rooms, she said that when she was a little girl, Dr. Venkataswamy constantly dragged her and her cousins to temples.

"You need to build a vision," he would tell her, "as if you were building a temple. It takes a focus on that vision, many generations to build it, no single source of leadership. It must be lasting and it must be done for the people."

Dr. Venkataswamy and John Gardner are no longer alive, but both of them created legacies that will long outlast them, for their visions for change were based not on their own egos but on contributing to the world in a way that released the energies of millions of people. Doing this gave both of these great men deep senses of purpose, meaning, and happiness. As I look to the next generation and the one after that, we are well advised to also look back to those who came before us and imparted such wisdom.

Build a vision for the people and recognize that no single source of leadership will make it happen: This is our challenge for creating a future in which every human being can participate. Just imagine the inventors, scholars, teachers, artists, and entrepreneurs who will grace the human race once this happens. The first step for each of us is to develop our own moral imagination, the ability to put ourselves in another person's shoes. It sounds so simple, and yet it is perhaps the most difficult thing we can do. It is so much easier to pretend that others are different, that they are happy in their poverty, that their religion makes them too difficult to engage in real conversation, or that their faith or ethnicity or class makes them a danger to us.

Each of us needs to develop the courage to listen with our whole heart and mind, to give love without asking for thanks in return, and to meet each person as a chance to know a new individual, not as a way of reaffirming prejudices. Our work should remind us all that the poor the world over are our brothers and sisters.

But empathy is only our starting point. It must be combined with focus and conviction, the toughness to know what needs to get done and the courage to follow through. Today's world needs more than humanitarians. We need individuals who know how to listen and who have real and tangible skills to share. We will succeed only if we fuse a very hard-headed analysis with an equally soft heart.

There is cause for optimism. Look at the progress in the world over the past 20 years, let alone in the time since my grandmother was born. More than 300 million people have been lifted out of poverty in the past quarter century alone. Think of the democratization of the globe by the Internet, which makes it so much harder for despots to shield their people from the enticements of the free world. Consider our ability to communicate without the intermediation of government. Remark on the tremendous strides made by women across the globe in both the political and economic arenas. Look at young people the world over who are willing to get involved in enterprises whose bottom lines are more about change than strictly about profits. There is reason to believe that people everywhere can lift themselves up, but they have to be given the tools to do so. We can only open doors so that they can walk through them.

Today we are redefining the geography of community and accepting shared accountability for common human values. We have the chance to extend to every human being on the planet the notion that all men are created equal, and this will require global structures and products we are only beginning to imagine. Though the average citizen cannot, of course, match the enormous gifts made by successful entrepreneurs such as Warren Buffett and Bill Gates, each of us in his or her own way can contribute something by thinking—and acting—like a true global citizen. We have only one world for all of us on earth, and the future really is ours to create, in a world we dare to imagine together.

ACKNOWLEDGMENTS

After the Rwandan genocide, in an effort to understand what happened there, I started writing this book as a letter to myself. It turned into a 10-year love letter of sorts, one written by my pen but infused with the help and wisdom of individuals much wiser and more thoughtful than I could ever be. Thanks to everyone who touched this book in some way.

Endless gratitude goes to the women of Rwanda, my friends, who spent hours upon hours talking to me, telling me stories, trying to help me understand an almost incomprehensible situation and doing it with grace and love. The women of Duterimbere, and most recently Dativa Mukeshimana and Anne Marie Mukarugambwa, spent days discussing the organization's history and future plans with honesty and a true desire to contribute. You reaffirm my faith in the strength of Rwandan women, and I thank you as well as the borrowers we visited over the years, who are all struggling to make better lives against all odds. Jovithe Mukaziya, Revocata Umawutara, and Jeanne d'Arc Uwanyirigira, have been my guides and friends for each of my five trips back to that country over the years. The team at UNICEF, as well as Stephen Lewis, who was country director when I visited, always facilitated my stays and made me feel that I had a second home. Indeed, I've benefited from kindnesses large and small in Rwanda, for which I am grateful.

The book *Leave None to Tell the Story,* written by Alison Des Forges with the important organization Human Rights Watch, was very helpful to me and deserves tribute here and for recording Rwanda's tragic history of the genocide.

Many thanks to Anthony Romero and the Ford Foundation for encouraging me to return to Rwanda after the genocide and supporting those early trips through a grant from the International Institute of Education. Without you, this book would not have been possible.

Even before there was a book, there were countless drafts, especially about Rwanda, and there were no two people like my sister Beth and my mother who "accompanied me," as the Rwandan women say so beautifully, until the book was fully written. A forever thank-you.

To my amazing editor, Leigh Haber, you opened my heart with your questions and comments and helped me discover my voice. I am humbled by your clear thinking, precision with words, and deep caring. Thank you.

Patricia Mulcahy, you have been a true comrade in arms and wonderful partner, helping me shape this book with your generosity, intellect, and spirit. Thanks, too, for introducing me to the best agent I could imagine. Marly Rusoff brought integrity and gutsiness and a powerful sense of solidarity that I will never forget. Thanks to you, Marly. And thanks to Michael Radylescu for his hard work.

Thanks to the terrific women at Rodale for all of their true support, especially the wonderful, generous and understanding Shannon Welch, Beth Davey, Beth Tarson, and Trina Perrineau.

Thanks to Sunny Bates, Antonia Bowring, Karie Brown, Peggy Clark, Katherine Fulton, Leslie Gimbel, Jessi Hempel, Saj-Nicole Joni, Afshan Khan, Otho Kerr, Geraldine Laybourne, Emily Levine, John House, Bruce Nussbaum, Bilge Bassani, Elaine Pagels, Chee Pearlman, Andrea Soros, Cyndi Stivers, Dan Toole, Keith Yamashita, and Emory Van Cleve for reading so many drafts, making introductions, helping me move forward. Seth Godin, you are a brilliant light who gave me strength—and a mantra to keep it simple even if I couldn't. I am awed by your generosity. Dominique Browning, you helped turn the stories into a single narrative, teaching me more than you know along the way. An enormous thank-you.

MY DEEPEST THANKS GO to the entire Acumen Fund team, always and every day, for the work you do with so much discipline, grace, joy, and passion. It is one of the greatest honors of my life to work with each and every one of you, and I thank you heartily for your support. Special thanks to Mariko Tada for insights, care, and all you did on so many levels; to James Wu for your tireless patience, endless copying, and help with juggling appointments; to Molly Alexander, Catherine Casey, Nadege Joseph, Ann MacDougall, Brian Trelstad, and Yasmina Zaidman for reading drafts and giving feedback; to Katharine Boies for your great energy and assistance; and to Aun Rahman, Varun Sahni, Nthenya Mule, and the country teams for taking such exquisite care of me and helping me find a sense of home and insights in each of your countries. This book is in so many ways from and for all of you and those you inspire.

Enormous thanks to Acumen Fund's amazing board members past and present. Margo Alexander, our board chair, took me under her wing, introduced me to possible editors, read early drafts, and always believed.

Thanks as well to Angela Blackwell, David Blood, Hunter Boll, Andrea Soros-Colombel, Stuart Davidson, Roberta Katz, Bill Mayer, Cate Muther, Bob Niehaus, Ali Siddiqui, Joseph Stiglitz, and Tae Yoo. To my brother Michael Novogratz, thank you for the unwavering support you've given for so long with so much heart.

It goes without saying that I send my deep appreciation to all of Acumen Fund's investees, including those not mentioned in the book. All of you are powerful models for change and I'm proud to work with you. Thanks especially to the teams at A to Z, Drishtee, IDE India, Jamii Bora, Kashf, Saiban, TRDP, and WaterHealth International for your hospitality, candor, and openness. We'll change the world together.

THANK YOU TO ACUMEN FUND'S founding partners: the Alexander Family Foundation, the Apex Foundation, Hunter and Pam Boll, the Cisco Systems Foundation, Jerry Hirsch, Jill Iscol, Charles and Roberta Katz, the Kellogg Foundation, Laura and Gary Lauder, Jennifer McCann, Cate Muther, the Novogratz Foundation, the Phalarope Foundation, the Sigrid Rausing Trust, the Rockefeller Foundation, the Sapling Foundation, Lindsay and Brian Shea, Andrea Soros-Colombel and Eric Colombel, the TOSA Foundation, George and Patty Wellde, and William Wright II. Thanks to our stewards, Abraaj Capital, Peter and Devon Briger, the d.o.b. Foundation, GAIN, Lehman Brothers, Jim Leitner, Polly Guth, the Lundin for Africa Foundation, the Aman Foundation, Raj and Asha Rajaratnam, Amy Robbins, Niklas and Catherine Zennstrom, the Bill & Melinda Gates Foundation, Google.org, the Skoll Foundation, and the Woodcock Foundation. No one builds an enduring institution alone, and you have helped in so many ways. And thank you, too, to the Stanford GSB and the Aspen Institute for the inspiration and sense of community I always receive.

My greatest thanks goes to my family, who taught me to love the world: my parents, Barbara and Bob; my siblings, Robert, Michael, Elizabeth, John, Amy, and Matthew; and my in-laws, Sukey, Cortney, and Tina. And finally, to my darling Chris, for challenging me and supporting me, for reading through endless drafts and always improving them, for your patience, your kindness, and your love. You are my rock.

MY UNCLE ED PASSED away last year, but it is to him that I will always be indebted for the blue sweater and everything it continues to mean.

INDEX